P9-AES-089

# How to Be Heard

# How to Be Heard

## Making the Media Work for You

Ted Klein and Fred Danzig

*Macmillan Publishing Co., Inc.*
NEW YORK

Macmillan Publishing Co., Inc.
866 Third Avenue, New York, N.Y. 10022
Collier-Macmillan Canada Ltd.

---

Library of Congress Cataloging in Publication Data

Klein, Ted.
How to be heard.

Includes bibliographical references.
1. Mass media—United States—Handbooks, manuals, etc. I. Danzig, Fred, joint author. II. Title.
P92.U5K5     301.16'1'0202     73-14109
ISBN 0-02-563900-5

---

First Printing 1974

Printed in the United States of America

*Because this book, in its own way, makes common cause with the national citizen's action movement founded by John Gardner in 1970, the authors humbly and respectfully dedicate it to him.*

# Contents

# Foreword

THIS IS A BOOK for those who want to be heard, but do not know how to begin or where to begin.

What we write may be used to fight some aspect of what we call "the system" or to uphold and strengthen it.

This is not a guerrilla text. It will provide both "establishment" and "antiestablishment" organizations with the keys that unlock the secrets of the media.

With this book, anyone—acting alone or with the help of others—should be able to construct an information program and communicate the information to the public.

We are aware that by itself this book will not help a great deal if the reader fails to apply the contents to a fair and reasonable communications program. This book must be regarded as the first step toward the utilization of the media. We do not offer much comfort or help to those who hope to learn how to coerce a program director into providing them with free time on a network TV newscast. But we do offer advice on how to find the TV program director, what to tell this individual when you contact him, how to present the needed facts so that informed decisions can be made on whether or not to put a network at the disposal of a spokesman for your group.

It is very possible that with the information we present here, some of our readers will one day be able to face a TV camera and literally be seen and heard by millions of viewers across the country.

Bear in mind that it takes a tremendous amount of patience and persistence to achieve repeated exposure by the media. A one-shot appearance on a local TV program is hardly worth very much effort. A story carried by a wire service can be printed in a thousand newspapers, but most people will not see it. Those who want to be heard must keep at it, so that a continuing presence begins to make itself felt through media. At times, this task requires that one forget about ordinary courtesy and quiet good manners, important though these may be. One must be sure of what to say and not give up the effort to say it.

We all know that it is possible for one person to achieve monumental changes through the strength of one's will and the force of the story being told. We are aware of a Hitler, of a Stalin, and of the changes they wrought. But remember, too, that Christ and Buddha also managed to get heard even though they relied for the most part on word of mouth to build their movements and their "organizations."

Ralph Nader accomplished much virtually alone, with a book, *Unsafe at Any Speed*. However, he has a highly developed understanding of how to get heard. He does not need a book like this, because he has become a "media person," sought by the media for his opinions. Nader probably has already achieved more change on the part of the corporate and legislative establishments than all the members, and all the rhetoric, of an organization like Students for a Democratic Society (SDS), which also knows how to deal with media.

A few men and women challenged and defeated the legendary park- and road-builder, Robert Moses, possibly for the first time in his more than fifty-year career, when they succeeded in getting the federal government to declare Fire Island a national seashore and thus foil a highway scheme. To do this, these people had to reach a large number of residents—voters—who live in Nassau County, New York. They could not have succeeded without a skillful utilization of the media.

One man, John Banzhaf III, was able to get most of the TV

and radio stations in the country to give the American Cancer Society and other antismoking forces "equal time" to warn against cigarettes. He did it all by himself, with virtually no money and, in the beginning, no special influence with media. He simply made it his business to get heard.

It takes perseverance, courage, and understanding of the media to do what these people did. The system we have in the United States permits exploitation of the media; in fact, the system is set up for it. And the media do not mind telling your story, despite what you might be led to think. The media, by and large, are interested in presenting new ideas and new stories to the audiences out there. The search for new material is constant and is vital to media success.

Do not let yourself get carried away with ideological biases in evaluating the media. You are, no doubt, aware of the controversy surrounding the press. How accurate are newspapers? TV news shows? The debate rages and no one knows the answer.

Those who feel wounded by certain coverage will take one side; they often will claim they were misquoted or misrepresented or perhaps just lied about to suit the bias of the reporter, editor, or publisher. The "Eastern liberal press," according to its critics, is the captive of the left and does its best to slant and twist the news to render middle-of-the-road, or more conservative viewpoints, silly and useless. Reporters for wire services that supply most daily newspapers with stories, and the papers' own reporters, are regarded as mostly "liberals," Democrats, or anti-Republicans who were educated in "Eastern" journalism schools dedicated to the undermining of "establishment" systems and institutions.

And then we come upon surveys to show that these same reporters are from all parts of the country, not home-grown Easterners at all.

There is very little hard information on newspaper accuracy. An organization called Accuracy In Media, Inc. (AIM) established in 1969 by Abraham H. Kalish, a retired professor of communications, contends that the *New York Times* and a few other leading news organizations do in fact often lie, twist facts, or simply report inaccurately. In some instances, AIM can make one of its charges stick, much to the dismay of many who read the *Times* and accept its reports as gospel. And then a conservative magazine, *National Review*, which is spiritually on the side of Kalish, publishes a detailed analysis of major stories that the *Times* published and concludes that the paper is, after all, fair and accurate.

In the February 3, 1973 issue of *Editor & Publisher*, Gerald L. Grotta, associate professor of journalism at Southern Illinois University, quoted a study by Charnley and Berry that found that accuracy in newspaper reporting was far from 100 percent. In fact, the studies to date have shown that when the question was whether or not a given person's quote was correctly reported, the accuracy score ranged from a low of 37 percent to a high of 71 percent.

Techniques used to establish accuracy vary. One that is common is to send a published article to the person quoted and ask whether the reporter did an accurate job. Of course, it is possible for a statement to be made by a person, recorded by a reporter, and written into a story accurately, only to have the speaker, on seeing the words in print, refuse to acknowledge authorship. (And we will not dwell on those who deliberately mislead reporters and then condemn them for being inaccurate).

There is no lesson to be learned from all this other than that newspapers are not 100 percent accurate. But newspapers can keep coming back to a story, so that in time an accurate story emerges. The more you can do to document a story, write out the facts, and see that the reporter reads them as you do, the better the chances that your story will be printed satisfactorily.

When you consider the speed with which news is gathered and disseminated and the many different ways in which errors can occur, one must conclude that our reporters are, generally speaking, remarkably accurate and, perhaps more important, eager to be fair.

Another point to remember about media has to do with people. The saying is, "Names make news." It is true. People like to know about other people. We are a nation of joiners. And if you represent a minority, even a minority of one, you can attract attention to your cause by letting the media know your views. Often, the more controversial the story, the easier it is to get attention. And when you have generated some attention, you can generate some support.

As you prepare to use this book, we suggest that at first you avoid dipping into it. For the most effective approach, we suggest a cover-to-cover reading. This is because some details about one aspect of communications—the press release, for example—turn up in chapters on newspapers, wire services, and news conferences, where the detail may more properly belong. To have attempted to cover every eventuality in the chapter on the press release would have tripled the size of this book through repetition.

Not long ago, Arthur Ochs Sulzberger, president and publisher of the *New York Times*, told a graduating class at Montclair (N.J.) State College that the public does not understand the free press. Nor does it recognize the fact that attempts to stifle it are dangerous to our society. "Debate—boisterous debate—is the lifeblood of a free society," he said.

There is no question that the individual citizen, by using his knowledge of the press and by using the press, can give his ideas credibility. There is something about words in print that makes them believable. The better you understand the inner workings of the media, and public opinion, the easier it will be to be heard. This book provides a blueprint to almost every part of media. If you use it properly, you will be heard.

Our society thrives on "news." Yet, much of what we read in *news*papers, *news* magazines, and *news*letters and see and hear on *news* broadcasts is made up, unreal, often a part of a carefully worked out campaign to gain some advantage for the people responsible for delivering the message to the reader or viewer.

By knowing how to be heard, you may never again be one who accepts all that is labeled "news" as objective truth. At the same time, you should emerge from your reading with a healthy new respect for, and understanding of, the power that we *all* can command in dealing with media. This, in turn, is of vital importance if we are to combat those who believe the people are best served by elected officials, private business interests, or public groups who should not be observed or questioned as they make decisions that affect all of us. In this land, more debate of the issues, not less, is best.

# Acknowledgments

TO HELP EXPLODE the myth that individuals with ideas are, in this society, powerless, we have written this book. And to help the reader put it to its proper use, we offer this paraphrase of Sir Noel Coward, who addressed himself to "the public" where our version refers to "the press."

> "Consider the press. Treat it with tact and courtesy. It will accept much from you if you are clever enough to win it to your side. Never fear it nor despise it. Coax it, charm it, interest it, stimulate it, shock it now and then if you must, make it laugh, make it cry, but above all, dear pioneers . . . never, never, never bore the living hell out of it."

We take the responsibility for all the mistakes. There are many who have helped us put this book together. To them we can only say thanks, and mention their names.

In addition to Sir Noel, this book has benefitted from the counsel of a large number of people—colleagues and friends in media. We are particularly grateful to Ray Bouley, Jim Lawrence, Tom Zumbo, Howard Geltzer, Pete Willett, Mario Cuomo, Barbara Curry, Diane Bianchi, Helen Conlin, Dan Cooper, Sam Convissor, Dominic Crolla, Margaret Cushing, Don Davis, Dr.

Michael Fry, Elizabeth Geiser, Marie Heinz, Walter Kemp, Bill Kitay, Frank Koch, Irv Markowitz, Milt Moskowitz, Bill Nelligan, Les Norins, Bob Schreiber, Art Shapiro, Gil Simon, Leo Orris, Ed Tuohy, Piet van Keep, Russ Wilks and Dave Zimmerman. Our manuscript typist, Carmen Elliot, deserves special praise for what she did with what she got.

And a deep bow to Crain Communications' weekly publication, *Advertising Age*, which sets a glowing example of giving all viewpoints a chance to be heard and can teach so much about *how to be heard.*

# 1

# Television

## HOW TV PROGRAMS ARE PRODUCED

IF YOU PAY ATTENTION to television in your community, you are already familiar with the channels that reach your home. You should also become familiar with the newscasts, the locally produced news shows, whether "live" or on tape, so that you know when they are aired and what their formats are.

Study the TV listings and watch as many of these shows as you can. Look at the credits that follow each show. Jot down the names of the producers, executive producers, news directors, writers, and reporters for each show. And pay special attention to the assignment editor's name. This is the most important name on the list for you. It is the assignment editor who is the key to getting your story on television. Well before the producer of the news show enters the scene, the assignment editor has developed a story lineup and has sent out film crews, correspondents, and film editors. Once the producer shows up at the office, he can direct the news desk as to which aspects of a story are to be used. He will work with film brought in by the crews earlier in the day, and by the time this film is being screened for him on the control room monitor, it is virtually assured of a spot on the newscast. In live coverage of a news event, the producer can be found with the director, seated in a control room, deciding which of the various pictures to air. For the regular news show, in which film plays an important part, conferences on coverage can also include the news director, his assistant, the assignment editor, and the producer.

An essential ingredient in their planning is the wire-service daybook. This moves on the Teletype to subscribers and lends a certain cachet to the scheduled events of the next day. Check first with the local wire-service bureau or the one nearest your community, and get your event listed on the daybook (see Chapter 5). The daybook is studied by the assignment editor, news director, city editor, and community affairs director. They will try to determine the all-important picture possibilities in the daybook events, so you must present your item to the daybook editor in graphic, highly visual, descriptive terms. The producer or any of his staff members may already be aware of the picture possibilities through your prior contact with them, but having it reinforced on the wire service daybook will help your cause.

If anyone in your group knows these people, or knows someone who knows them, use that "in" as a wedge for an introduction. If your group knows none of the individuals who put together the news shows or public-affairs programs, make your telephone call "cold" and ask for the assignment desk. Ask the station for the name of the producer of the specific program you want to be dealing with. There is usually a news director or news department producer for all news programs. And they have secretaries. The secretaries are trained to block telephone calls from people like you. They must hold interruptions to a minimum, since the producer is usually busy enough trying to put together his show. He does not want to be interrupted by strangers who want to chat with him about a story idea. In general, the best time to make your telephone call is in the morning, before eleven o'clock and in midafternoon, around three o'clock. Do not bother calling at five o'clock, because that is when the daily panic is setting in for the news-show people.

You are better off if you can locate the person in charge of a given show. Once you have the name, you can ask for this person. Sometimes, a program will have more than one producer. Your best bet is to ask for an individual whose title most closely corresponds with your needs. If you aren't sure, try calling another department at the station, and ask for advice on who you should be trying to contact. It's surprising how an "inside track" can be found by dealing with someone inside the company who enjoys helping someone who obviously needs help.

You must also realize that busy producers have buffers, or screeners, who handle their calls. You may find that you seldom, if ever, book your story by talking directly to the producer. But the producer's experienced telephone-screeners can get the job done, so don't turn these people off.

Bear in mind that there is a big difference between national and local newscasts. The networks—American Broadcasting Company (ABC), Columbia Broadcasting System (CBS), and National Broadcasting Company (NBC)—run separate network and local news operations. There are separate news directors, assistant news directors, producers, assignment editors, reporters, and so on.

Do not expect the network to cover your local story. If used at all, it will be used on a local news show, meaning that you can't expect a Walter Cronkite, a Howard K. Smith, or a David Brinkley, to cover your story. (If your story should prove to have national significance, however, network crews and local crews—each assigned by separate shops at a given network—will most likely show up to cover the story and work side-by-side.) Another possibility for broader coverage of a local story is the "feed," where a local station that is affiliated with a network feeds the segment to other stations.

To learn the names of the key people at stations in your area, their network affiliation, or their group membership, check with the *Broadcasting Yearbook* in your library. This volume provides, (radio and TV) station information, Federal Communications Commission (FCC) rules, ethnic program information, and the like and is published by *Broadcasting* magazine, 1735 De Sales Street N.W., Washington, D.C. 20036. On the local level, you must deal with local stations.

Here are the contacts for the TV and radio news media in New York network offices (before sending anything by mail, it is a good idea to check by telephone to make certain that the lists are still valid):

ABC NEWS
7 West Sixty-sixth Street
New York, New York 10023
(212) LT 1-7777

| | |
|---|---|
| President ........................ | Elmer Lower |
| Vice President, Director, Radio News .. | Tom O'Brien |
| Assignment Desk | |
| Television Manager ................ | Ed Kinney |
| Radio Manager ................... | Mike Stein |
| | Mark Richards |
| Executive Producer, Evening News ... | Av Westin |
| Senior Producers, Evening News | |
| New York ........................ | David Buksbaum |
| | Richard Richter |
| Washington, D.C. ................. | William Lord |
| Director, Films ................... | Jack Bush |
| Director Daily Electronic Feed ....... | Sid Byrnes |
| | Chuck Novitz |

NBC NEWS
30 Rockefeller Plaza
New York, New York 10020
(212) CI 7-8300

| | |
|---|---|
| President ........................ | Richard Wald |
| Vice Presidents | |
| TV News Programs ............... | Donald Meaney |
| Sports ........................ | Carl Lindeman |
| | Robert Mulholland |
| General Manager, News Operations ... | William T. Corrigan |
| General Manager, News, Radio ....... | James Holton |
| | Robert Kimmell |
| Director, Editorial Assignments (Assignment Desk), Radio and Television ... | Mark Landsman |
| Executive Producers ............... | |
| Nightly News, Television .......... | Les Crystal |
| "Today," Television ............... | Stuart Schulberg |
| Special Programs ................. | Lucy Jarvis |
| | Fred Freed |
| | Lou Hazam |
| | George Murray |
| | Robert Northshield |
| "Meet The Press," Washington, D.C. .. | Lawrence F. Spivak |
| Senior Producer, Nightly News, Television, Washington, D.C. ....... | Herb Dudnick |
| Washington Bureau News Chief ...... | Frank Jordan |
| Film Librarian .................... | Robert Butterfield |

CBS NEWS
524 West Fifty-seventh Street
New York, New York 10019
(212) 765-4321

President .......... Richard S. Salant
Vice President, Radio News .......... Emerson Stone
National Assignment Editor
(Assignment Desk) .......... Peter Sturtevant
Executive News Editor, Radio .......... Tony Brunton
Executive Producers
News Special Events .......... Russ Bensley
Morning News, Television .......... Richard R. Clark
Evening News, Television .......... Paul Greenberg
Executive Producer, "60 Minutes" .......... Don Hewitt
Documentary Producer .......... Perry Wolff
Radio Special Events .......... Charles R. Reeves
Radio Public Affairs .......... Peter Wells
Senior Producers
Morning News, Television .......... Harry Briggs
Helen Moed
Evening News, Television,
Washington, D.C. .......... Edward Fouhy
Producer, Health .......... Shirley Wershba
Researcher, Morning News, Television . Carolyn House Ferguson
Film Librarian .......... Neil Waldman

United Press International (UPI) AUDIO
220 East Forty-second Street
New York, New York 10017
(212) MU 2-0400, Extension 481
In Washington: (202) 393-3430
In Chicago: (312) 321-0553
In Los Angeles: (213) 656-4644
Recording phone for radio: (212) TN 7-3995

UPITN
460 West Fifty-fourth Street
New York, New York 10019
(212) MU 2-0400

Vice President, Broadcast Services,
Radio .......... Peter S. Willett
General Manager, Television .......... Burt Reinhardt
Assistant General Manager, Television . Reese Schonfeld
UPI Daybook (Metropolitan) Editor .. Thomas D. Zumbo
Newsfilm Librarian .......... Lou Tetunic

Bear in mind that the morning assignment editor generally is determining coverage of stories that will appear on the 6:00 P.M. news. The afternoon assignment editor comes on duty at 2:00 P.M. and he is chiefly concerned with preparing fresh material for the 11:00 P.M. show. Plan your news event accordingly. In terms of news-show production, very little generally occurs before 11:00 A.M., except updates and aftermath stories of fires, crimes and disasters. Plan your event for 10:00 A.M., generally. Remember that while news conferences at noontime are popular, producers abhor what they term "talking heads," or film showing someone talking. Rarely, if ever, does a speaker rate two-minutes of film that shows a talking head. The rule of thumb is one minute for such excerpts.

Before you decide that you want to try to get TV coverage for your event, organize your material into a brief presentation. Mail it in. Call afterward. Address it by name to the assignment editor.

The first sentence should have the most important element of the story in it. Hang this "lead" sentence on a "news peg," and present it in terms that are visually appealing to one who deals with the visual side of news.

Once you have worked out your lead, you can proceed by presenting the facts in a logical fashion, aiming at one and only one goal: getting the assignment editor and the producer to book you on the program, to send a camera crew to interview your group's spokesperson, or to cover the event itself.

Bear in mind that in a large city a minor neighborhood issue is not going to carry much weight unless it is presented in a larger perspective—and visually. That is, the small issue must be made part of a larger concern so that it relates to the entire audience.

The size of a program's audience is going to guide much of what you will or will not see on your TV screen. Most stations pay for audience audits on almost a second-to-second basis. Unless he is successful in holding his viewing audience, a producer will be replaced. If a succession of producers fail to turn the rating upward, the show will be replaced.

## ORGANIZING YOUR PRESENTATION

Get your presentation down on paper. All the reasons why the producer should give you valuable air time in which to tell your story to his audience. Remember, it is *his* audience, *his* program, *his* fifteen or thirty minutes.

Regardless of whether you contact him by phone or mail, you will have only a few seconds to grab his attention. Be aware of the two-minute rule. A good news show will be made up of segments that devote no more than two minutes to any one story. And the two minutes can be divided up between scene-setting, your side of the story, the other side, the newsman's narrative, and summation.

Often, the newswriter decides which segment of the soundtrack, or "sound bite," is airworthy. The producer will set the time limits and the correspondents "cut" their own pieces to fit. After twenty seconds, the producer is tempted to cut to another story, because the attention span of his audience may have been stretched to the breaking point by that time. This is why you must practice telling your story effectively, persuasively, in only fifteen seconds.

In your meeting or conversation with the executive producer or reporter, don't get into the business of reminding him that the airwaves belong to the public, that he has an obligation to cover community news, that you know the man who owns the station, or that your uncle is one of the station's major advertisers. These are good ways to turn him off. Remember that program executives want to keep their listeners tuned to their station so that the sponsors' messages will be seen by as many people as possible.

Here is an example of a request for TV time. Let's assume that you want to convince an assignment editor or producer to interview a member of your organization. Let's suppose that your group opposes community control of schools. You have mailed in your brief letter requesting the interview. You haven't heard from the station. Two or three days have gone by since you sent the letter. You place a telephone call to the assignment desk or the news director. Your call should start with a statement and end with a request (see page 151 on how to find the name of the person to whom the letter is addressed and the phone call directed): "Mr. Smith, I am *Ted Frederick*, representing the *Citizens Committee for Appointed Boards of Education*. We would like to send a representative of our organization to tell *your audience* why they should *support* the appointed school boards and *not* support parents who want to run the schools." (The italics are the words the assignment editor, or his assistant, listens for—who you are, what you want, why he should give you valuable air time).

The first response might be, "Didn't we get a letter from you on this?" You acknowledge the letter and proceed with your "pitch." Perhaps the morning newspaper carried a story about your group. Much of the evening news is based on the morning newspaper headlines. Mention the timeliness of your proposed interview.

If the editor or his aide is interested, be ready to answer a few questions. You may be asked to write a summary that deals with some points not contained in your earlier letter. If it is requested, send in a new summary. Also, be prepared to tell him the name, address, apartment number, telephone number, and other essentials of your spokesperson, with a promise that this person will be available at a moment's notice to come to the station or meet a camera crew for a filmed interview. Supply the editor with the names of your group's telephone contacts, making certain that the spelling is correct.

Your follow-up summary should be sent by messenger. Don't send it to the station in the hope of seeing the editor unless you are invited to do so. Usually, the editor will want to see your summary and talk it over with his staff. They will decide whether to give your opponents a chance to be heard on the issue, or perhaps they will enter into the spirit of the story, see its possibilities as you do, and begin to plan for more than just a minute or two of time on the newscast.

The written pitch should be the fact sheet (see page 140) and a covering letter that restates why you feel your message is important and newsworthy. This material also should provide a telephone number where you or an alternate contact can be reached at any time of the day or night. (Some decisions to use a story are made at the last minute, and in such cases, a telephone interview—without video coverage—can be used. The call to you may come on a Sunday afternoon at three o'clock for use on the six o'clock news show).

If you have a request that fits in with local community news, try to contact the community affairs producer. Ask the operator at the station for his name and then ask to be connected. If you represent a political candidate, then you should ask for the news producer. If you wish to request time on a station in order to present an opposing view of an editorial that was broadcast by the station's management, you should ask for the general manager of the station. Opposing views of broadcast editorials are often a good route to take, since stations are obligated to carry them. As soon as you learn the name of the executive to whom your request should be made, ask for him. Usually, the operator just rings an extension without ever answering you. Identify yourself to the next voice you hear and ask for the person whose name you have been given or for the producer. And then you do your number.

Some tips: Don't use the first name of the person who comes to the telephone. Be formal, reserved, very brief, and not too pushy. Remember that it's *their* station and that *they* decide who gets on it. Tell your story. It's better to read it from your fact sheet if you are nervous. Some very experienced public relations executives are not afraid to refer to a prepared "script," or fact sheet, once they are connected to the key individual in media. And if they can do it, you should feel free to do it, too—especially if you believe that your nervousness will cause you to forget parts of your pitch. After the first few sentences, pause. Let the other person think over your request and make some comment before you roll ahead with another thundering set of facts to bolster your case.

The producer, assignment editor, or station executive, may want to test you with some questions that will help him evaluate your request. Some commonly used attitudes include these: "Why should our audience be interested?" "How many people are in your organization?" "Do you know [here he mentions the name of someone who opposes your point of view]?" "Would you be willing to appear with him?" "Write me a note about this." "We did a school story [or story that seems to parallel the one you are pitching] last night. Sorry." You must be prepared with an appropriate reply to each comment.

If you don't succeed, you must keep trying, again and again. Each time, you will have to look for another natural news peg, or "hook," for your story. Remember that a turn-down today does not necessarily mean that you will not be called tomorrow or that you won't ever get booked on the show. Events have a way of altering decisions. Stay on top of your story and look for a way to freshen up your topic by relating it to the latest developments. As you endeavor to update your story, pointing out to what new heights of importance it has escalated because of current events, you will always strive to make your story newsworthy.

If the station has booked your opposition or you feel that it is ignoring your request for air time, then either you have been making mistakes in your approach or what you have been putting forward just isn't of sufficient interest to grab the producer's imagination or excite his news judgment.

At this point, you must try a new pitch. Develop a new leading statement, or have someone else try to contact the people who are not returning calls or responding to letters that request air time. Remember, this is not a business for bashful people. You must persist and come on strong in order to make the most of the precious seconds and minutes that you are hoping to obtain for your story. Work on the visual and audio potential of your story. Make it dramatic, challenging, and informative. If you can't seem to get the required results, find someone who might have better luck. That's what it's going to take to get booked on a TV news show.

Keep in mind that the TV news team will not be interested in showing how the fire department rescued your cat from a tree. But if there is a stronger human-interest aspect to the story, your request will take on added weight. Perhaps you can offer a feature idea: show how many man hours the fire department spends in rescue activity—activity that is not related to putting out fires or preventing fires. Your story takes on wider interest in this way. And perhaps in this new context, your particular cat can be shown getting rescued from the tree.

Suppose that you are fighting to have a new traffic light

installed at a neighborhood crossing. Certainly, this is not the most unique kind of local action; these battles have gone on since cars and people began using the same roads. Perhaps you can interest the TV news producer to film a story about what goes into the installation of a traffic light. The surveys, the different agencies that become involved, the manufacture of traffic lights and poles can all be part of the story. Using your particular neighborhood as the focal point, this case history could deal with the matter effectively.

A playground is needed in your community? How about a story on neighborhood playgrounds, new equipment, and the question of swimming pools, using your area as the story center?

If your community is a speck in the larger sea of city life, you must not expect the same degree of attention in media that serves a wider community. Attention to local issues diminishes in direct proportion to the size of the audience reached by the medium.

Always think in broader terms when you anticipate that the local aspect of your story might be considered too narrow or too local. If you are involved in a hot issue, one that has a history of attracting attention and generating emotion, then you are offering "hard" news, and it will not be necessary, for the first go-round with media, to dress up your story.

If you have been given several opportunities to appear on TV and you have had some success in making your points, you cannot expect your welcome to last indefinitely.

You will have to come up with fresh story angles in order to maintain the interest of media. If you find that you can't generate new angles, then perhaps you must recognize the fact that you have saturated your market; you have arrived at a point where you must forget about further exposure on TV and move on to other methods of developing your story for your potential audience. Remember that news- and talk-show producers must constantly ask, "What's the hook?" What kind of hook can you give them to hold the attention of the audience?

The interview is one method of approaching a story, although you must remember the bias against talking heads. Try to come up with visuals that present your story more directly. One picture is worth many words, but it must be a usable picture—one with news quality—for the TV reporter to include it in your interview segment.

Any slides that you bring along should be 35-mm color slides mounted in cardboard (the way they come from the processor) or in glass. You will need to work with a photo finisher to do this. As for identifying your organization, this can be handled by the graphics department or graphics director on the show. It may be a "lower third" identification, appearing as an overlay on the bottom of the TV picture as you talk.

Remember that the TV screen is not vertical; anything you bring along to get before the camera should be able to be shown on the horizontal (preferably 11 by 8½ inches). Otherwise, it may not fit the screen.

If you have your own film footage, be sure it is 16-mm color film. Usually, silent footage is best, since the TV host can then ask you to handle the narration. Bring all the film you can and let the shop choose what it wants. (One minute of air time uses less than a hundred feet of film.) Don't try for fancy effects in your film work unless you have professional guidance. The cost of shooting a minute of film can run from under a hundred to several thousand dollars, but this is money well spent if your film crew is good.

TV tape supplied to the station by outsiders is increasingly useful for public-service programs but is still quite rare. Don't go to the trouble and expense of shooting in videotape unless you have been advised by a producer that there is a good chance the station will use it. Check with him before you invest any effort in this aspect of your program.

There are also commercial organizations that prepare slides and film footage for public service and paid announcements. They also send out the material to stations, ranging in number from one to several hundred. The average cost for this service varies from $1000 for a single 35-mm slide-and-script mailing to 200 stations to $7000 for a one- to three-minute TV newsfilm in color and with sound. It is best to seek professional help before trying to produce visual material. Most cities have this help available. In the New York area, among the companies that specialize in this service are Planned Communications; Worldwide Newsfilms; Joan and Joe Ziel; and UPITN Corp.

In your contacts with the TV news-show people, do not use Xeroxed or mimeographed letters or releases. Send your material as original copy, writing it as you would write a news story.

If you are planning a demonstration, let the station know about it. Usually, they will say that they will check it out. Many TV news-show directors and editors recommend "kills" on such footage, unless the demonstration is so huge—100,000 people or more—as to be of singular importance. The assignment editor may look at the daybook to see if anyone else is aware of the demonstration—in other words, to see if the event might attract other media.

You will proceed and have your demonstration late in the morning, around the lunch break, or in the early afternoon and hope for fair weather. If no camera crew appears, you can telephone the station and tell your contact—the producer, news editor, news writer, assignment desk—what's going on. Remind them of the gravity of the issue, but don't oversell the story.

If your demonstration is taking place inside a building, you are at a disadvantage from the TV standpoint, because special lights may be required. In smaller cities, cameramen work the lights and the sound along with the camera. In the large cities, the crew consists of a cameraman, light man, and sound man. They may find it difficult to maneuver into a small space in a building, although new portable equipment is helping to eliminate this problem. The outdoors, under sunlight, remains your best bet.

If you succeed in having the assignment editor send a crew out to film the action or to interview you outside a building, there are a few basic rules to remember: Preparation is everything. If you know your subject and have gone over it dozens of times to make your message concise and effective, it will be easy for you. You will have watched, by this time, scores of TV interviews, and you will have noticed things that you will do your best to avoid. Make notes.

Your interview will begin cold. No rehearsals are tolerated by the news teams. If you are concerned about the camera crew walking up and down, seeking out one of your "troops" for a spontaneous interview, make sure you have thoroughly briefed each member of your group on what to say, or make it clear to each demonstrator that they are to refer all questions to the group's spokesperson. The spokesperson should be the most articulate member. In response to questions, don't ramble. Be precise. You should be well groomed, if possible; sloppiness in demeanor and appearance can detract from your message.

Before all this occurs, however, you should prepare for your TV interview or statement by having a member of your group play the role of the interviewer, the devil's advocate, or both. Don't assume that the TV interviewer is going to fawn over you. Don't look for the kid-glove treatment.

During the actual interview, as you respond to questions, don't worry about the camera or the mechanics of filming. Be yourself. Talk to the newsman, not to the camera, because if you talk to the camera, your concentration on the lens can bring about a "preachy" look on your face. The newsmen prefer the talking-to-the-reporter-at-your-side approach because it's more in line with actuality, with *cinéma vérité*. There may be some movement around the camera crew, some conversation going on in the perimeter; don't worry about it. Talk to the interviewer. Concentrate on what he's asking you and on what you are saying. And don't ever, ever tell any camera-crew member how to do his job. If you find something happening that might make for an interesting shot, call it to the attention of the reporter parenthetically, not as if you are his director.

Be aware of that two-minute rule, but remember that if you're lucky, you'll get twenty seconds on that evening's news show. Remember that the interview, when it airs, may be rolling over the picture of a picket line, so that the viewer sees the demonstration but doesn't see the speakers. When you've had your say, stop talking.

Now and then, you may see on a news show this scene: The interviewee has finished saying something and the reporter, unprepared for a short answer, perhaps, pauses while he puts together in his mind the next question. The camera may stay on the interviewee. This sort of awkwardness isn't common. It happens when the film editor hasn't tightened up the film sufficiently, perhaps because time was too short. Normally, such pauses are edited out, along with embarrassing mispronunciations.

The microphone that is held under your chin as you speak is for maintaining the sound level. That is why it is moved from one chin to another during an interview. Many newsmen prefer to hold the mike in one place, usually between themselves and the interviewee. But at an airport, at a noisy demonstration, or at a construction site you'll have to shout into the mike to be heard. Wind blowing can create background noise. And slogans that are superimposed on the screen or waved behind the speaker can distract the viewer.

Most often, the spot where the interview takes place will be selected by the cameraman. Leave this decision to the expert unless you know what you are doing. The cameraman will try to pick a fairly quiet spot, but sometimes, he will want to shoot the event live, with the reporter adding comments to the soundtrack ("voice-over") later at the studio.

We said earlier that you should be well groomed, if possible. Think of the audience you are trying to reach. If you're interested only in a community that you know very well and you know they know you, you can get by with jeans or whatever you are known to prefer to wear. But by and large, remember the larger audience. Remember Middle America. Conservative suit. Light blue shirt (not as essential now as it once was for color but still a good idea). (For technical reasons, avoid houndstooth or other loud patterns, which tend to wipe out the picture.) Otherwise, darker suits are best; they are sober and do not distract attention. Never, never wear a shirt that is darker than your tie. Most TV is still seen on black-and-white sets, so the dark shirt with light tie can make you look like a villain.

If you want people to contact you, be sure to ask the producer or interviewer if you can give a "commercial" on how viewers can get in touch with you or your group. Generally, it's best not to work in a "plug" unless you have cleared it in advance with the reporter. If you surprise him, he may cut the segment or kill the entire interview. Discuss with them the chances of showing a phone number, or mailing address, in a lower-third treatment.

Help the interviewer invest the interview with a beginning, a middle, and an end. If the interviewer isn't too good at the job, you can take over the interview for him and make sure that you deliver your prepared closing. The interviewer may want to chat with you for a few minutes before telling his cameraman to roll.

Makeup? Forget it. There's no makeup in outdoor interviews, and in a studio, there will be someone to apply it. If you try it yourself, you'll look weird.

Wear a hat if the weather makes it necessary to do so, but otherwise try to be bareheaded. And if you must wear a hat, avoid one with a brim that casts a shadow across your face.

Be soft-spoken. Be sure of your facts. Have information at your fingertips. Let comments pass if they will take the discussion into side issues that you previously decided were less relevant. Don't be a name-caller. Don't polarize the issue. Be dignified, credible, confident. Always be polite. Smile naturally. Look them in the eye. Stop talking when you've had your say.

Sometimes the cameraman will have a question written on a card, and he will hand it to you—often not giving you much time to think about your reply—record your answer, and depart. If you are being covered during a meeting or demonstration, you may never know that you have been filmed. Portable videotape recording units make this more possible than ever. Videotape can record the action at low light levels; film needs brighter lights.

Keep all jewelry to a minimum, or leave it home. Avoid wearing bangles, bracelets, and especially necklaces and beads. There are several reasons for this: The sound engineer may not get an adequate level on you when you start to speak and not realize, until too late, that your necklace rubs against the neck microphone, or "lavalier mike." This can make a funny noise and he may shut off your mike, tell the interviewer or moderator (by way of the floor director) that he should cut down on his questions to you, because you're not coming over clearly. Also, the beads or necklace can be glary and "burn" the picture, to the annoyance of technicians and the viewing public.

It sounds silly, but the age of the knee-high sock for men coincides with television's emergence. The ankle sock makes shin skin visible, and this is a TV no-no.

Do not try to wow the audience with a "way-out" wardrobe because all that will be recalled about your TV visit will be your getup. This is acceptable for ego-trippers, but if you are seriously trying to serve a cause or advance a point of view, you won't want ego to intrude.

Some time ago, Abbie Hoffman, at the time a leader of the

hippie movement, turned up at a taping of CBS-TV's "Merv Griffin Show" wearing a shirt that was patterned after the American flag, with stars and stripes as the motif. Rather than show Hoffman in this getup and risk criticism, CBS decided to carry only the audio portion and blanked out Hoffman. This could be done because the show was on tape, and Hoffman was sitting in a chair to Griffin's right. Viewers saw Merv Griffin talking to a blank half-screen. The result was interesting. The viewer, not at all distracted by Mr. Hoffman's mannerisms or wardrobe, could devote full attention to his remarks. The "blackout" did him a favor. Moral: Don't let your wardrobe overwhelm your words. The message is your medium.

Remember, don't answer at length. Keep your statements short. You won't be on very long, so get your message quickly out of your mouth. Rehearse it. Don't look around for the monitor or at your friends, husband, or wife nearby. Always bear in mind that you may be on even though you're not talking. Certain TV directors like to take very, very close, or "tight," shots of listeners as well as speakers. So try to stay cool and look "together," even though you may be in shreds inside. When you are on television, you are on. Period. It is an *intimate* medium that shows all.

Try to keep your voice modulated, even when provoked. If there is a "loudmouth" around, don't let it be you. Always keep your voice "under" the loudmouth's decibel count. In that way, you stake a claim to being the voice of moderation, of rational discourse. Also, if you tend to gesticulate while talking, your gestures should be small ones, contained. Small movements are all that the intimate TV screen can handle. Your smallest movement or gesture will usually be out of the picture frame in some tight or medium closeups.

You will learn from watching the TV news shows what the different approaches are. A favorite technique is to begin a segment of news coverage with the wide "establishing" shot, which shows, or establishes, the general scene from a distance. Then, once the who-what-when-where-and-why is passed along, visually and aurally (by the reporter on the scene or by voice-over), the camera moves in for medium closeups and, occasionally, extreme closeups (or ECU's). The medium closeup, or "two-shot" (reporter and interviewee), is supposed to give the viewing audience the "feel" of the action that has been described. Producers seem to discourage opening a segment with an extreme closeup, because it requires too much in the way of mental adjustment for the viewer before one figures out what is happening.

Being prepared to make a statement doesn't mean that you will always get a chance to deliver it on television. When you are shut out in this way, it's usually your own fault. Here's how to avoid that situation: Your request has been approved and the camera crew is at the scene. The anchor man of the news show had his producer talk to you, and then he came out to see you himself. After interviewing you in person and after you recite for the umpteenth time the reason for your concern and your need to be on television, the reporter tells the cameraman that he is ready.

Now, instead of asking you the ordinary questions you were led to believe were coming, he throws you a curve: "Tell me; how long has your organization been associated with this left-wing cause?"

A cool professional wouldn't bat an eye, wouldn't respond to what is obviously a low blow. But let's assume that you're not an actor or actress, you're flustered and even angered. You have fallen for an old trick. The TV news team has used this approach to get a better story. Sure, it's not fair, but this can be the way the interview starts. You must be prepared for this sort of gambit. The best defense is your offense, carefully organized. (You don't want to be left on the cutting-room floor.)

You can respond with something like this: Laughing, you say, "Yes, I suppose some people may think of us as a left-wing organization, just as in the early days of our country, Washington and Jefferson were thought of as far-left radicals, too." Then you simply ask your own question and answer it and go from there. The producer probably will recognize that you weren't fooled by his capricious opening gambit and will run your spot more or less as you want it.

What about the hurly-burly of sidewalk interviews, where viewers see as many as ten or twelve newsmen pressing around a person, pushing microphones toward the subject and shouting questions?

If the subject is well prepared, he can still bear down on the central issue, as developed for his TV appearances. He can also try to set the pace. If the questions are flying thick and fast and a commotion is occurring, the subject can quiet the reporters merely by opening his mouth and uttering a word or two: "Gentlemen, let me just say. . . ." The reporters will hush in order to hear his words. Once the quiet sets in, the subject can deliver his prepared pitch. Once he pauses, the questions will begin again.

The subject will try to control the situation by selecting the question to which he will respond. He will look at the reporter who asked the question. He must ignore the cameras and microphones that surround him and speak to his questioner, if possible. He will work hard to maintain composure, to come in "under" the tone of his questioner, speaking more calmly. If he begins to shout excitedly, he will not be understood, and the TV viewer will shrug at this performance and write him off as just another troublemaking street freak who ought to be locked up.

If he is able to smile at a time like this, the subject will smile naturally. But if smiling comes hard, he will forget about acting and concentrate all the harder on his sentence construction and choice of words and on listening to his interrogators.

Generally speaking, a noisy street interview by a cluster of reporters occurs spontaneously and involves the relatively unknown demonstrator. Community leaders, people of good reputation who are known to reporters, are treated with more consideration. They do not generally get badgered even after they have explained that they cannot say anything more. This is not written as criticism. Reporters are human, and much as they try to overcome their biases, even as they strive to report fairly, they respond differently to different people. A Nelson Rockefeller gets treated one way; a long-haired, denim-clad militant gets treated another way. Similarly, a pretty woman with a smashing smile will get more courteous treatment from the media than a loud-talking, tough woman, even though the latter may be miles ahead in brainpower, commitment, and experience.

All who hope to appear on television with some regularity must bear in mind that their options are constantly being reviewed for renewal. Those who are reliable "performers" (i.e., not obscene or blasphemous) or lucid, fairly well disciplined spokespeople for a point of view will find that they are being absorbed into the media. They will eventually get invitations to appear on shows even when they have nothing new or special to say. When that happens, they will also be given suggestions on how to make their story fresher and more compelling.

When a person becomes used to working with the TV crews, he will also find the field producer giving direction and getting fancier with production values as they deal with him. Rather than just do the simple interview as a two-shot, he will ask the person to converse with the interviewer so that extra footage can be filmed to cover a voice-over commentary. In such scenes, the subject is seen by viewers to be conversing earnestly with the reporter, although the conversation cannot be heard. The same approach applies to the cut-away question. Usually, they're talking about the weather, how they feel, or what time the show will be aired while the camera takes the "cover" shot.

What happens when the interviewer goes off on what you, as the interviewee, consider a diversionary matter? Don't be shy. You can say, politely, "I'd like to really talk about" the main issue. The interviewer should respond by opening that door for you, at best. At worst, he will continue his diversionary probe. If you fail to return to what you regard as the main issue, despite repeated attempts, you can let the viewers know that something is amiss and that you're not getting a chance to talk about what you regard as the main point. Chalk up that interview to experience. Try to get booked on another show.

After that interview is over, you should talk to the reporter and explain why you felt the interview went badly for you. He might agree or disagree, but at least you will have established a relationship that could lead to a better experience the next time.

If you are being interviewed by a reporter who moves the microphone back-and-forth rapidly, you should understand that he is after a fast-paced interview. Crisp questions. Crisp replies. You may be able to adapt your long, previously prepared responses and statements to this pace and deliver shorter, to-the-point statements. But if you feel uncomfortable with this pace, you might try to slow things by speaking more slowly. Or you might remember to make your central point every time the mike comes around to you again.

The process might go like this:

*Reporter.* What is your group doing here today?

*Interviewee.* We want the mayor to know that we need a new playground in our neighborhood . . . (mike is pulled away).

*Reporter.* Are you all residents of this area?

*Interviewee.* We need a new playground because the nearest one is one mile away . . . (mike is pulled away).

*Reporter.* Do you all come from this neighborhood?

*Interviewee.* Yes, we do. But we're here today to tell the mayor that there are 1100 school-age children in our community who have no place to play . . . (mike is pulled away).

*Reporter.* How long have you been asking for a playground?

*Interviewee.* Two years. Our wives must take our children across some heavily traveled roads to reach the nearest playground. . . .

The pattern is to respond to the question as briefly as possible and then add a sentence that builds your case as briefly as possible.

Concentrate on your story. Don't budge. In some cases, for any number of reasons, the reporter might hold his microphone under your chin too long, for a few extra "beats" after you have finished. Perhaps he doesn't realize that your statement is complete, and he expects you to continue. The inexperienced person will feel obliged to keep talking as long as the microphone is in front of him. He fears dead air even as the most experienced broadcaster does. And so he adds a few lines, such as, "And that's how I feel about it. Really. That's what I think. You can quote me. Heh, heh." And so on.

If the microphone lingers and the camera keeps rolling, simply restate your main theme all over again. Sum it up. Be a stuck record. It's better to repeat than to dilute your story by what could be seen by viewers to be an indecisive fadeout. The film editor at the studio can tighten your segment by trimming the repetitious dialogue, of course.

When an interviewer asks, "Do you think a demonstration of this sort will accomplish your goal, or is it liable to be counterproductive?" you are being invited to discuss tactics.

Why use this precious, hard-to-get TV time to discuss the subject of strategy and tactics? Simply revert to your basic statement. Respond in this fashion: "Our demonstration is intended to focus attention on the need for a playground in our neighborhood. We know that a playground is badly needed. Our polite letters to the powers-that-be haven't accomplished anything. We have waited seventeen years and nothing has happened. We need a playground now, not five years from now."

If the interviewer asks another diversionary (to you) question, such as, "What about that little fella there? Is he your son?" you can respond with, "This lad is here with us to demand that we get a new playground before someone gets hurt, or killed, in crossing highways."

Don't be shy about pressing your case with media. Don't worry about being considered a pest. Keep at it until you get your chance. Remember that you have a lot of competition and that if you hold back, you'll be skipped over.

If you are turned down by the TV people, do not become discouraged or bitter. Prepare yourself for another try.

Remember that preparation is everything. And remember, too, that not everything that happens in the coverage of news is spontaneous. For example, during the 1972 presidential nominating conventions, the TV floor teams were constantly being approached by agents and principals of all political shadings who, mindful of the huge audience "out there," wanted to be interviewed. The practice is not followed only by the downtrodden. Jay Rockefeller, the West Virginia Democrat who was beginning his gubernatorial campaign, had his press secretary put a card into the hands of CBS newscaster Roger Mudd that noted Rockefeller's availability for an interview. Writing in the publication (*MORE*) after the Democratic convention, J. Anthony Lukas noted, "Obviously, a lot of people came to Miami Beach primarily to get television's attention. Once again, television was not just the Medium, not just the Message, but the Prime Mover of it all."

During an early-morning convention commentary, economist John Kenneth Galbraith told NBC's "Today" show host, Frank McGee, "You people really have to do something to keep the convention alive or you have no justification."

A leading member of the Senate was reported by CBS to have contacted the podium at that same convention and asked for permission to speak on a night when the party's platform was under consideration. Asked which plank he wanted to speak about, the senator replied, "Oh, I don't know. What do you have going around midnight?"

## THE STUDIO INTERVIEW

The half-hour discussion show devoted to your cause? Don't get your hopes up. Time is too valuable; the station is interested in holding an audience and in selling its time. The subject must be of overriding importance to the general audience before an entire half-hour show will be devoted to it. The trend is to do perhaps ten or fifteen minutes at most as part of a "magazine" format.

You achieve a breakthrough by going directly to the producer. You make your presentation on the basis of what the program will mean in terms of public service and general interest. The station manager or the program director also are proper targets for this presentation.

If you can collect lots of names on petitions, you might help convince management that there is some interest in the subject and that you're not merely a one-man show. The petition approach is heavy-handed, but in some cases it can help. Perhaps you can also bring in numerous newspaper clippings that are related to the issue. These can help convince the station's management that your story has an ongoing interest.

Stations are under a great deal of pressure to do more public-interest programming, also called public-service programming, and this fact is of great value to you. Also, be sure to help the station's management understand the other side of the story so that they can develop both sides for the program.

The regular studio interview is more readily attainable than the half-hour show. Once you are booked for an interview at the studio, double-check the time and place to make certain there is no slipup on either side. If you have some film, tell the station that you want to air it during the program. The control room needs to know such things in advance so that a projectionist will be on hand to run the visuals.

Some time before the program, sit down with a friend or associate who knows your subject as well as you know it. Let this person serve as a devil's advocate. Go over every possible question that could be asked, especially the ones you hope nobody asks, the embarrassing ones. Know your answers and be prepared to defend them.

You may find that the producer's researchers have done their homework, too, and that the producer now knows your strengths as well as your weaknesses. He will, if he's smart, try to book an opponent to appear on the show with you. (The theory at work here is that two scorpions in a bottle make for a better show than one scorpion.) Don't be surprised if you walk into a program that is loaded against you.

If you see a TV show that presents a one-sided point of view in an issue that concerns you, you have reason enough to telephone and ask for time. If you're in politics, you can ask for equal time. If the issue isn't political, just ask for a chance to present an opposing viewpoint. The equal-time provision of the communications law is not one for amateurs to play around with. Better to rely on your facts and charm and the judgment of the producer, but if you are not sure of a specific question that is involved, get the advice of a lawyer.

Strange as it may seem to the layman, some producers—especially in educational television—will let an outsider help with the production of an entire TV program. This is best accomplished when you have a point of view that is controversial. You can call the producer and suggest that you can supply a guest (yourself or a spokesman for your point of view) and then suggest one, two, or three others whom you know to be on the other side of the question.

Naturally, you'll want to be sure that your presentation is strong and well prepared before you suggest that the opposition be invited in. But the fact that you are willing to be objective in the interests of producing an informative TV show may help to persuade the producer to book you. Especially if he likes controversy.

Work with the producer of the public-affairs program, the panel talk show, the interview program, or press-conference program to help develop a topic that will include a representative from your group. Amass your facts and figures to show why the subject is of general interest. If you can assure the producer that your spokesman will make news—legitimate news—with a statement during the course of the show, your chances of being invited will be assured.

Remember that the producer of the TV show is looking for publicity for his show; he wants his show talked about, written about, and viewed by ever-enlarging audiences. He's not going to be interested in presenting some nice people who specialize in conversation that puts large numbers of people to sleep. He's going to be interested in presenting a speaker who will make news. His station or production company may employ publicists, or "show handlers," who generate press releases based on the show's subject matter. If you have something newsworthy to say and if you say it during their show, you will be doing them as much of a favor as they are doing you.

There are talk shows scheduled for daytime and nighttime slots, aired locally, regionally, and nationally. Start local. The cable-TV, or "open-channel," route, is excellent basic training for the neophyte TV speaker. These appearances on small-audience channels can be parlayed into appearances on stations with larger audiences, just as you can parlay a newspaper article about your cause into a "calling card" that gets you booked on a local TV show. Many TV appearances are generated by the morning newspaper headlines.

At the beginning, you will not have much of a chance to get yourself booked onto a Johnny Carson-type network show. You might have a better chance of enlisting the support of a well-known personality, one who is making the rounds of the talk shows or is periodically booked on these shows because of his or her entertainment value. Try to arrange a meeting with a personality in this category of public life so that you can explain your project. You may find the celebrity is willing to "plug" your project during a TV or radio appearance. The celebrity, if he detects some publicity value in becoming more closely identified with your cause, can pick it up and run with it, making it a personal crusade and leaving you to wonder where you fit in. But you're not on an ego trip, remember; you're simply looking for media exposure for your cause.

But be careful about selecting the celebrity-spokesman. If it is someone who is "overexposed" in terms of "cause" appearances on the tube, your project may be diminished more than it is enhanced. Try to single out a fresh celebrity as your surrogate advocate, one who is not tainted by a political stance (if your project is nonpolitical), one who will see—and make use of—your cause as a handy hook on which to gain TV guest appearances and interviews with print media. This celebrity will benefit by appearing to be more than a performer who can talk only about a motion picture, TV show, or record album.

## THE NEWS CONFERENCE

The TV newsroom is a crowded and busy place. Much of the footage produced for daily audiences concerns news conferences.

To gather this footage, the station deploys its crews. Coverage is limited by logistics and personnel. Depending on union rules, the size of each crew varies from one to three people. Where the union is strong, one member of a crew doesn't move without the others.

At the press conference, if you are the principal speaker, you will be addressing a mixture of broadcast and print reporters, each with different methods of working. You will have to give repeat performances after or before the conference, for the benefit of the radio and TV reporters. Repetition must not diminish your enthusiasm. You must keep your freshness throughout these reruns.

Often, the postconference conference can be bunched for all the local radio and TV news shows. These affairs are seen on TV as taking place in a hallway of a hotel, often, with a cluster of microphones in front of the speaker. The cameras record the scene as he speaks for all the TV and radio stations simultaneously.

As for the TV coverage, the TV camera crew is first asked to film the outside of the room or building, for use in establishing the scene of the conference. A "wraparound" can have the reporter introducing the event and, when it is over, supplying a brief concluding remark as to the significance of the event. There also may be cutaway shots of the audience or cutaway questions asked by the reporter to no one in particular. These cutaway questions allow the writer and the editor, back at the studio, to jump from an early point in the interview or press conference to a later point—from question 1 to question 6, for example—while maintaining continuity. The cutaway shot may include a scene of reporters taking notes or footage of charts near the speaker. These scenes are spliced into the film while the voice-over moves on to another point, thus covering the scene changes without missing a beat.

The TV reporter usually doesn't have to write the copy that the studio newscaster will read to introduce the segment, because the studio newswriter often handles this by working from wire-service copy. The forty seconds or so of film footage that emerge from all this activity include background, provided by the reporter.

Remember, the TV station turned up at the news conference because of an advisory in the wire-service daybook. This leads to a situation where the print media—the wire service—establish the importance of a story and TV reacts to it. The pecking order at the TV station finds the assignment editor in a key position, keeping tabs on the available film crews and reporters. Each news show's producer is concerned about content and pacing: How many commercials will there be? How much time will they take? What kind of film do we have? What's the timing of each bit of news film? Any possible problems? If so, the producer will see that they are resolved. He wants to know who the reporters are for the day's show and what they are wearing. (More and more TV reporters are asked to wear blazers with their station logo for the crest. It has happened that reporters who lacked a blazer on the job have found themselves "buried" in the day's newscast.) The show will plan to include sports, a light feature to leave them laughing, and weather. These segments also are measured, but they can be telescoped if a truly major news story occurs.

The news director worries about the budget as much as about the flow of news and his coverage of it. When a major story breaks, the station may send out its truck with a reporter, who will usually have read wire copy on the story before starting for the scene, have been briefed by the assignment desk, and have been in radio contact with the newsroom while traveling to the scene of the story. When he arrives, the camera crew sets up and he delivers his "spiel." The opening shot may be of him facing the camera, microphone stem firmly in hand, explaining the occurrence. Then he will interview some of the people who are involved and still available.

## TV SPOT ANNOUNCEMENTS

Most TV stations maintain a department of community affairs, whose responsibility includes deciding whom to interview and which free public-service spot announcements are to be aired.

It is usually far easier to get an announcement on the air than to get on the station yourself, especially if your presentation is visually attractive.

The most frequently used public-service announcements run for ten seconds. That's about 12 words. A twenty-second spot runs 35 words; a one-minute spot uses about 120 words. If you can supply slides, consider one slide for each ten seconds. Don't count on getting the slides back. And, unless you're very lucky, you won't get a report on whether the station used the material or at what hour. One way to try to overcome this problem is to send a postage-paid card along with the spot announcements so that the station manager can have the essential data filled in and mailed to you. But this approach is still not successful in most cases.

## CABLE TELEVISION

The availability of community cable television is on the increase. Thousands of communities are now receiving TV network and local programs via cable. Cable-TV companies in the 100 major markets are required by the FCC to provide at least one free public channel for a variety of community public-service purposes, such as coverage of local government, neighborhood meetings, school programs, and virtually any other project that involves bona fide community residents.

The cost of production is to be borne by the user. The FCC also says that the channel—termed the public-access channel—will spin off yet another public-access channel once it becomes 80 percent saturated with public-service programming. In this way, overcrowding is expected to be avoided.

If there is no cable television where you live, you can count on getting it in the near future since it has been estimated that by the end of the 1970s, almost 90 percent of all American homes will be wired into a cable-TV system.

Despite its relatively small audience, the public-access rule has sent ripples throughout television. Organizations have been established around the country to help people prepare their programs for cable-TV presentation. Colleges have set up workshops. In New York City, a nonprofit organization called Open Channels, Inc., formed in 1971, provides technical assistance and training to groups seeking exposure on the cable-TV public channels, an outlet that is ideal for most causes or projects. Besides providing an electronic soapbox from which ideas can be tested in the marketplace, these units provide instruction and, in general, offer excellent basic training for the novice TV performer.

The newspapers still do not supply readers with detailed program schedules for cable-TV stations, and the stations are generally unable to issue program listings on their own, so viewers often must tune in on a pot-luck basis. Again, monitor the cable-TV channels serving your community so that you can determine how best your group can fit its presentation into the schedule. It is usually not difficult to get on a cable-TV program and the exposure is invaluable in gaining TV experience. The cable-TV station is to the commercial station as the farm team is to the major league baseball team, one might say. You must remember, of course, that the cable-TV station's audience is quite small when compared to the major commercial stations in a community.

To get booked on a cable-TV station, note the names of show producers that appear on the "crawl," or list of credits, that follows each program. If there is no crawl, write or telephone the station and seek an appointment. The station may be housed in one room, where a section is set aside for the "studio" and the tiny TV camera is fixed on a tripod.

The principal medium for cable-TV programming is videotape. A one-hour program can cost from $600 to $1000. A sampling of some cable-TV programs, taken from Channel 10, the Sterling Manhattan Cable Television channel in New York City, offers discussions and interviews with authorities in the fields of drug abuse, the environment, law enforcement, prison reform, media, the need for black community involvement, and a variety of shows about funding techniques and problems, franchises, minority attitudes, and the like.

In Reading, Pennsylvania, a city of about 83,000 persons,

American Television & Communications Corp., in partnership with the School of the Arts Alternate Media Workshop, New York University, has conducted a pilot public-access TV project that involves many Reading residents. These people were given an opportunity to learn about videotape equipment, how to use it, including postrecording processes and editing. The cable-TV public-access movement is rapidly growing, and any group of citizens would do well to make use of this opportunity.

Many cable-TV companies are building and equipping studios for news shows, talk shows, and interview shows. Because older video-tape equipment still weighs about 140 pounds per unit, it is difficult to maneuver outside the studio. Portable videotape recording (VTR) equipment is gaining popularity. A twenty-one-pound VTR unit, with battery-operated camera, can be taken into the streets or to anywhere people can go.

To demonstrate how such portable equipment can open up informational programming, a check of the Santa Cruz Community Service Television Project shows a schedule that would include, on videotape, an ecological history of the Monterey Bay area; introductions of new people in the community, permitting them to share their experiences with their new neighbors; coverage of the weekly board of supervisors meeting; a program on "A Day in the Life of a Santa Cruz Peace Officer"; a report on a volunteer community-renovation service; a disaster-relief service; community-message service; and student VTR productions. The list is a basic one for community service and easily suits groups that seek to express viewpoints not otherwise aired on commercial channels.

A periodical called *Radical Software*, devoted to alternate video equipment, public access, and video theater, provides a generous perspective on the uses to which VTR equipment can be put. In Video Theater (i.e., closed-circuit video-tape programming) tickets are sold. This would be the electronic age's version of the early motion picture theater.

Noted *Radical Software*, "The only potential for any semblance of fairness is to provide each citizen with an amplifier for the expression of self to others. There can be no better report on housing than the Spanish or broken-English statements of a Puerto Rican telling and showing his or her East Harlem living condition of a rat-infested, garbage-stinking, two-room, fifth-floor walkup."

This kind of programming is, of course, no longer relegated to alternate TV channels. Commercial stations are turning to coverage of this sort and will pursue sidewalk-staircase programming in the future.

*Radical Software* stated that a first-year budget for an alternate video station amounts to about $35,000, which can be reduced in future years as "community support through advertising and services is realized."

Some cost breakouts are as follows: equipment, $5000 for two portable half-inch videotape units and support systems and $6000 yearly for 100 hours of tape; and personnel, four full-time staff members at $5000 each "with a support video producers' collective who are compensated for work performed only and who share profits of tapes which prove to be lucrative."

Lending impetus to what has been termed the "open-channels" movement is the portability of the equipment. Wrote Andrew Kopkind in *Boston After Dark* (July 11, 1972): "A number of events and developments have come to make do-it-yourself video less of a novelty, if not yet an institution. First, technology has advanced and production organized to make a reliable, versatile and fairly inexpensive video system available for about the price of two quality stereo layouts or a used VW bus in good condition: i.e., the survival equipment of the hip bourgeoisie."

Other inputs that should help the growing open-channels movement, Kopkind notes, are "a surplus of bodies in the particular age, class and educational categories open to the new technotoys," and "the promise, prophecy and probability of mammoth Cable TV and video cassette industries have indicated a demand for production skills and programming software."

## HOW THE PROS HANDLE TELEVISION

"The biggest mistake in my political life was not to learn how to use television," said Hubert Humphrey after he lost to Richard Nixon in 1968.

The professionals make certain that they surround themselves with professionals who know how to use television. Perhaps if this book had been available in 1968, Humphrey would have had fewer regrets. Another book that would have helped him—except that it couldn't have been written before the 1968 election—was *The Selling of the President 1968*, by Joe McGinniss. Besides entertaining us with behind-the-scenes descriptions of the Nixon campaign, the book serves as a practical guide to the use of television for opinion-molding and image-protection.

Many persons made the mistake of looking at the McGinniss book as a compilation of negative aspects involving packaged politics, because Nixon placed himself in the hands of the technicians, ghost writers, experts, and pollsters who could guide his words and actions through the campaign.

In 1972, Humphrey, having shed his queasy attitude toward packaged politics, entered the business with everything he had. Longer hair. Wide lapels. Flared trousers.

Now we know the rules: To achieve dignity, energy, and a superior reflective capacity, a public figure ought to be carefully filmed in a studio, on a set that contains full bookcases, perhaps a heavy brown desk, a window, and drapery between the bookcases and behind a desk to add psychological "lightness." Backgrounds for TV sets show wooden panels because they have "clean, solid, masculine lines," we were told in the McGinniss book.

We also learned that the subject's most comfortable posture on the set must be utilized. If he prefers to lean against a desk or sit on part of the desktop because this pose makes him seem informal, so be it. We learned that nobody should stand in front of the subject while the filming goes on, unless that person is absolutely vital to the production. To crowd in on the subject is to open the possibility of distracting him, of causing the subject to shift his eyes. There must be no still photographers with flash bulbs around the set. The cue countdown should be conducted immediately under the camera, directly in front of the subject. Again, this is so the viewer doesn't see any eye-shifting.

A second or two before the on-the-air occurs, before the red light on the camera begins to glow and the tape machine emits its beeps, the subject receives a warning signal to begin to move, to avoid a "frozen" look as he goes on the air.

Reading from cue cards (or "idiot" cards) can be supported best by the use of sentences that are brief. We learned from the McGinniss book that it's wise to use cue cards or a mechanical prompting machine, since viewers assume the subject is reading anyhow.

Why all this attention to detail? In politics, candidates are not supposed to betray uncertainty or insecurity. They must come across with conviction and directness or, they think, they will evaporate in a mist of carelessly prepared dialogue.

When Senator Thomas Eagleton, the 1972 vice-presidential candidate, was being pressured to leave the Democratic ticket, he attempted to make himself completely accessible to media, especially television. The thinking was that if the public could see his display of candor and personality and hear him explain the history of his emotional problems in his own way, his cause would prevail and he would remain on the ticket.

On the Sunday before he was dropped from the ticket because it was felt that his psychological history would have become a campaign issue, Senator Eagleton went on CBS-TV's "Face the Nation."

Reporting on this appearance, a *New York Times* reporter wrote, "According to his aides Mr. Eagleton went to the studio a half-hour before broadcast time determined to make two points —to reemphasize his determination to stay on the ticket and to spell out in greater detail the circumstances of how the Vice-Presidential nomination was offered him earlier."

He made sure that he set aside a quiet block of time in which he could ponder the possibilities and put together a strong statement. Eagleton was able to make his points in different ways during the program. The same news story noted, "Sen. Eagleton's answers were informal, sometimes almost joking and self-deprecating."

It would seem from all this that Senator Eagleton used media to serve his purpose as best he could. But there was one unforeseen hitch. The panel moderator, mindful of the importance that manifestations of tension played in considering Eagleton's case, told the audience that the senator was perspiring and that there was a slight tremor in his hands. (As there might be with any guest after a half-hour of pressurized give-and-take under studio lights.) Eagleton, hoping to salvage himself from what was implied, noted that he is the sort of person who perspires even on Christmas Eve. He added that he actually felt "very comfortable and very relaxed."

The point here is that there are unpredictables in such formats. Nothing should be taken for granted, which is why it is a good idea for the subject to get his aides together for a no-holds-barred question-and-answer session the day before the program. Football coaches are known to schedule tough two-hour scrimmages before an important game in order to give the team a feeling that the Big Game itself will be a breather—only sixty minutes long.

The McGinniss book also teaches us that candidates must speak up; they mustn't chew their words. Do not think you must come across like a Walter Cronkite or Howard K. Smith on camera. You're not a professional newscaster, and you're not expected to sound so polished that your audience will be bowled over by your presence.

It's a good idea, however, to work on your enunciation as much as possible. Work with a cassette tape recorder. Listen to yourself. Conduct interviews with your associates and tape them. Conduct critiques afterward. Remember to avoid "urrs" and "ahhs" or "tic words" that betray nervousness through constant use. Don't use words with which you're not completely familiar. If you're not a lawyer, don't try to sound like one. You're not going to escape sounding like yourself, so don't fear speaking naturally. The main thing is to organize your material, master your facts, and sound off clearly.

Also bear in mind what the purpose of your appearance is. Are you simply there to explain something or to make a point? To be informative? Are you trying to persuade an audience to support your cause? You must be prepared to sort out the many threads that run through your story and focus on the main ones, the key points, the specific aim. Use the reporter's questions to prepare: Who? What? Where? When? Why? How? Gather the material that will develop your points. You may want to put together charts and diagrams or slides and photographs. By constantly working over your material, by noting how the general public responds, you can fine-tune the presentation. Repetition helps tighten your presentation and enables you to make your points more effectively.

Although we warn against twitching and twaddling, we must also point out that there are exceptions. The late Edward R. Murrow, besides being a chain smoker, sweated profusely on camera and habitually pumped a leg up and down while speaking. Bad form? If an unknown tried it today, he'd flunk the audition.

Rather than discuss the impact on a society when it confuses style for substance, we say that for our purposes, in this book, we are attempting to professionalize the layman. Appearances by public officials and laymen on television are generally compared with the performances of professional actors and actresses or comedians, rightly or wrongly. This being the case, we say get ready to do the best you can when you get your chance to "perform" in media.

Marshall McLuhan has noted that the success of any TV performer "depends on his achieving a low-pressure style of presentation." McGinniss, in his book, wrote, "The harder a man tries, the better he must hide it. Television demands gentle wit, irony, understatement: the qualities of Eugene McCarthy. The TV politician cannot make a speech; he must engage in intimate conversation. He must never press. He should suggest, not state; request, not demand. Nonchalance is the key word. Carefully studied nonchalance."

In the 1972 Democratic presidential primary campaign, Senator Humphrey was mindful of his reputation as a nonstop talker and sought to keep that tendency under control. Nevertheless, he came on strong during his first TV debate with Senator George McGovern during the California race. For the second debate, Humphrey did an about-face and pursued a softer, friendlier approach. Even after all his years in the public eye, Humphrey was still struggling to find a comfortable TV presence. McGovern, on the other hand, is by nature more informal, gentle, and easygoing in conversation. When he felt the need to press too hard, to appear dynamic and hard-driving, he fared poorly on television. The performer, then, "must talk to one person at a time," wrote McGinniss. "He is brought into the living room. He is a guest. It is improper to shout."

McGinniss also suggests that the politician should never admit a professional knowledge of television. "He should express distaste for television; suspicion that there is something 'phony' about it. This guarantees him good press, because newspaper reporters, bitter over their loss of prestige to the television men, are certain to stress anti-television remarks."

Such advice has lost a good deal of its steam since it was written. Knocking television is boring. Print-media reporters have grown more sophisticated. They do not automatically regard as the "good guy" the politician who tells them how great they are and how lousy the TV people are. They tend to react to such a gambit in the way they reacted, in pre-TV days, when a politician would say to them, "I used to be a newspaperman myself." This attempt to massage the taut muscles of professional brotherhood is a mistake, and so it is for the politician who tries to play one medium against another these days.

Perhaps a public figure should approach media in this fashion: "Being in the public eye as I am, I suppose I've got to be a bit of a ham. And I'll only start worrying about media when they stop paying attention to me. Frankly, it's part of my job to do this—appear on television or talk to reporters of all kinds—and they are professionals who know what they're doing. I can't complain about the way they do their job and I hope they can't complain too much—or too loudly—about the way I do mine." Enough of the "one is better than another" nonsense. Remember Harry Truman's advice: "If you can't stand the heat, get out of the kitchen."

While we caution against the McGinniss view of print-versus-broadcast competition, we don't hesitate to commend some of the other accumulated wisdom that fills his book:

If you're going to be witty, let a pro write the words.

Give the speaker words to say that will show his *emotional* involvement in the issues.

He should be presented in some kind of "situation" rather than cold in a studio. The situation should look unstaged even if it's not.

"It's not the man we have to change, but rather the *received impression*."

"Stay away from gimmicks." Never let the speaker wear a hat

he doesn't feel comfortable wearing. You can't sell the idea or candidate like a product. With a product, all you want to do is get attention.

When the question of an appropriate campaign photo was under discussion, it was feared that too broad a smile could mar a serious tone. But not to smile is to flirt with looking like a funeral director. A Nixon advisor, Leonard Garment, saw the humor in this dilemma and said, when *the* picture was selected: "So it's a cheerful, grim, serious, and optimistic picture." To which aide Frank Shakespeare added, "And youthful."

Studio lighting: If the lights are too high, they show shadows under eyes, on faces. Better to lower the height of lights and eliminate the shadows. Keep the front key spots low.

Eye contact: Remember the home audience and the head-on camera.

Movement: Don't use arms too much and too predictably.

Avoid closeups, if possible. The director controls the shot, of course, but before air time, discuss matters and see if he will agree to go no "tighter" than a medium waist-shot.

Use visually interesting locations. (But not a location that will distract the viewer with motion or unusual appearance.)

Get a suntan (if nature hasn't provided you with one already).

Camera rehearsal should be limited if the subject tends to perspire easily. (For Nixon, studio air-conditioning was turned up full at least four hours prior to air time. All studio doors were kept closed.)

For panelists: Avoid complicated, multipart questions. They slow the pace and are difficult to follow. Better to ask a follow-up question.

Arie Kopelman, an executive with the Doyle Dane Bernbach advertising agency, which briefly handled the Humphrey campaign in 1968, said, "A candidate can't be too smooth. There have to be some rough edges that cling to the surface of the country and find their way into the nooks and crannies. If a communications effort is too smooth it becomes just that—a communications *effort* on the candidate's behalf rather than a projection of the candidate himself. . . . In the end, communications skills alone can't do it. I don't think it's possible to merchandise a vegetable. I think that eventually the man must show himself."

In TV circles, the feeling is that the auricon camera never lies. It pulls out the hidden *persona*, revealing the "true" image.

## WHAT TO BEAR IN MIND ABOUT TV

It is difficult for any outsider to grasp every aspect of a commercial TV station's dynamics when approaching that station with a request for air time. And, conversely, station personnel will not grasp every aspect of your group's dynamics when you make your approach, assuming that you are not known to media at the time.

With these gaps in communications as a constant, it becomes desirable for you to be aware of the general ground rules under which the TV and radio stations must operate.

The FCC licenses and supervises radio and television, issuing licenses for three-year periods. Before granting a license, the FCC checks the applicant's financial qualifications, personal and business history, the standards of programming that the applicant states will prevail once the license is approved (ratio of news and public-service programming to entertainment programming). The FCC also wants to know the technical details of the proposed station. In recent years, license-renewal applications increasingly have been challenged in markets where groups of people have felt that an incumbent station management failed to serve the community properly.

The FCC also supervises "fairness" disputes or "equal-time" requests. The broadcasters, besides functioning under the FCC's rules, also have their own codes, to which members of the National Association of Broadcasters (NAB) subscribe. The code lends support to the public-access advocates with such statements as, "Commercial television provides a valuable means of augmenting the educational and cultural influences of schools, institutions of higher learning, the home, the church, museums, foundations, and other institutions devoted to education and culture."

The code also asks that TV broadcasters be "thoroughly conversant" with the community's cultural and educational needs and desires; "affirmatively seek out" responsible and accountable educational and cultural institutions of the community; and provide for "reasonable experimentation" in the development of programs directed to cultural and educational advancement.

Responsibility to the community also flows in the opposite direction, from the community and its representatives to the station. Related to the public's use of the airwaves are bans on "profanity, obscenity, smut and vulgarity," prohibitions against attacks on "religion and religious faith," and bans against "excessive or unfair exploitation of others or of their physical or mental afflictions."

Despite these prohibitions, however, in major cities today it is possible to air free discussions on every imaginable topic, with language suited precisely to the topic and the intensity of the discussion. Usually, a station announcer will broadcast at the beginning of the show a warning advising those who might be offended by the language used, to tune out. Certainly, the days when we were startled to hear someone use "hell" or "damn" during a radio or TV appearance are behind us.

On the subject of community responsibility, the NAB code also contains this: "A television broadcaster and his staff occupy a position of responsibility in the community and should conscientiously endeavor to be acquainted fully with its needs and characteristics in order better to serve the welfare of its citizens."

Broadcasters also are required to have "an affirmative responsibility at all times to be informed of public events and to provide coverage consonant with the ends of an informed and enlightened citizenry."

Where controversial public issues are involved, broadcasters agree to consider "on the basis of their individual merits" requests from "individuals, groups or organizations for time to discuss their views on controversial public issues." Such programs are to be identified as such. Broadcasters also agree to use their "best efforts" to apportion time fairly among representative religious groups in the community.

# 2

# Radio

IN EARLY 1973, just after his inauguration, President Nixon started using radio as his major form of communicating with the American public. His aides reported that the president liked radio far better than television. The reasons for this are simple.

Radio is a less forceful medium; in the McLuhan sense, it is "cooler" than television, and because it is cooler, it is calmer. A talk on radio has a different, less strident appeal. It is somehow warmer, more intimate. In a radio message President Nixon doesn't have to submit himself to questions as he does in TV news conferences. A radio speech is a perfect medium for a politician who wants to be heard but not questioned. The "fireside chats" of President Franklin Roosevelt will never be forgotten.

Radio permits you to read your prepared text without *looking* like you are reading, because no one sees you do it. On radio, you can bring to a studio experts who can silently stand by and feed you notes answering questions that may be telephoned in. Radio lets you signal an interviewer that you don't want to answer a question.

Via duplications of audio tape, a radio information program

can be sent across the nation to stations at a cost a fraction of that of doing a TV program on film or video tape.

With telephone hookups to broadcasting equipment you can literally telephone a story across the nation to many cities on an "exclusive" basis. Long-distance telephone calls from a remote place can put you on a radio network, via UPI or Associated Press (AP) radio or PBS (Public Broadcast Service), in a few seconds, no matter where you are.

The top TV-news executive producers listen to radio when they get up before they look at the morning newspapers, because they know radio news is ahead of television or print. A short radio spot on a local morning news program can become a feature on the TV evening news.

If you have a news story, using radio may be the best step you can take to get heard. Don't forget that a major difference between radio and television is the degree to which each relies on sound. Radio doesn't care what you look like, only that you sound interesting. You can sound handsome or beautiful. It provides a great opportunity for the person who has a command of the language and can use his voice well. The radio lets the listeners decide what the voice "looks" like, often to the benefit of the person speaking.

Today radio is getting more and more powerful as a source for news. In all parts of the country it is radio that consistently beats television and print at being first to bring news stories to the public.

Some stations have very few opportunities for permitting the public access to the station's listeners. Some don't have any programs as such at all. A few disc jockeys may have live broadcasts, but the news shows may be completely automated, with only one or two engineers at the station who play recorded cassettes. The news broadcasts may be patched-in via telephone or special circuits, so that the station doesn't even have an announcer. These stations offer no hope for a local group unless it can get on one of the Sunday programs set aside for public access. Listening to the station will tell you just how it is operated.

There are some stations that broadcast nothing but news. These are the easiest to work with if you learn the techniques needed. The first thing to do is listen to the stations, and then decide what kind of programming they have and how you can use it. Some stations' only contact with the community they serve is via a "community bulletin board," where the announcer will read ten-second spots telling about a local cake sale, a PTA meeting, and such. All it takes to get announcements on this kind of station is to represent a charity or other nonpolitical cause and send in announcements about ten days before the event you want to promote. The average station will run the announcement once or twice the day before the event, not more. If you are plugging a charity like a United Fund Drive or a League of Women Voters voter-registration campaign, there is a good chance that an individual station will run the announcement every day, more than once, for a week or more. To do this, you have to write a convincing letter to the station's community-affairs director asking for the station's help.

After you have received the free time, be sure to write a thank-you note to the station, telling them that you appreciate the time given. This will do wonders when you go back and ask them for help another time.

Because sound is so important, be sure your spokesperson has a good voice. A good voice is defined as one that is interesting to listen to. A professionally trained voice with clear enunciation sounds professional; thus, hiring an announcer to read your comments may not be a good idea. The voice you select to represent your views should be clear, memorable, and believable. Naturally the quality of the voice is secondary to the intelligence and capability of the person who has it. If there is a choice to be made between several voices, listen to each on tape recorder or telephone to test which one comes over as more believable and understandable.

The booking process on radio is the same as it is on television. You write or call the person who is in charge of guests. The major difference is that there are fewer and fewer radio programs that interview guests; thus, there are fewer people to work with at the station.

Radio is much easier to work with than television when you have a "hot" news announcement. Chances are that it will be used if you know how the system works. When you call the station, there is a good chance that you will be taped for broadcast at that time via telephone. This will be done by the person you talk to. The interview will be edited and perhaps played three or more times in the next few hours. If the station is affiliated with other stations, your interview may be shared with them.

To get a news announcement or opinion on the air, you should write a short statement of ten or twenty words that will interest the interviewer when he gets on the telephone. What you say should involve a subject in the news at that moment. Call the station* and ask for the newsroom. Identify yourself and then give your statement.

If you have done your job well, you may spend the next few minutes being interviewed or may perhaps be asked to come to the station for a lengthy interview.

Frequently your call will be screened by a news researcher or reporter before you are given a chance to talk to a newscaster. It is possible that the entire conversation will be aired as it was recorded, but most often a producer will edit your remarks.

You will have to listen to the station to find out what you said. If the editing leads you to believe there was some change in your meaning, call the producer back and explain your point of view. You may get another chance.

## RECORDING A NEWS STATEMENT

If you have called the station, passed the screener, and now are to be interviewed by someone on the station for later broadcast, take these hints: Remember you are being recorded. Sometimes you will hear a "beep" every few seconds indicating that your telephone call is monitored. (This may or may not be the case, so even if you don't hear a beep, always assume that your voice is being taped when you call a radio station news room.)

Don't call to arrange for an interview without organizing your statement. Wait until the interviewer says, "Go ahead, we are now ready to record you."

Then give a short statement explaining your point of view or

* Often the number of the newsroom is not listed in the telephone book. You will have to do some homework to get the number of the newsroom (after hours and on weekends the switchboard is closed). Having the unlisted newsroom number lets you get to the news editor directly, and once you have the number, you are more often accepted as a legitimate source.

announcement. Don't talk for more than thirty seconds—that's less than thirty words. Don't be surprised when the announcer or interviewer breaks into a sentence. He will do this if he doesn't understand what you said or understands it very well and wants you to repeat it to make sure his audience does too.

If he asks an unfair question or one that will be hard to answer, just ignore it and continue to say your piece. Try very hard to rehearse what you want to say with a friend before you call. Get a tape recorder, so that you can listen to the way you sound and to what you say.

If you possibly can, try to see the news producer at one local station before starting out to book a series of radio programs. A few minutes with a professional can save a great deal of time and money. You can explain what you are doing and why you feel you should get free time to be heard. If you are fortunate enough to get someone locally who wants to help, your job will be a lot easier. Try this before doing it on your own.

## GETTING HEARD

Let's assume you are the spokesperson for a group of people in your town advocating senior-citizen housing. The mayor makes an announcement that there will be a hearing the next evening at a regular town council meeting. Perhaps he hopes that there won't be enough time for people who are opposed to his views to get there in numbers or in time to be heard.

You want as many people to be there as possible. Your committee has been called, and everyone you can reach says that they will come; but you want to show the council that there are many people in the community who want senior-citizen housing. You want a tremendous turnout to influence the council members.

Call the radio stations that have news announcements. Ask for the news department:

"Hello, I'm Ted Frederick, chairman of the West Orange Senior Citizens Housing Committee. An important public meeting has been called by the mayor for tomorrow at eight o'clock in the Municipal Building." Pause here, waiting for him to ask why it's important. "We are asking your help in telling your listeners about this because the meeting was called at the last minute and there isn't time for us to reach all the people who we feel will want to come to the meeting." Pause again.

The producer will say, "Okay. I'll tape your message," or he will ask you to bring in or send the exact text of your announcement. If you possibly can, do what he asks, making certain you know his name and the correct name of the person to whom you must send the announcement. Then ask him when he thinks he will air the message.

If he does air the announcement, be sure to write a letter thanking him for his help. If he doesn't, write asking why he decided not to use what you said. You may learn something for the next time.

## INTERVIEWS AND TALK SHOWS

Many radio stations do almost no in-depth interviews during the week; their lengthy talk programs are usually aired on Sunday and often recorded in advance. Some are actually the sound track of a TV interview used the same day on a TV station.

To get on a panel or radio interview program, your approach is best made by letter, with a succinct query to the correct person. Call the station to find out who is the producer of the program you feel is right for your message. There is no better way to get ignored than by writing or calling the wrong person. Do your homework.

The written query should be short, but long enough to tell your story.

Here is an example of a written query requesting time on a radio interview show for the authors of this book:

Ms. Nina Kaufman
The Betty Groebli Show
4001 Nebraska Ave., N.W.
Washington, D.C. 20016

Dear Ms. Kaufman:

Fred Danzig and Ted Klein have written a book which may complicate your life but will probably help many of your listeners better understand how you book guests.

The authors, both working writers with news and radio experience, have written a book, *How To Be Heard*, which if used, will help many individuals gain access to the media—your program included.

They are available for interviews in Washington any time during the next few months. The book will be published in August. Enclosed is a fact sheet about it, and a copy of the book on its way to you.

If you would like to discuss booking Danzig and Klein, please call.

Cordially,

## WIRE SERVICES AND PROGRAM PACKAGERS

Often a radio news program is completely made up by clipping bulletins from a wire-service teleprinter. The announcer will sometimes do this himself just before going on the air.

Therefore, to get on a radio station that uses only wire-service news, your story will have had to be on the wire—another important reason why a wire-service use of your story can mean so much.

If you are fortunate, a telephone call to the Associated Press newsroom in your city will result in a 100-word story on the main, or "A," wire (see Chapter 5 for more information on wire services). This story will be written a few minutes after you give it and then relayed across the country to radio and TV station newsrooms.

Shortly after you hang up you may be able to tune in almost any radio station with an all-news format and hear your story. The stations that operate with regular newscasts on the hour or half-hour use less news.

Depending on the judgment of the person you contact at the wire service, the news editor of the radio station, and the time of day your story moves on the wire, you may or may not get exposure for your message.

A good time to get on the wire with a news story is often late at night, when a station is getting ready for its morning newscast. If you know the telephone number of the wire service or the newsroom of the station, your call can result in radio newscasts throughout the morning of the next day.

There are still many stations that depend on outside packagers for many radio interviews and public-service programs. When you call a radio station and ask for the producer of a given program, you may get the name of a company that does this work.

Some programs are produced by local or national service organizations, trade unions, religious groups, and other organizations with an interest in being heard. Usually the name of the producer is given at the end of the program. Listen before you call.

You can learn a great deal about how the program is put together just by listening to it. Then plan your approach.

## SPOT ANNOUNCEMENTS

Many organizations with a national story to tell will pay for professionally produced radio spot announcements. The same people who make the TV spots and news features will be able to syndicate a radio feature (see page 12 for their names and addresses).*

You should not attempt to package your own radio spots without professional help. In most cities the local radio stations know who does this sort of work. A call to, or lunch meeting with, the news director of a station that you feel does a good job is a worthwhile investment to make.

Here is an example of a 20-second spot from the National Institutes of Health. Note the style: upper-case type, and ellipses used for pauses. This announcement was sent to all stations in the country; the only cost was for postage and printing.

NATIONAL INSTITUTES OF HEALTH
PUBLIC SERVICE ANNOUNCEMENT

RADIO COPY (20 SECONDS)

* The cost for a syndicated radio spot recorded and sent to hundreds of stations is about $700.

DEPARTMENT OF HEALTH, EDUCATION, AND WELFARE
PUBLIC HEALTH SERVICE
NATIONAL INSTITUTES OF HEALTH
BETHESDA, MARYLAND 20014

NATIONAL INSTITUTES OF HEALTH
PUBLIC SERVICE ANNOUNCEMENT

20 SECONDS

| VIDEO | AUDIO |
|---|---|
| Color Slide, Allergy Research--An Introduction Booklet, with NIH Address | ALLERGIES....CAN MAKE LIFE MISERABLE.... AND SCIENTISTS....ARE SEEKING WAYS.... TO PREVENT....AND TREAT....THEM. A NEW PAMPHLET....ALLERGY RESEARCH.... IS AVAILABLE FROM....THE NATIONAL INSTITUTES OF HEALTH....FREE. WRITE.... ALLERGY....NIH....BETHESDA....MARYLAND.... 20014. |

FIG. I

FIG. 2

ALLERGIES . . . . CAN MAKE LIFE MISERABLE . . . . AND SCIENTISTS ARE SEEKING . . . . WAYS TO PREVENT AND TREAT THEM. A NEW PAMPHLET . . . . *ALLERGY RESEARCH* . . . . IS AVAILABLE FROM . . . . THE NATIONAL INSTITUTES OF HEALTH . . . . FREE. WRITE . . . . ALLERGY . . . . NIH . . . . BETHESDA . . . . MARYLAND . . . . 20014.

Example of TV Public-Service Spot Announcement

The script (fig. 1) and a single slide (fig. 2) were sent by a HEW information office to all TV stations in the country. This is an excellent example of the best format and technique to get on the air with an announcement.

## TALK SHOWS USING TELEPHONE CALLS

"Call-in," or "dial-log," radio invites all listeners to call in and deliver opinions or information to the station's audience. The format usually centers around a host, or hostess, who handles the calls, usually on a "tape-delay" basis so that offensive comments can be caught and killed before airing. The subject may be sports, politics, or a wide range of news topics.

Listen to these programs if you have them in your area. In the large cities where such formats abound, you will hear the same people again and again as they make the rounds, from one program to another and from one station to another.

When you call, you will probably hear a busy signal. This can be frustrating, but if you call often enough, someone—probably the show's producer—will finally answer and ask you what you want to discuss. This procedure can be called censorship, but it also represents a "show biz" quality, since the producer wants to present an interesting, lively program and may feel that your subject needs further thought before he puts you through to the listening audience. By screening the callers, the producer gives himself some alternatives for a change of pace and should, if he knows his business, enhance the entertainment value of the show. In any case, be patient. Use your time to formulate your comments. Take a deep breath every few minutes to calm your nerves and steady your voice. And when you hear the words, "Hello. You're on the air," turn off your radio and start talking. Try hard not to repeat yourself; when you finish, if there are no questions, thank the host and hang up.

You may prefer to have your message written. Read your twenty or thirty words. Then stop talking. If the person likes what you say and is interested in hearing more, he will question you. If he doesn't or feels that you are too long-winded, he will cut you off. So your first ten words are very important.

## LISTS TO USE

Every classified telephone book has the listing for local radio stations. In Appendix II we have printed a list of educational stations. The best source for information on what program is on, and when, is the station itself. Many are now organized to send lists of programs to interested people acting in the public interest. A telephone call or letter to the station manager will usually result in a prompt reply. Once again, listen to the station several times before calling or writing. You may decide that there is no one on the station with whom you want to talk. That knowledge can save you time and effort.

Community organizations can often get a radio station to help them when a TV outlet will not. For example, each year for the past five years, radio station WMTR in suburban Morris County, New Jersey, has joined with the local Kiwanis Club to hold a radio auction. In 1973 a total of $8500 was raised by the Kiwanis for their Youth Activities Fund.

The listener-supported FM radio stations in New York (WBAI); Berkeley, California (KPFA); Los Angeles (KPFK); and Houston (KPFT) take a great interest in community activities, as do almost all educational stations (see Appendix II for the national list of stations).

By presenting yourself to the usually accessible station manager, you can talk over what it is you want the radio station to do. If all you really need is announcements of meetings, mail them. It doesn't make much sense to go to him with a request for a radio interview unless you have thought out your appeal and are prepared to suggest a program format that fits in with the station's operating philosophy. Listen to the station before approaching the management to ask for air time.

Some stations just will not put anyone but their announcers on the air. For them, send announcements. Some radio stations will only use one- or two-minute recorded interviews or read all news from wire-service copy. Some actually will go out and record entire meetings.

The news directors or managers of many educational radio stations will send a recording crew to a meeting—or use a telephone hookup to cover a meeting live. All it takes is advance planning and a willingness to spend the time talking to station managers to arrange this sort of coverage.

In those areas where there are only a few stations and they do not schedule news programs or public-affairs or talk shows that make use of interviews with guests, you will have to content yourself, perhaps, with responding to a station editorial, if possible.

If a station carries an editorial that endorses or opposes a candidate for office or takes sides in a public issue, the station must offer those who wish to respond with an opposing viewpoint a "reasonable opportunity" to respond within twenty-four hours.

If the editorial is carried within seventy-two hours of election day, the station must follow the response procedure "sufficiently far in advance of the broadcast to enable the candidate or candidates to have a reasonable opportunity to prepare a response and to present it in a timely fashion," according to FCC rules.

If a station carries an attack upon "the honesty, character, integrity or like personal qualities of an identified person or group" during its presentation of a controversial issue, the FCC requires that "within a reasonable time and in no event later than one week after the attack," the station get in touch with the person or group. The subject must be notified by the station of the date, time, and name of the broadcast; be provided with a script or tape, or an accurate summary if a script or tape isn't available; and be offered "a reasonable opportunity to respond over the licensee's facilities."

Exceptions to the personal-attack provisions are attacks on foreign groups or foreign public figures; personal attacks made by legally qualified candidates, their authorized spokespersons, or those associated with them in a campaign; and bona fide newscasts, bona fide news interviews, and on-the-spot coverage of a bona fide news event. The target of a station editorial, however, must be notified, supplied with text or tape, and given an opportunity to respond over the air.

If your group is convinced that the station in your area is not serving the local community properly, you can write letters to the station, to the network with which it is affiliated, and to the FCC. You can file petitions against license renewal. You can try to arrange meetings with the station management. You can try to wrest the station away from its present management by filing a competing application for the license.

Remember that a station must keep its license-renewal application on hand for public inspection. Compare the station's application with those from other stations in your area and in other parts of the country. There are instances in which citizens' groups have improved programming after simply sitting down with the station management over a period of time and working out new program formats.*

Citizen groups seeking to improve broadcasting standards in a community can obtain assistance from the following groups:

American Civil Liberties Union
22 East Fortieth Street
New York, N.Y. 10016
(212) 725-1222.

Anti-Defamation League of B'nai B'rith
315 Lexington Avenue
New York, N.Y. 10016
(212) 689-7400

Broadcasting and Film Commission
National Council of Churches of Christ in the U.S.A.
475 Riverside Drive
New York, N.Y. 10027
(212) 870-2567

Institute for American Democracy
1750 Pennsylvania Avenue
Washington, D.C. 20005
(202) 466-8428

National Citizens Committee for Broadcasting
4101 Nebraska Avenue, N.W.
Washington, D.C. 20016
(202) 244-3500

Office of Communication
United Church of Christ
289 Park Avenue South
New York, N.Y. 10010
(212) 475-2127

* A superb book to use in connection with this rather technical aspect of community participation is *Guide to Understanding Broadcast License Applications and Other FCC Forms*, by Ralph M. Jennings. This paperback consists of detailed explanation of broadcaster rights and the public's rights; reprints official FCC forms; and offers step-by-step procedures to deal with gaining access to the airwaves in the event that a local manager or station management has not been receptive to airing all aspects of a community's "problems, needs and interests."

Citizens Communication Center
1812 N Street N.W.
Washington, D.C. 20036
(202) 296-4328

Action for Children's Television
46 Austin Street
Newtonville, Mass. 02160
(617) 244-5941

Black Efforts for Soul in Television
1015 North Carolina Avenue S.E.
Washington, D.C. 20003
(202) 547-1258

NAACP Legal Defense and Educational Fund
10 Columbus Circle
New York, N.Y. 10019
(212) 586-8397

Mexican American Legal Defense and Educational Fund
145 Ninth Street
San Francisco, Calif. 94103
(415) 863-5345

National Mexican-American Anti-Defamation Committee
1356 Connecticut Avenue N.W.
Washington, D.C. 20036
(202) 833-2667

Stern Community Law Firm
2005 L Street N.W.
Washington, D.C. 20036
(202) 659-8132

# 3

# Newspapers

NEWSPAPER COLUMNS ARE OPEN. They beckon to you. They beckon simply by being there, not by overtly begging you to send in your press release (see Chapter 8). Following are some examples of the uses to which they may be put.

A woman in a suburban community learns that a land developer is about to develop a lovely wooded area near her home. She takes it upon herself to meet with local officials to discuss the possibility of the park district purchasing the tract in order to preserve the land. She is told that she first must prove that people want the land preserved in its natural state. Together with a friend, she forms an organization, Friends of Brook Park. The organization's creation is announced by means of press releases to area newspapers. Petitions are circulated. The petition project also is reported to the newspapers. Thousands of signatures are collected on the petitions. Before long, the effort is being given a good chance of achieving its purpose.

A woman in another community hears about an organization called Friends of Children of Vietnam, which aids Vietnamese children who have been orphaned, left homeless, or injured during the war. She decides to set up a local chapter. Where to begin? She chooses a date for a public meeting at the village library, reserves the room, and sends a press release to the newspapers in the area to publicize the meeting. In her press release she explains that the plight of child victims of the Vietnam war and fund-raising efforts on their behalf will be discussed. A good turnout gives the project impetus. Plans are immediately made for a garage sale, art sale, and cake sale. The newspapers print the releases. The effort is on its way to success.

In Evanston, Illinois, students become concerned that millions of people seemingly want to learn, while other millions have something to teach them. How to get these groups together voluntarily? The six students form the Learning Exchange. They distribute leaflets that invite people to sign up. Those who want to learn, those who want to teach, or those who just want to get together to discuss topics of mutual interest are enrolled. The organizers get newspapers and radio stations to publicize their project. Posters are placed in stores, libraries, and coin laundries. The project takes root and grows.

The examples are endless. In each case, there is an idea that is given expression by means of a press release. This chapter will tell you how to work up a press release and get it printed.

## ORGANIZATION

The newspaper's organizational table is, for our purposes, relatively simple: editors and reporters. If you live in a small town or a neighborhood that is served by a local newspaper, chances are you can deal directly with the editor of the paper. The staff usually consists of the editor and one or two reporters. There are others, too, but you will be concerned chiefly with developing contact with those who actually write the stories for the paper.

A major city newspaper will have editors, associate editors, a managing editor, news editor, Sunday editor, city editor, assistant city editor, telegraph and cable editors, makeup editors, editors for various departments (sports, finance, drama, society, photography, religion, television, real estate, books, art, film, dance, music, the family, furnishings, fashions, and food), state news editor, copyreaders, rewritemen, reporters, photographers, artists, clerks, office boys, copy boys, messengers, and librarians.

The suburban or neighborhood paper will telescope roles. An

editor and a good reporter can do it all, including the photography, if necessary.

Read your papers carefully. Get to know the names of the by-line reporters and feature writers. Check the papers' deadlines for editorial copy and pictures. Bear in mind that the earlier you can deliver copy before the deadline, the better your chance of getting it printed.

The larger newspapers with department editors should present no special problems when it comes to determining the proper desk, or reporter, for your contact work. There are a growing number of consumer-oriented features and news stories in the papers today. This aspect of journalistic coverage will become more apparent as the so-called consumerism movement becomes more sophisticated and more widespread. Many newspapers also include ecology editors in their tables of organization, but at present this assignment is usually given to the reporter who shows the keenest interest in it.

## USING THE TELEPHONE

If your organization deals with school matters, you will naturally direct your press releases and telephone calls to the reporter or editor who covers that beat in your community. You may already know that person, but if not, simply call the newspaper and ask. The switchboard can guide you to the proper desk. Be polite and patient as you seek out the proper party. When you are connected and the reporter gets on the phone, do not waste time. The reporter is busy and doesn't have time for small talk with strangers. Say what's on your mind. Explain who you are and what you want. The reporter will ask questions while taking notes. If your call is simply to give notice of a meeting, tell the reporter who is holding the meeting, what's on the agenda, the names of any guest speakers, the place, time, date, and any other information about the meeting that makes it newsworthy. Explain why the meeting is important. You may have a statement from the head of the group that can be used in the article you are asking the reporter to write. The quotation is important if a subjective viewpoint is expressed in connection with the call to the membership. Proper journalistic style in such news items requires attribution for any subjective expression.

When it appears, the story may take this form:

> Midtown, May 3—The Midtown Concerned Parents Association will hold a public meeting to discuss the forthcoming $6.5 million school construction bond issue in School District 1 on May 11 at the Midtown High School auditorium at 8:30 P.M.
>
> Charles Jones, association president, said details of the bond issue will be analyzed at the meeting by School Superintendent James Smith and architect Walter Brown of Brown & Brown, the firm that designed the proposed new elementary school. Admission is free. Refreshments will be served.

If ever your meeting has an admission charge, or if a collection of funds will be made at the meeting, it is wise to include this information.

The above news item is a routine one. Small newspapers are filled with them. There should be no problem in getting it printed, in one form or another. (Many newspapers automatically relegate such "advances" to a calendar-of-events column.)

Supposing that the bond issue, involving increased taxes, is a controversial matter in the community and the local newspaper has assigned one reporter to the ongoing story. You have spoken to this reporter on the telephone to call attention to the meeting. It happens that the reporter is preparing a lengthy story, or "take-out," on the bond issue. Your notice may end up as a sentence or a paragraph somewhere in that story. Do not get upset if this happens. Not every piece of information that a newspaper prints gets a prominent display beneath its own headline. Alert editors try to combine stories in order to save space and to make the paper a more convenient package for readers.

It may turn out that your modest announcement actually triggers a larger story. Suppose that the bond-issue controversy is a heated one and the school superintendent has come under attack for not making public details of the construction program. Suppose that there have been calls for him to inform the taxpayers more fully. Your news item, by including the fact that the school superintendent is going to be at this meeting, can escalate the meeting into one of greater news value for the community. The reporter may decide to handle the story in this manner:

Midtown, May 3—School Superintendent James Smith, under fire for allegedly avoiding questions on the District 1 school construction bond issue, has agreed to appear at a public meeting on May 11 to discuss the details of the controversial building program.

The story may go on to supply background material about the situation in which Smith has found himself. The reporter may have spoken to Smith and included some quotes from him in the story. Your Midtown Concerned Parents Association may be mentioned at the tail of the story. So it goes. Don't complain. Look at it this way: The heavier emphasis on the "news" treatment of the story should build attendance for the meeting. And that, after all, is your goal.

In taking this information over the phone, the reporter should be given a telephone number in case the need arises to verify material or add information to the story.

## NEWS RELEASES

If your meeting is a regularly scheduled weekly or monthly one, you should handle the publicity by mail or by delivering your release to the newspaper by hand, dropping it off on your way to or from work.

Being aware of the newspaper's deadlines, you will get your release to the newspaper office as far in advance of publication day as possible.

The papers that you deal with will be more receptive to your stories if you supply useful information in complete form. Your press release should include a name, address, and telephone number for the reporter's follow-up questions. If possible, provide alternate names and numbers. If the contact named on your release is not able to be at that number for periods of time, arrange to have another person receive the call and supply information, or find out the needed information and relay it to the reporter. Promptly. Reporters who are racing deadlines—and you must assume that they *always* are racing deadlines—do not like to be told that the person listed as the contact isn't around and won't be back for a few hours or will call back tomorrow.

If the required information isn't available from anyone but the contact whose name appears on the press release, make certain that you leave a telephone number at the listed number so that the person who is fielding the reporter's call can tell the reporter something like, "We can have someone call you right back. Or would you rather call another number where [the contact] can be reached?"

In other words, show that you mean to cooperate quickly and that you are treating the reporter's call on a priority basis. A few minutes' time can make the difference between your story's making a deadline and getting into print or missing a deadline and possibly missing with it your only chance for newspaper publicity. If your story is held over to the next day, or the next week, your story may lose its news value, or get crowded out again by fresher news stories. Always remember that speed counts in dealing with the newspaper people in your community.

The telephone and the typewriter are the reporter's basic tools. If you have a news event to report, call up those whose deadlines are nearest at hand. In a major city, calling the local news bureau of the wire services should get the news out quickly. The wire services will disseminate the news to client newspapers and radio and television stations (see Chapter 5).

When dealing with local activities, of interest only to local media, be prepared to handle your publicity program by telephone. The press release can be sent over by mail or delivered by hand by way of confirming the information you have provided in your telephone call. You may find that you can give pertinent information on the telephone and offer to send additional material, "backgrounder" or "fact-sheet" material, by mail.

## *Style*

Release material should be typewritten and double-spaced, on one side of the paper (see Chapter 8 for more information on releases). Such detail may sound ridiculous, but you would be surprised at what passes for releases if you could look through a newspaper's mail one day. Often, newspaper copy editors will "pencil down" a release, attach a headline to it, and send it to the printer without changing a word or comma (by "pencil down," we mean the editing process: marking paragraphs, standardizing the style, and so on).

Your release also should make certain that full names are used, not only one initial and the surname. Double-check spelling of all names. Include proper affiliations for those who are mentioned in your press release, unless you are bunching up a list of committee members. It's good practice to double-check the date and day of the week in your release.

In assembling your release, begin with this:

From: Name
Address
Telephone Number (or the name of the contact and the contact's telephone number, if different from yours).

One-line caption, or headline:

M.C.P.A. HOLDS PUBLIC MEETING
TO DISCUSS BOND ISSUE

Now, the main copy for your release. Ask yourself who, what, when, where, and why and write down your answers:

Midtown Concerned Parents Association
Public meeting
Friday, May 11 at 8:30 P.M.
Midtown High School auditorium, Oak Street and Maple Road
To discuss details of the $6.5 million school construction bond issue.

Putting all this together, you now have your press release lead:

> The Midtown Concerned Parents Association will conduct a public meeting on Friday, May 11 at 8:30 P.M. at the Midtown High School auditorium, Oak Street and Maple Road, to discuss details of the $6.5 million school construction bond issue.

Subsequent paragraphs of your press release should elaborate on the what, who, and why by noting the guest speakers, the reasons for the meeting at this time, and other details about the meeting, including the information that admission is free.

You might want to include some of the questions that will be answered at the meeting as well as some background about the bond issue. Do not try to slant your release by ignoring the fact that there is opposition to the bond issue. Be objective and fair.

If the editor senses that your press release has "touched all the bases" fairly, he may be inclined to "pencil it down" and take it to the printer. If he senses that you have loaded the release with one-sided opinion, he will give the release to a reporter for a rewrite job.

## WHEN YOUR STORY ISN'T USED

If your notice doesn't appear in the paper, you can call up the editor. Since your item didn't run, you'd like to know if it was because of the mails (nondelivery) or because it was improperly prepared. You just want to make sure he at least received it. If the editor is unfamiliar with the release, he may refer you to someone else. Stay with it until you establish that the story was received by someone at the paper. You may be told that, yes, the release arrived and it was fine. It was just that space was tight today, or this week, and since the meeting is still two weeks off, it was decided to hold it in favor of more timely stories. Your item was squeezed out, perhaps, by a more important story. You may be told that your story is now in the "holdover," or "carry-over," the galleys that contain surplus stories from this issue of the paper. These galleys are supposed to be used for the next issue, and they usually are. After all, the story is in type; the paper has an investment in it, and if the story doesn't run, the cost of setting the type will have been wasted.

Whatever the reason, don't get angry. Don't argue. Be courteous. Think before you speak. The newspaper office is a busy place and the people in it have better things to do than argue with people over "routine" releases that haven't made an edition. At the same time, your polite and persistent interest in the ultimate fate of your release will help to endow it with something of a priority. The old saying "The squeaking wheel gets the oil" happens to be valid. If you content yourself with sending in releases and never seeing them in print and if you fail to find out what went wrong, you are not serving your committee's publicity needs effectively. You must show an interest, overcome your natural reticence by talking about the lively interest in the subject matter on the part of many readers, and in that way improve your batting average. But remember, do your "pushing" with good humor, good sense, and good manners. Don't get paranoid about failure. You are dealing with people at the newspaper who may not know you except as a voice on the telephone. They can help you or hurt you. Don't give them any reason to hurt you.

Suppose that the local papers you are dealing with have taken editorial positions on the issue that you are supporting. The editorialists have blasted your efforts and yourself. You might believe that the news columns of the papers will either be closed to you or, if open, will slant your material in order to support and strengthen the editorial viewpoint.

Most of the time, your fears will prove to be groundless. In fact, it may be that the paper will bend over backward to give your views publicity just because it wants to avoid the charge that it is slanting the news in order to support its editorial stand.

But let us suppose that you're right: the paper *is* giving your group a raw deal. You have overwhelming "evidence" of this. You must first present your evidence to neutral observers and ask them for an opinion. If others, removed from the situation, agree with your judgment, then you must pursue a program that will remedy the situation by opening the paper's news columns to you.

You can proceed in a number of ways. Try to arrange a meeting with the publisher and the editor so that you can exchange views and see if they will agree that something should and will be done. At this point, you won't ask them to change their editorial position. All you're asking for is access to the community through legitimate news stories that they will print in their news columns.

If the publisher and the editor will not meet with you and reject your premise, take your plight to others and try to enlist their help. Perhaps a friend, or a friend of a friend, one who may know the publisher or the editor, can be consulted. Perhaps they will intervene. Or perhaps a highly regarded public official who is friendly to your cause can be persuaded to intervene on your behalf.

Should your tactful efforts fail to change things, you will then have to seek alternate means of reaching the community. Advertisement? Sure, if you have the money and if the paper will agree to run it. Another route would be to print and distribute flyers, put up posters, conduct mailings and perhaps a telephone campaign, too. If radio and television are available to you, concentrate on them.

It is a painful situation when a community's only newspaper fails in its responsibility to be fair to the varying opinions held by its readers. But we know that situations of this sort occasionally occur. There are cases in which residents in such communities have banded together and published their own newspaper, pledged to fair treatment for all voices. This is a costly, difficult, and time-consuming task, however, and more properly belongs in a separate book. Before you choose the route of starting your own paper, try everything else. Again and again, if necessary.

## PROBLEMS AND HOW TO SOLVE THEM

The "slanting" of news is a perennial problem for media. "Admittedly, the ideal of objectivity is hard to realize," wrote Lester Markel, a retired editor of the *New York Times*. He added, "Lapses into non-objectivity are more easily, and much more frequently, achieved by editing tricks and word manipulation."

Editing tricks and word manipulation. A single-column, one-line headline over a one-paragraph story located at the bottom of a page deep inside the paper isn't quite as attention-grabbing as a three- or four-column headline over a twenty-inch story up front. And while you may be pleased with your story's position, or "play," in the paper, your pleasure may turn to anger if you sense that the story has been written from a standpoint that clashes with your own. You may end up wishing that the well-placed story was handled as a one-paragraph item deep inside, where it could cause you less damage.

The newspapers that you deal with will probably have editors and reporters on the staff who consider themselves disciples of "advocacy journalism." These newsmen believe that if a writer makes his biases clear to the reader, it is permissible—indeed, imperative—that he become a partisan in a cause. Objective newswriting—if there be such an animal—can "get in the way" of truth, the advocacy journalists believe. Where does this professional schism leave you? Just let the newspapermen work out the rules and techniques by which they must do their work. Your role is to supply them with facts as background material, to make yourself or your group available for questions and "on-site inspection," to tell the truth even if it hurts, and generally to try to help reporters in their work.

## WRITING HINTS

Your role also involves writing a news release that is professionally acceptable. There's really no great mystery to it, of course. The width of the newspaper column makes it important that the writer remember to stick to short sentences and short paragraphs. Otherwise, a lengthy paragraph that comes from a typewriter will appear far longer when squeezed into the narrow column of type. Try to avoid long sentences and long paragraphs, because they look too formidable and discourage readers.

Also remember to keep it simple. Do not try for fine writing or cuteness. Don't talk about a "convocation" when you mean a "meeting." Or "conflagration when you mean fire." In some places, policemen are fond of telling reporters that they "apprehended the perpetrator." Avoid this kind of writing. Your writing should be more to the point.

To achieve brevity, read and reread what you have written. Look for the "water" in your sentences and squeeze it out. If you write, "Among the speakers who will be present at the meeting to address the audience are . . . ," you can squeeze the water out with, "The speakers' list includes. . . ." If you write, "He attended the University of Connecticut, from which he received a Bachelor of Arts degree in June, 1963 . . . ," squeeze it down to, "He is a graduate of the University of Connecticut."

If you are assigned the job of writing up your organization's last meeting for the local newspaper, organize yourself as follows: Begin with the lead. State the result of the action or meeting. Answer these questions: Who met? What happened? When did they meet? Where? And, when pertinent, Why? and How?

The rest of your story will build from the lead paragraph, or paragraphs. Your first paragraph doesn't always have to include answers to all of these basic questions. You can deal with them in subsequent paragraphs.

If the Midtown Concerned Parents Association met last night, you do not begin your story with, "The Midtown Concerned Parents Association meeting last night at the Midtown High School auditorium was called to order by Charles Jones, association president, at 8:42 P.M." You are *not* writing the minutes of the meeting. You *are* arranging the minutes into a news story format. For example:

> Midtown, May 12—The Midtown Concerned Parents Association has called on the District 1 School Board to add a remedial reading program to the high school curriculum.

In examining the foregoing lead, you will see the who and what but no when, where, why, and how. On to the second paragraph:

> Charles Jones, association president, said during a well-attended public meeting last night at Midtown High School that next year's budget could handle the estimated $40,000 cost by eliminating such "frills" as uniforms for 18 pom-pom girls, new furniture for the teachers' lounge, and a course in dog training.

The second paragraph tells us when, where, how, and a bit more about who, but leaves why for the next paragraph.

Leads are varied. Sometimes the why is the key to the story, as in this version:

> Midtown, May 12—Citing below-grade reading levels among Midtown High School graduates, the Midtown Concerned Parents Association has called for the speedy introduction of remedial reading classes.

The how lead for this story might run as follows:

> Midtown, May 12—The Midtown Concerned Parents Association wants "frills" such as pom-pom girls' uniforms and a dog-training class removed from next year's school budget so that a remedial reading program can be introduced at Midtown High.

In writing of this sort, you can decide on how to position the central action. The key is to keep the central action in the lead. Once the central action—in this case, the call for a remedial reading program—is placed in the lead, subsequent paragraphs can elaborate and add support as they follow, each one a separate unit. Do not worry about transitional sentences to link paragraphs. At the newspaper, the copy editor may elect to switch paragraphs up or down, and your carefully developed transitional sentences can slow him down. If space is short, the copy editor will want to "bite" your story from the bottom. That is, he will cut from the last paragraph and work upward until the story fits the available space that he has set aside for it.

If your lead has supplied the central action, identifying the event, place, and time, your second paragraph should finish up the remaining questions. Your first two paragraphs, then, should be so tightly written that if all that follows them is cut, the broad sense of the story will not be lost.

## "NO COMMENT" AND "OFF THE RECORD"

"No comment." When you read those words or hear someone utter them during a television newscast, you're supposed to think that you are dealing with a professional, one who knows how to handle the media.

The expression has a number of meanings or interpretations: "I don't have to tell you anything" (emphasis on "I" and "you"). "I'm under wraps; my lawyers won't let me say another word." "Are you kidding, Mac? I'm not going to answer that one." "Who the hell do you think you are, hitting me with that dirty question?"

These interpretations point up what a troublesome phrase "No comment" can be. The best thing to do with it is to avoid using it.

If a reporter asks, "Has the Midtown Concerned Parents outfit folded up?" you may be tempted to respond, "No comment." What you are telling him, then, is that he's on to something. You are encouraging speculation about the demise of the organization. You said, "No comment," because you didn't want to give a flat yes or no answer or you think any discussion of the association's future is premature. Or you want to fence with the reporter and try to lead him off the trail of his story without lying to him. Clearly, the "No comment" response isn't good enough.

Let's assume that when the question was asked, you knew that the association was having its troubles. There's no money;

some members have resigned; internal strife is paralyzing activity. Now the word is out, and the newspaper is on to it. Now the reporter is putting the question to you. One wrong word and it's all over. If you say something like "I can't answer that. You'll have to get in touch with Charley Jones, the president," then you are, in effect, fueling the rumor. No, you haven't denied anything emphatically, unequivocally, vehemently. The reporter is encouraged to continue his pursuit. The story lives.

Why not try to handle this crisis in another way? Like stalling for time. You ask the reporter where he heard that rumor. He responds with, "A little birdie told me" or "We have our sources." This nonresponsive reply to your nonresponsive reply is another way of telling you to quit stalling. The ball is now back in your court. What are you going to say now?

If you say, "No comment," it means that an official of the Midtown Concerned Parents Association would not comment when asked if the organization had closed up shop. To most reporters, "No comment" means "You're on to something but if you crack this one, you'll have to do it without my help." It can also mean, "Whoops! The news is out! Well, he's not going to pin it on me."

Depending on how well you know the reporter, you should try to work out some terms of cooperation. You can tell him, "What I'm going to say to you next is entirely and completely off the record. Do you understand?" Listen to the response. Make certain that he understands that you are prepared to take him into your confidence, but first he must pledge not to use what you are about to tell him. At least, he must not use the information until you both agree on how it will be used. At this point, assuming that there is truth in the rumor, you can no longer expect the news to be suppressed. You can, however, work to present the story in a manner that is more sympathetic to the members' cause. You can tell the reporter, "I don't want to lie to you; I never have and I never will. You know that you're on to a story here. But this is the deal: We've been having our troubles. We're having a meeting tonight, as a matter of fact, and we think we will have something for you after it's over. It may be that we will continue in operation after a reorganization. It may be that we'll just fold our tents and quietly steal away. But all this is off the record for now. There's just no way to predict what will happen at tonight's meeting." And then you ask him, "Now, what kind of a story are you planning to write?"

What you have done with this approach is to open a dialogue and remove the tensions of an adversary relationship. You're asking him how he's going to write his story. Who knows? As you discuss his approach and work in the nuances, the imponderables, and the alternatives, the reporter may decide that his story isn't ready to be written as yet. He may decide to hold off until the meeting takes place and you can get back to him. At the meeting, of course, the association's leadership will discuss how the press should be handled. You will have gained valuable time.

Another way to respond to the question, "Has the Midtown Concerned Parents Association folded up?" is with another question: "What do you want me to say? First, I'd like to say I wish you hadn't called. I'd like to say it's absolutely not true. But it so happens that we're having our problems. No, we haven't dissolved. Maybe we will; maybe we won't. Maybe we'll ride through this period and come out of it better, stronger than ever. So your question is a tough one to answer. I really don't know how to answer."

Take your time with the reporter. Get into a discussion of the situation, to whatever extent that you can. If you choose to be terse or hostile, you may be sorry.

The discussion that you hope to start with the reporter may bring the picture more clearly into focus for him and for yourself. Let the reporter know that what you are saying is entirely off the record. Repeat this to him several times so that he doesn't get the impression that only the first few sentences or exchanges were off the record. Don't be afraid to discuss what you will say for the record and what must remain off the record. Be frank. Take the reporter into your confidence. If you lie, you're through. Any news story that follows will make clear that you lied.

Put yourself at the reporter's service. Fill him in completely so that he understands as much as you do. Then, if he elects to write a story immediately, there is a good chance that it will be written with some depth and insight. Possibly a soupçon of sympathy. That's all you can hope for.

If his story is hard-nosed and one-sided and cuts your group dead, you can at least go back to your associates and fill them in on what happened. If your associates can keep the organization together, the earlier news story will soon be overshadowed by the later one. Nobody said the media are in business only to protect your personal interests or to massage your ego.

## TELL IT STRAIGHT

Candor is good for you. If you are prepared to set aside your personal feelings in a matter that concerns you directly and can manage to give the reporters your most objective views of the matter, you stand to gain in credibility and attention. If the bond issue on which you have been hard at work seems to be a losing battle, you may find it helpful to respond in that way to a reporter's question. You can say, in a one-to-one conversation, "Well, please don't quote me. This has got to be off the record. The answer is no, I don't think we're going to approve the bond issue." You then go on to explain why you have reached that conclusion. This background material will emerge in the story that reports the defeat of the bond issue, assuming that your forecast is accurate. If you truly do not think the vote will go against you, then you shouldn't be making such forecasts. In any case, don't try a touchy backgrounder like this on an off-the-record basis if you have more than one reporter for an audience.

What good does it do to provide a reporter with a backgrounder? It gives the reporter an expertise that he otherwise might not have when he sits down to write his story. You help to make him look good. You may benefit from this. Someday. Somehow. Have faith.

Another expression that you should be wary of is "off the record." There are times when individuals will tell a reporter something off the record that is actually a fact. As such, the information is very much a part of the record. Don't tell a reporter something off the record if it has already appeared in the news.

Off-the-record material is best reserved for subjective discussions, in background briefings in which the ground rules are clearly set forth and agreed to by all the reporters in the room. You may find yourself referred to as an "informed source," an "industry source," or a "source close to the situation," while your name is not used. These instances occur when the reporter writes a speculative article that attempts to present an in-depth roundup of a situation.

"Not for attribution" is similar to "off the record." It means that you are supplying some background information to the press but that the stories that appear are not to attribute the information to you. This, too, is a tricky technique. Sometimes it turns out that only one person is privy to the information that is made public through a not-for-attribution briefing, and that person is you. It may be best to use the not-for-attribution approach only if problems will arise if attribution occurs. You must ask yourself whether it *really* makes a difference if you provide attributable or nonattributable information.

There is another technique that may come in handy: "overkill," or telling the reporter more than he wants or needs to know, drowning him with background, much of it inconsequential. He'll start off by taking notes on your narrative, but soon his eyes will film over and he'll be trying to get rid of you. This technique is used in very special cases. If you would just as soon not see very much publicity about something, you might use the overkill technique. By being so eager to press information on the reporters, by appearing to thirst after a "big story" on the item under discussion, you may turn off the reporter and find only brief mention, or none at all, in your paper the next day—just what you wanted.

## MAKING YOURSELF USEFUL

Help the newspaper cover the news. If your organization holds a routine meeting at which a guest speaker shows films of African game, you shouldn't expect the newspaper to send a reporter to cover the session. Cover for the paper.

Write up the meeting and deliver it to the paper as quickly as possible, within twenty-four hours if you can manage it.

You may be able to supply a photograph to the paper (see page 120 for more information on the use of photographs). It will usually be appreciated if it is clear and has some animation. A word of caution: If you decide to send photographs to more than one publication, make sure you send out different photographs to each. The same cast of characters can be shown, but try to have them arranged differently in each. The photograph should preferably be an eight-by-ten-inch glossy, but Polaroid pictures can be used if they are clear. Make certain that your caption is accurate as to spellings, affiliations, and the left-to-right order. Write the names in full. Do not write on the back of the picture. Pressure from your pencil or ballpoint can break the glossy film surface and render the picture unusable. It is better to type your caption information on a separate piece of paper and attach this paper to the bottom of the picture with a strip of Scotch tape (place the tape on the back of the picture, not the front).

If your group needs to have its name before the public in order to generate interest, recruit members, raise funds, or perpetuate an image of action or movement, then you will want to look for feature-story ideas. Feature stories, in this instance, would deal with human-interest elements and would entertain and, perhaps, instruct.

You can help develop feature-story ideas by examining the backgrounds of the members. Perhaps a key figure in your group is best known for achievements in another field or has an unusual hobby or business. If you sense an unusual story, you should try to interest the newspaper reporter. The reporter may turn down your suggestion or may see another possibility for a story and agree to meet with, and interview, the person you have in mind. Sometimes a suggestion may lead to a larger story. If you present as a feature-story possibility the fact that the chairman of your group is a well-known bird-watcher, the reporter may discover that there are hundreds of bird-watchers in the community who meet regularly. His story may be about this group, and your original story may be just one part of it. But you may be pleased, nevertheless, to see "your" bird-watcher recognized in the story that ultimately emerges. The story may even refer to his activities with your group.

Persons in your organization may have special recipes to offer the local paper's food pages. You may form a softball team or touch-football team, and you'll want the sports editor to know about it.

## LETTERS TO THE EDITOR

Any newspaper worthy of the name will publish letters to the editor. If the paper carries an editorial about a subject of interest to your organization, write a letter. Praise the editorial or criticize it. Take a middle view; offer some additional information. Or use an editorial on one topic to justify your letter on another topic. You may find it useful to have different members' names on your letters if you are dashing off a series of letters during a brief period. But always get permission from your associate whose name is being attached to the letter.

Don't use the paper's letters column to gripe about the way the newspaper reported on a meeting that your group sponsored. If you're unhappy about the coverage, be patient. If the situation persists, try to meet with the reporter who is writing the stories and explain your concern. If the headline jars you, bear in mind that the reporter usually doesn't write the headlines. The headline is written by the copy editor or someone on the copy desk who edits the copy turned in by the reporters. When you first read a newspaper's account of a meeting that you attended, a talk that you delivered, or a statement that you made, you may grit your teeth and groan. It just doesn't *sound* like you when you read it in cold type. Or the meeting was really more significant than the news story makes it out to be. They just didn't grasp the dimensions of the story. Or the quotes were telescoped together; they're incomplete, or a bit inaccurate. You may want to call up the reporter and chew him out. Don't. Cool it. If you solicit opinions from acquaintances who weren't at the meeting, who aren't as close to the story, you may find that they come away from reading the story with a positive feeling about the meeting. In other words, maybe the story isn't as bad as you first thought it to be.

If some time passes and you get a negative feedback as a result of the article, you can call the reporter. Give him some news to report. And during your conversation, mention the write-up. Tell him that you appreciate his efforts but that there's something about the story that is bothering you. Several people have commented to you about it, and you'd like to pass along their views. You can then review the way the story reads and let the matter rest. Don't harbor resentment. If your resentment revolves around a minor point, think twice about bringing it out. If it's important enough and you mention it to the reporter, he will take extra care the next time to word his story more carefully.

## CALLING CAN MAKE THE DIFFERENCE

Don't write a letter to the editor about the episode. There's an old saying that the paper always has the last word. Don't burn your bridges in the newsroom. Remember that newspapers are a hurry-up production. The writing is fast. The production is fast. And they are read fast. Errors occur. If a story is incomplete today, it can be filled out tomorrow. The story can unfold. You can help it unfold by developing every angle of the story and calling the reporter's attention to every one.

Suppose that the news story about your school association erred by referring to the "50" members instead of the "500." Don't demand an immediate correction and make a fuss. Your committee will meet again, and there will be an opportunity in subsequent stories to correct the figure.

Sometimes the problem is more subtle; it involves personalities and hurt feelings. Let's assume that a news story quoted one of your members at length and led to embarrassment because the committee chairman wasn't mentioned at all or was mentioned in an off-hand manner. Or perhaps the views of the member, given as representative, were actually at odds with the official committee position. Perhaps this situation arose because the chairman wasn't available to the reporter when the story was being prepared. The reporter simply called someone else for comment.

To help soothe ruffled feelings, ask the person who was quoted in the story to telephone the reporter. The person can thank the reporter for the story and then explain that he thinks some aspects of the issue under discussion were inadvertently misrepresented. Emphasize that it wasn't the reporter's fault. Your associate then could ask the reporter to help square things by calling the chairman, who is now available. He should explain to the reporter that the article, through no fault of the reporter's, created a problem. Tell him what the problem is all about. Don't be reluctant about swallowing your pride; it helps clear the air quickly and enables everyone to get back to work on the business at hand.

The committee chairman, if called by the reporter, can develop his views without doing violence to the other committee member's explanations. One device for minimizing differences of this sort is to say, "Sometimes, in trying to clarify an issue, we tend to simplify it a bit too much, and this is probably what happened in this case." The chairman then can go on to clarify, interpret, explain, and, one hopes, set the record straight. If the reporter appears annoyed when the first call is made to him and lets you know that he's not interested in mediating personality clashes, don't press the matter any further.

If you must deal with more than one newspaper, then you may find yourself inadvertently getting caught in a competitive fight. Rather than play favorites—assuming you have no special reason to do so—play it as an even break for all. Send your press releases and your advisories to both papers at the same time. Call each paper as soon after the other as possible. If one paper then chooses to do nothing with the news you are providing, while the other one uses it, you can't be accused of having withheld the story from one paper in order to give the other an exclusive.

If your group holds a meeting, write it up immediately and get the story to the newspapers within twelve hours. Don't hold off writing the story until the next week because you want a certain weekly newspaper to have the story, too. A week-old story isn't going to get printed in a daily newspaper.

Occasionally, you will come up with a special angle for an exclusive story. It is then proper to decide that one newspaper should have first refusal. You telephone and try to interest a reporter in handling the exclusive story. If he turns down your idea, try another newspaper and so on. Make it clear each time that this is exclusive, that the other papers in the area will not have it. And make certain that you keep your word. Peddle exclusives to one publication at a time.

Don't promise an exclusive to any news medium unless it is truly exclusive. The dictionary defines "exclusive" as "excluding all others; shutting out other considerations, happenings, existences, occupations, etc . . . not shared or divided; sole; single. . . ." Nothing can generate ill will faster than the arrival at a newsroom of a release slugged "exclusive" that has appeared in yesterday's editions of the rival newspaper. Never assume that reporters do not read the competition.

In some cases, a publicist will offer an exclusive to one paper and get it printed. Then he will go to the rival paper and promise to give them an exclusive on the same story. How? By saying, "Well, the story that ran in the other paper wasn't the whole story. I saved the best part of it for you." You shouldn't have to work that way.

Another no-no is sending out a mimeographed press release that is marked "exclusive." Newspapermen believe that mimeographing and exclusivity are contradictions. Who would take the trouble to mimeograph one copy of anything? On the other hand, a Xerox copy of a press release can bear the "exclusive" slug and not give rise to skepticism because, as a practical matter, an original copy of a release may be sent through a copier in order to produce file copies quickly. But mimeographing? Don't give the newsroom crew the opportunity to question your credibility.

Once you elect to provide an exclusive story to any one news outlet, you must be prepared to deal with the displeasure of the excluded media. There are times when you will find this risk acceptable. Weigh the pros and cons carefully.

Ideally, your group should be generating enough news to keep everyone happy in your community. You may even be able to dish out exclusives to all in turn. But keep track of your exclusives. Make certain that you don't begin to play favorites unless you do so by design.

## FREQUENCY OF RELEASES

You should issue a release every time you have some news to report. What's news? News from your organization would consist of any timely decision, action, plan, or program that would be of interest to the newspaper's readers. It should be a first report. That is, if elections are held today by your membership, the results are news. The results couldn't have been reported anywhere before this. But if the elections were held two months ago and you are only now getting around to issuing a press release, don't waste your time. The reporter will ask, "When was the election?" If you tell the truth, you're dead. If you lie and he finds out that you lied, you're dead. "Timeliness": remember the word.

There is no hard rule to follow when considering the question about the frequency of press releases, because frequency depends upon the organization's work and goals. Some groups may find that they must issue many press releases during a day. A political campaign, for example, requires a steady flow of releases and the flow increases as election day nears.

At times, where a group functions in a community that has both morning and afternoon newspapers, it becomes necessary to issue separate releases for each. If your news item bears today's dateline and made the afternoon paper, make sure tomorrow morning's paper gets a version of the same release. It is likely that the morning paper may not wait for your release. On seeing the story in the afternoon paper, the morning paper will work to update the story. That is, it will assign a reporter to develop a new lead that advances the story to the next step or develops reaction to the story you generated. The same thing would take place if the morning paper broke with the story and the afternoon paper went after an update on the story. Be ready to handle the calls.

There are clubs and associations that don't do much except elect officers and set up new committees once a year as they go about their rather private business. Releases from such organizations follow an obvious and predictable timetable. If they suddenly get bitten by the publicity bug, they can generate extra "ink" by "milking" the information. Instead of issuing two releases a year—one when new officers are elected and another when committee chairpeople are appointed—the club can stretch things over a longer period.

One release will tell about the election of officers, as always. The next release will tell about the appointment of a new ways-and-means committee chairperson. A photograph of the new appointee and a biography accompanies the release. The third release tells about the appointment of a new program committee chairperson, with picture and biography. A fourth release follows. It deals with the hospitality committee's new chairperson. And so on. The releases are doled out rather than bunched. This technique helps keep your group's name before the public. If your group is conducting an active program, then there is no need to milk publicity in this manner. You will want to get the election and appointment releases out of the way as quickly as possible so that your next releases can get down to the main business, the meetings and programs.

The milking technique usually works best in smaller communities, where the paper may be more dedicated to the "names make news" concept of journalism. Bigger papers probably won't have the space to give over to news stories, and pictures, of committee chairpeople.

## HOLD FOR RELEASE

Another technique in press-release management involves the "hold-for-release" item. The technique is used when a news item regarding your organization must not appear in print prematurely. The news item itself, however, will take place on schedule. You can, therefore, distribute the press release well in advance of the release date. The release is captioned, or slugged, HOLD FOR RELEASE ON [DATE]. or NOT FOR RELEASE BEFORE [DATE]. Often, texts of speeches are delivered to media in advance of delivery in order to give newsmen more of an opportunity to study the text and prepare their summary news stories or commentaries.

The hold-for-release technique makes sense if your organization is about to conduct a routine annual election of officers. The new slate is known in advance. Delivering the story as far in advance of the actual election, together with photos of the new officers and their biographies, gives the papers a better chance to treat the story with added care and, you hope, gives it a bigger and better play than it would get if the material arrived late. Since you don't want the election results to appear in print before the voting takes place, you type, in capital letters or red ink, the HOLD FOR RELEASE ON [DATE] line. You may also decide to add a note to the release that calls attention to the release date.

Where you must deal with morning and afternoon or evening papers, you would slug the morning paper release, FOR RELEASE IN A.M.'S OF [DATE]. This means the story can be released the night before, when morning papers are produced. The late news shows (11:00 P.M.) on television and radio make use of news that is being released in morning papers, because by that time of night, the morning papers, bearing the next day's date, are rolling off the presses.

You would send a different version of the release to the afternoon paper, slugging it, FOR RELEASE IN P.M.'S OF [DATE]. If your news item is scheduled to break during the afternoon, not during the morning, you should slug the releases as follows: FOR RELEASE IN P.M.'S OF [DATE] and FOR RELEASE IN A.M.'S OF [DATE]. In the former, the news is for afternoon papers and newscasts. In the latter case, the news is for morning papers bearing the next day's date. Each release should consist of the same basic information, but handled in such a way as to make the stories read differently. Otherwise, morning and afternoon papers would be identical. And that would never do.

What happens if you send out advance stories on an event, all duly slugged with the proper release-date information, and for some reason, the event doesn't take place (for example, a blizzard causes a cancellation or the indisposition of your guest speaker leads to a change of program)? These things happen. When the paper decides to make use of the story but must put the story to bed before confirmation can be obtained, the copy desk will use the phrase, "In a speech prepared for delivery last night. . . ." Or, "The election, scheduled to take place last night, saw the departure of. . . ." These precautions are designed to minimize embarrassment over reporting an event that doesn't take place.

# 4

# Magazines

THERE ARE THOUSANDS OF MAGAZINES in this country, many of which have an enormous impact. Rachel Carson first published her book *Silent Spring* in *The New Yorker*. When *Time* or *Reader's Digest* devotes a page or two to a person or a subject, millions and millions of people suddenly know about it. A place or point of view that may have been obscure the week or even the day before publication suddenly has national prominence.

The mass circulation magazines for the general public are not doing that well. Many in publishing believe that *Life* and *Look* didn't really die but were killed by editorial neglect and marketing stupidity. Nonetheless there are magazines with circulations under 100,000 and over 10 million that are widely read and have great impact on public opinion. The important point to remember is not the circulation of the publication. It still is possible to place an article in a magazine and have the entire nation wake up to a new view on an important issue. The examples since Rachel Carson's book, published in *The New Yorker* over ten years ago, are many. *Ramparts*' article on the CIA was widely reported.

The *Bulletin of the Association of the Atomic Scientists* had enormous impact on public opinion when it was first published. Not because so many people read or even understood the articles, but because several mass communicators for daily newspapers and TV stations would read an article in it and then popularize it via their media.

Not long ago a short article on cold allergy in the *Journal of Allergy and Clinical Immunology*, circulation about 5000, was picked up by *Time* with a circulation of over 3 million. The *Reader's Digest* specializes in finding (and often placing) articles in smaller publications that it will abstract for the *Digest* reader. The average issue of the *Digest* runs to thirty or so articles, of which one-third are written for the *Digest*. Two-thirds usually are from other publications, including some few have ever heard of, such as *Empire* Magazine, *Guideposts, Bridge World*, and *Contemporary*.

There are influential magazines in almost every field of human activity, from art and architecture (about thirty different publications) to women's interests. There is hardly a better place than a magazine to gain national prominence. The publication's circulation has little to do with impact after publication.

Aside from the many consumer publications there are thousands of specialized interest publications that come out weekly, bi-weekly, monthly, quarterly, or annually. The best list of them by subject is printed each year in Bowker's *Literary Market Place*, an annual available in most libraries.

## GETTING AN ASSIGNMENT FOR AN ARTICLE

Even if you have a story that may well be interesting enough for a specific magazine, you should know that there is no easy way of getting into print. Your best bet is to try to interest an editor in assigning a staff or free-lance writer to do your story.

If you are skilled enough to write the article on your own, there is a very small chance you will have it used. You can try, but your best bet is to get the editor interested enough to assign a writer or to find a writer on your own who is known by the editors and who can get an answer to a magazine article idea.

## USING WRITER'S DIGEST

*Writer's Digest*, a magazine sold at most newsstands, by subscription, and available at most libraries, is a treasure house for anyone interested in getting an article into a major magazine. If you really can write, you can try a direct approach to the specific editor who can buy your article. Reading the publication does help, but *Writer's Digest* gives solid hints on which publication is working on what kind of article. *Writer's Market*, an annual book published by *Writer's Digest*, has excellent articles on how to place magazine articles with specific information on each publication's requirements.

## WORKING WITH A STAFF WRITER

For a staff writer to be assigned to work with you, an editor must first get interested enough to spend the publication's time and money on your idea. To accomplish this, you should carefully study several recent issues of the publication. See if they have ever done an article on the same subject; if one appeared recently, chances are the publication won't want to repeat itself. If the article you have in mind does not fit in with their editorial format, no matter how good an idea it is, you will not be able to get it assigned.

### APPROACH #1—*You want an editor to assign a staff writer to do an article.*

Once you know the publication and understand how the editors direct their writing, write a short letter to an editor. Explain in some detail the scope of your interest and the essence of what the magazine article would be about. Offer yourself as being available for an interview, send clippings of newspaper articles about what you or your group have done, and so on.

If you don't get an answer immediately, don't be too concerned. Most magazines work by editorial committee and will be planning articles three, four, or even six months in advance. Thus, a monthly woman's magazine will be finished assigning articles for a June issue before December of the year before. (It takes three or more months from the time they actually finish editing an article before it appears. For an article that appeared in the January *Ladies' Home Journal*, the writers had to be finished with their copy by September.) Keep this in mind. You should not suggest an idea that is time-limiting to a monthly publication unless you have considered the time it can take your idea to be translated into an article.

Weekly magazines like *Time* or *Newsweek* move very fast. They will run a news story a few days after they get it. But feature articles are often held for two or three months before use.

Often before an editor assigns a staff writer to you, the editor will assign a researcher to interview or call you. The researcher will use a standard approach designed by the magazine to get enough information so that the editors can decide if they want to take the next step, assigning the writer and/or photographer.

It is extremely important that you level with the researcher and supply everything asked for. If the researcher doesn't think you are honest or have a story or if he believes you are just a publicity hound, the assignment will be killed well before any writer gets involved.

When you meet or are called by the writer, start all over again to sell your story. Don't assume just because you have passed the editorial review for the idea, met with a researcher, and supplied reams of material that you are sure to be in the next issue. (Remember never to send original material to a writer, editor, or researcher. If the material is lost you are out of luck and really have no way of getting it back.)

Bring to the interview detailed fact sheets. All pertinent information that you feel must be quoted should be supplied in writing. If you don't do this, there is a good chance the article will miss making an important point. Remember there is no guarantee that you will ever see the article from the interview or from material you gave until it is in print.

## APPROACH #2—*How to get a free-lance writer to do an article*

The Society of Magazine Writers lists several hundred professionals throughout the country who are available for free-lance assignments. For a list of these writers send $15 for the annual membership list to the Society of Magazine Writers at 123 West Forty-third Street, New York 10036.

There are three major ways that you can get the services of

a professional writer. One is to employ him as a ghost-writer. The writer's name does not appear on the article: yours does. The article is your property, and you can change it any way you wish and do anything you want with it. In accepting payment for the article, the actual writer gives up all rights. Depending on how much time it takes him to complete an article, $200–$1000 is fair. Anything mutually agreed upon in advance is acceptable, and the respective rights of the collaborator and the ghost-writer are entirely dependent upon the terms to which the parties agree.

Another way often used to place a magazine article is for the writer to decide to do an article on his own for a publication. If he is assigned to a publication as a staff writer, you can't pay him for it; he is paid by the publication. In this situation all expenses connected with getting the story are paid for by his publication. He will be grateful for an idea for a story that he can do.

The third way that you can get a professional writer to by-line an article in a magazine is to reimburse him for any out-of-pocket expenses he may incur in getting his story ready for submission. In many instances a free-lance writer will accept travel expenses, payment for extensive research, and, of course, the fee paid by the publication. *The amount you pay may not have anything to do with whether or not an article will be used.* Often a professional writer will be grateful for an idea that he can sell to a major magazine. You may not owe him anything and will in fact gain his gratitude for the idea.

### APPROACH #3—*Stage a press conference or a seminar where several writers from different magazines are invited at their own expense to cover the sessions.*

The seminar held for science writers described on page 175 attracted several magazine writers, including a staff writer from *Vogue*. On the basis of material she collected at the one-day meeting in Chicago, the writer was able to do three short articles over a period of several months. All the expenses of her trip from New York to Chicago were paid by her publication. The Academy of Dermatology provided her with one modest lunch and audio-cassette copies of the presentations she was interested in.

APPROACH #4—*Distribute well-prepared backgrounders to magazine editors.*

The well-prepared background article with a complete bibliography, names of experts to consult, and several ideas for articles is an excellent stimulus to a magazine editor. The backgrounder (see page 83) will be used to get a writer to do an article, or as a beginning project for a researcher.

## IMPORTANCE OF OBJECTIVE RESEARCH

If you supply research to a magazine writer, make sure it is objective. You will kill a story idea with an editor or free-lancer and waste your time and money if you don't give him both sides of a story. Before he writes, the writer will want to know what it is you are selling. Don't play games and attempt to hide the "commercial."

Suppose you want to get an article in a national magazine that discusses the need for more medical information on contraception for high school students. If you are also a member of a local planned-parenthood group, don't hide this from a writer you may meet or seek out. You also have to face the fact that abortion is often a method of contraception. This may well turn off some writers, but they won't trust anything you tell them unless you acknowledge that it is a problem.

The best approach (that which will get an article in print) is hard to zero-in on unless you know the writer and the market he writes for. Don't do all the work. Have a well-organized file folder ready, and be sure it is easy to read and all photos are marked carefully. Remember, send only copies—don't take a chance with original material.

## MERCHANDISING THE RESULTS

Once an article appears, you have to get permission to reprint it. You can't make copies of anything that appears in print in a copyrighted publication without the written permission of the owner of the rights, usually the publisher and, sometimes, the author. The question of obtaining permissions depends upon the respective rights of the author and the publisher and these may vary depending on the contractual arrangements between them. This will rarely be denied if your purpose is worthy and you explain it to both. You do run a risk of a lawsuit if you make and distribute reprints without permission. This is important when investing time in working with a magazine. If you find out that the publication will not give you the right to reprints or will not sell them to you, you may decide it isn't worth the effort and expense involved. Often it may be that an article in a smaller publication that will provide you permission to reprint may be worth more than an article someplace that never gives permission.

# 5

# Wire Services

THE WIRE SERVICES ARE of vital importance to newspapers and TV and radio stations.

The largest of the wire services, AP and UPI, distribute news, film, tapes, and photographs to their clients around the world.

If you manage to interest the AP in carrying your group's story on its national wire, you could theoretically reach about 5650 newspapers and radio and TV stations. Realistically, however, you will find yourself dealing with a local wire-service bureau and hoping to land your story on a local wire, one that covers the area in which you reside.

Most of the time you will be dealing directly with the local TV or radio stations and local newspapers in your community. And even if there is a wire-service bureau in your community, you may not need to deal with it very often. The chances are that you will not need to deal with the nearest wire-service bureau either, for it can be some distance away. If you seek broader exposure for your article, or press release, then send it to the out-of-town wire-service bureau. The bureau can put your story on the state wire, reaching all print and broadcast clients in the state. (The wire services usually offer clients a variety of wire reports, including the Metro wire, state wire, regional wire, national wires, business news wire, and sports news wire.)

If you send a press release to the wire-service bureaus nearest your home, you may find that the material is converted into a daybook listing. The daybook, as noted earlier, is an advisory of scheduled events for the day and plays a very important role in shaping the news coverage in your community.

Perhaps, in addition to being included on the daybook file, your press release may be given to a rewrite man at the bureau to be "boiled down" into a paragraph or two. This truncated story will then be filed on the local wire or on the state wire.

Routine items cannot expect much more attention from a wire service. And by routine items, we mean those that deal with subjects well above the level of local meetings with limited participation and interest, the social gatherings, fund-raising events, and so on. If your group is involved with efforts that pertain to state, regional, or national matters already in the news, your press release may be treated to a lengthier story by the wire service in order to add depth or balance to the larger story.

Because of the varied political leanings of the client publications and broadcasters, wire services have the reputation of being less than crusading, or muckraking, news-gathering organizations. They strive for balance, for objectivity, on the assumption that if the basic ingredients of a story or an issue are fairly presented, the crusaders and advocates can go on and generate newsworthy inputs from that point.

There has been a great maturing of wire services in recent years. They now report on abortion legislation, drug problems, the many other programs and tensions of urban life, including civil rights, crime, transit, jobs, and consumer issues.

To find out if a wire-service bureau is located in your area, check the telephone directory or call the newspaper office. One of the reporters will be able to tell you where the nearest wire-service bureau is located. If the newspaper is a member of AP, it also serves as an AP bureau, since AP is a cooperative venture and its members make their news reports available to other AP clients or members.

You can telephone the bureau manager and see if he or she will agree to a brief meeting. At this meeting, besides briefing the bureau manager on your group's program, you can supply names, addresses, and telephone numbers of your group's key contact people. Don't ask for special treatment or favors; don't press the media people for commitments by asking, "Are you going to cover the meeting?" or "Are you going to use the story?" Be professional. Tell your story, if you get the chance to do so, and then leave. Always bear in mind that the bureau chief and his staff are constantly racing a deadline; they have little time to waste. Competition for the wire is enormous.

## ORIGINS OF THE WIRE SERVICES

The AP is sometimes described as being the closest thing the United States has to a national newspaper. It is a cooperative news agency with some 4668 newspapers, radio and TV stations as members who participate in a mutual, nonprofit operation. AP, the oldest wire service, dates back to 1848, when a half-dozen newspapers created a news-gathering cooperative. A board of directors selects a general manager who administers AP operations from 50 Rockefeller Plaza in New York. The AP members pay assessments, levied on the basis of an operating budget. Extraordinary costs, such as those to cover a presidential election or a major story occurring unexpectedly in another country, are financed through special assessments. AP has about 3300 employes, half of them newsmen. There are about 170 domestic AP bureaus. Each morning, at wire-service headquarters, a telephone conference call with editors in Washington, Chicago, or Los Angeles helps determine, in outline, the stories that will be covered during the next twenty-four hours.

UPI is a privately-owned corporation that was founded in 1907 by E. W. Scripps, founder of the Scripps-Howard newspaper chain, and his associates. The company merged with William Randolph Hearst's International News Service (INS) to become United Press International in 1958 (INS was founded in 1909). There are about 2000 newsmen (including photographers) on the UPI payroll. UPI has 6550 subscribers.

Wire services have reporters who gather news; their stories are edited in their respective bureaus and put on leased wires to be carried directly into the offices of client papers and broadcasting companies.

The bureaus control their own production, generally, and move their stories on their local, state, or regional wire networks during "splits," periods of five, ten, or perhaps fifteen minutes in which bureaus can file accumulated copy that is usually of interest only to clients in their area. It has been estimated that about half of the AP copy that is sent into small-town newspapers comes from local member newspapers. There are mandatory stories, such as farm-commodity prices, that wire services must supply to certain clients. During splits, the bureau stories also are received at headquarters, and if a story from a bureau seems important enough, it can be relayed on the trunk lines and thus be given national distribution.

At UPI, more than 3 million words a day pass through the computer system in New York through seventy-two incoming and outgoing domestic and international circuits. The New York computer is linked by transoceanic cable and satellites with UPI computers in Brussels and Hong Kong to help service its subscribers.

For years, the wire services relied on Teletype machines to transmit copy at about sixty-six words per minute. Now they are using video terminals and high-speed communications links instead of Teletype. A story used to be written on a typewriter and then edited and handed to a Teletype operator to send out on the circuit. Today, reporters can compose on these video terminals, correcting and editing as they go along, and, when finished, see the story filed almost instantly into an information and retrieval bank. The editing and rewrite desks can retrieve stories for their wires, edit and rewrite them if necessary to include later material, and file the completed, freshly edited story back into the computer by means of a code number that determines on which circuit the story will move.

The wire services have Washington staffs to cover the White House, Capitol Hill, the many Federal agencies, the Pentagon, Justice Department, Supreme Court, and consumer matters. They have writers who specialize in sports, the arts, life-styles, family interests, and women's interests. They are constantly on the lookout for stories—news and feature material. They also supply "feeds" to radio and TV stations.

The wire service is of crucial importance to TV stations and smaller newspapers. The larger newspapers can manage to fill their pages with staff-written material, for the most part. But they will use wire-service copy as a measure against which the editors and reporters can gauge their own performance. In cases where a newspaper lacks a correspondent, the wire-service correspondent's copy will be used. Also used will be "filler" material from wire-service copy, to help fill some space at the bottom of a column.

The competition between the wire services is intense. Neither likes to see the other come up with a story that it doesn't have. If one service files a story that doesn't show up on the other's machine, the latter service will quickly hear about it (usually from a client) and will "effort" to match the competitor's story.

After the catch-up story is filed, the editors will conduct an informal postmortem—in telephone calls, a meeting, or a memo—to try to learn why the bureau was "beat" on that story. Usually, it boils down to the lack of manpower, which is a perennial and seemingly irremediable problem for wire services. Every time one wire service triumphs over the other in a major story, the winner proudly calls attention to its beat in messages to subscribers and possibly in advertisements in the trade publications.

If you decide to deal with wire services, it is important that you provide both with your releases. Don't play favorites. If both have your press release, you are doing your job properly. What they do with your release is up to them.

## THE DAYBOOK

Each evening, and again during the early morning hours, in major metropolitan areas, AP and UPI send out on their circuits the daybook. Newspaper editors, TV news departments, radio news desks, and even some magazine editors will make it a point to scan this listing, this "menu." From it, they pick out the stories that interest them and assign the reporters, photographers, and camera crews. By moving tomorrow's daybook at the tail end of today's day shift, the wire services enable clients to make up tomorrow's assignment list before going home. The wire services themselves assign staff members to cover the events listed on the daybook that seem to hold the most promise of a good story, photograph, or film feature.

There is frequently contact between the wire service news desk and a newspaper client or TV news department concerning which of the events listed on the daybook will be covered by the wire service. If the newspaper knows the wire service is covering an event, it will depend on the wire service to file something, and the newspaper editor then can assign his reporters to other things. The manpower problem is a constant factor in the news business.

The shape of the routine news of the day is, as you can see, determined by the wire-service daybook. The headline news of the day is usually an unscheduled event—an accident, violence, a crime, a fire. These occurrences are the tip of the news iceberg. Beneath this tip, crammed with the excitement of the day, is the massive hulk of bread-and-butter news, comprised of press conferences, luncheon meetings, promotional stunts, special ceremonies, awards and citations, special events, picketing, and so on.

In the book *News From Nowhere*, by Edward Jay Epstein, a table is included to show the importance of wire-service material to one TV network's news operation during one month, December 1968. Epstein noted that the AP and UPI wire services accounted for more than two-thirds—actually, 70 percent—of the assigned domestic stories, or 308 out of 440 stories used that month.

Public relations agencies were the source of 28 stories (6.5 percent); newspaper clippings led to 20 of the TV stories (4.5 percent); affiliates and local TV supplied 14 stories (3.2 percent); staff cameramen and free-lancers provided 8 stories (1.8 percent); and "others" accounted for 10 stories (2 percent). After the two wire services, the most productive source of news for the TV network were the producers of the TV news shows, who supplied 45 stories (11 percent).

The wire-service daybooks are vital, then, in determining the thrust of news coverage for TV stations and most newspapers. In television the assignment desks will look at the daybook list—which is sketchy at best—and try to determine the newsworthiness of the event, the certainty that the event will actually occur (so as not to waste precious time and money if a crew is sent out and bad weather or some other factor forces a cancellation), the potential dramatic values that can be captured on film, and the timing of the event (if it's late in the day, will there be time to film, process the film, edit it, and integrate it into the newscast?). These are the thoughts that run through the minds of producers and editors as they scan the daybook.

The same kind of thinking goes on at the wire service, in many cases, during the compilation of the daybook.

Here is what a daybook looks like. Notice the wide variety of activities that are included:

FROM THE UPI DAYBOOK FOR TODAY, THURSDAY, JUNE 28.

MEDICAL AMATEUR RADIO COUNCIL HOLDS SEVENTH ANNUAL MEETING, PLAZA HOTEL, 9:15 A.M.

COMMUNITY HEALTH FAIR, OUR LADY OF SOLACE SCHOOL, 2865 W. 19TH ST., BROOKLYN, 10 A.M.

EXECUTIVE SESSION OF CITY COUNCIL'S COMMITTEE ON INDUSTRIAL DEVELOPMENT, CITY HALL, 10 A.M.

BOARD OF EDUCATION HOLDS SPECIAL MEETING, 110 LIVINGSTON ST., BROOKLYN. (BOARD HOLDS PUBLIC HEARING ON PROPOSED SUMMER PROGRAMS), 10:30 A.M.

CITIZENS TASK FORCE ON REVENUE SHARING HOLDS PUBLIC HEARING, WESTCHESTER COUNTY BUILDING, WHITE PLAINS, 10 A.M.

75 RETARDED CHILDREN LEAVE FOR SPECIAL SUMMER CAMP, 200 PARK AVENUE SOUTH, 10 A.M.

DESIGN OF NEW SCHOOL IS PRESENTED, HAAREN HIGH SCHOOL, 899 TENTH AVE., 10 A.M.

LEGAL AID ATTORNEYS HOLD NEWS CONFERENCE TO ANNOUNCE PLANNED STRIKE NEXT MONDAY, 100 CENTRE ST., PRESS ROOM, 10 A.M.

CHRISTINE MARIE ADAMS, LOUISIANA SUGAR QUEEN, OPENS WORLD SUGAR FUTURES MARKET, 79 PINE ST., 10 A.M.

DR. SAMUEL WOLFE HOLDS NEWS CONFERENCE ON NEW PROGRAM OF COMMUNITY MEDICINE, TEACHING CENTER, LONG ISLAND JEWISH MEDICAL CENTER, NEW HYDE PARK, L.I., 10:30 A.M.

AMERICAN CIVIL LIBERTIES UNION HOLDS NEWS CONFERENCE TO LAUNCH CAMPAIGN TO HAVE PUBLIC HOSPITALS PERFORM ABORTIONS, 20 W. 40TH ST., 10:30 A.M.

NEWS CONFERENCE TO ANNOUNCE PLANS FOR A CARIBBEAN FESTIVAL IN THE CITY, NEW YORK HILTON, GREEN ROOM, 10:30 A.M.

SARATOGA SPRINGS SULKY DRIVER JIMMY ALLEN TEACHES SIX FEMALE CITY BALLET DANCERS THE ART OF SULKY RACING, LINCOLN CENTER PLAZA, 11 A.M.

NEW YORK STATE LOTTERY IS DRAWN AT CONEY ISLAND, STILWELL AVENUE AND THE BOARDWALK, BROOKLYN, 11:30 A.M.

WINNERS OF CITY HIGH SCHOOL POETRY CONTEST READ FROM THEIR WORKS, BRYANT PARK, NOON.

TRUMPETER MAYNARD FERGUSON PLAYS WITH SALVATION ARMY BAND, 33 W. 52ND ST., 12:30 P.M.

LEAGUE FOR INDUSTRIAL DEMOCRACY PRESENTS ANNUAL AWARD TO ACTOR FREDERICK O'NEAL, ESSEX HOUSE, 12:30 P.M.

A GROUP OF ELDERLY PERSONS CRUISE HUDSON RIVER, LEAVE FROM PIER 81, W. 41ST ST., 2 P.M.

PUBLIC AUCTION OF FRENCH, ENGLISH AND CONTINENTAL FURNITURE, CLOCKS, RUGS AND CARPETS, SOTHEBY PARKE-BERNET, 980 MADISON AVE., 2 P.M.

S. S. FRANCE DEPARTS FOR SOUTHAMPTON, PIER 84, FOOT OF 44TH ST., 3 P.M.

SGT. JOSE MENDOZA LOPEZ, 1944 MEDAL OF HONOR WINNER, RETIRES FROM ARMY, FORT HAMILTON, BROOKLYN, 3 P.M.

COUNCIL OF BETTER BUSINESS BUREAUS PRESENTS ABBY AWARD, SUMMIT SUITE, SUMMIT HOTEL, 4 P.M.

A SYMPATHY PICKET IS HELD FOR STRIKE IN ONEITA MILLS, S.C., 1303 SIXTH AVE., 4 P.M.

STATE DEMOCRATIC CHAIRMAN JOSEPH CRANGLE HOLDS NEWS CONFERENCE, 415 MADISON AVE., 23RD FLOOR, 4 P.M.

NEW YORK RESTAURANT PRODUCTIVITY DEVELOPMENT CENTER INC. HOLDS NEWS CONFERENCE, TWENTY-ONE CLUB, 21 W. 52ND ST., 4 P.M.

REVELATIONS MOVEMENT, PART OF NEW YORK COMMUNITY CHOIR, OPENS, VILLAGE GATE, BLEECKER AND THOMPSON STREETS, 6 P.M.

REP. EDWARD I. KOCH, D-MAN., SPEAKS TO COMMITTEE FOR BETTER TRANSIT INC., CITY UNIVERSITY GRADUATE CENTER, 33 W. 42ND ST., THIRD FLOOR, 6 P.M.

LATIN ROCK SINGERS MALO AND ESTHER DAVIS AND COMPANY PERFORM, TOMPKINS SQUARE PARK, 7 P.M.

WALTZ MUSIC IS PLAYED, BANDSHELL, CENTRAL PARK, 8 P.M.

DEMONSTRATION OF NEW TYPE OF SIREN FOR HOME PROTECTION, LOBBY, 812 W. 181ST ST., 8 P.M.

UPI 06-28 01:28AED

JERSEY DAYBOOK 6-28

FROM THE UPI NEW JERSEY DAYBOOK FOR TODAY, THURSDAY, JUNE 28:

BOONTON—1973 DOPE OPEN AMATEUR GOLF TOURNAMENT, BENEFITTING ANTI-DRUG ABUSE ACTIVITIES, KNOLL COUNTRY CLUB, 6:30 A.M.

ASBURY PARK—NEW JERSEY COUNCIL OF SENIOR CITIZENS CONFERENCE, CONVENTION HALL, 9:30 A.M.

NEWARK—FEDERAL JUDGE LEONARD I. GARTH HEARS ARGUMENTS ON SUIT SEEKING RELEASE OF $270 MILLION IN FUNDS APPROPRIATED FOR SUMMER NEIGHBORHOOD YOUTH CORPS PROGRAMS, FEDERAL COURT, 10 A.M.

ASBURY PARK—NEW JERSEY WEEKLY LOTTERY NUMBER DRAWN, PRESS PLAZA, COOKMAN AND LAKE AVENUES, 11 A.M.

WOODBRIDGE—MONTHLY MEETING OF THE N.J. HIGHWAY AUTHORITY, AUTHORITY HEADQUARTERS, 11 A.M.

NEWARK—JAZZ IN THE GARDEN, NEWARK MUSEUM, 49 WASHINGTON STREET, 12:30 P.M.

NEW BRUNSWICK—CONVENTION OF FUTURE FARMERS OF AMERICA, RUTGERS, 1:30 P.M.

PLAINFIELD—NEW JERSEY CONFERENCE OF MAYORS FROM MIDDLESEX, UNION AND SOMERSET COUNTIES, POLICE HEADQUARTERS, WATCHUNG AND 4TH STREETS, 8 P.M.

UPI NEWARK

UPI 06-28 01:32 AED

The one-sentence items on the daybook list come from press releases that range from a six-page single-spaced release from the Medical Amateur Radio Council to a one-sentence message from the Association of Legal Aid Attorneys announcing their press conference.

The Association for the Help of Retarded Children's press release was sent to UPI on June 25. It looked like this below the letterhead:

EVENT: 75 severely retarded New York City children departing, by bus, for special residential summer camp.
TIME: 10 A.M.
DATE: Thursday, June 28th.
PLACE: ASSOCIATION FOR THE HELP OF RETARDED CHILDREN
200 Park Avenue South (17th Street), NYC.

Camp Catskill, which is the destination of these campers, is a summer, residential camp, servicing 450 severely retarded children (in three separate sessions), who have been previously excluded from other camping programs because of their degree of retardation. There will be 5 in wheelchairs, several with Cerebral Palsy, and many on crutches. One third of the campers are being taken from State Institutions (i.e., Willowbrook, Letchworth Village, and Wassaic) and the remainder from communities in New York State.

The ASSOCIATION FOR THE HELP OF RETARDED CHILDREN, NEW YORK CITY CHAPTER, is coordinating this camping program in cooperation with the New York State Department of Mental Hygiene.

(The letterhead included the name of the Association's director of publicity, Miss Meredith Anderson, and the telephone number, along with the Association's address and, in red ink, the words *News release*.)

Another item originated from the New York Coffee and Sugar Exchange, Inc., 79 Pine Street, New York, New York 10005. It was in letter form:

Mr. Thomas Zumbo
City Editor (12th Floor)
United Press International
220 E. 42nd Street
New York, N.Y. 10017

Dear Mr. Zumbo:

We would appreciate your entering the following message on the UPI day book.

Louisiana Sugar Queen, Miss Christine Marie Adams,

opens the World Sugar Futures Market on Trading floor of the New York Coffee & Sugar Exchange at 79 Pine Street at precisely 10:00 A.M. on Thursday, June 28th, 1973.

If you have any questions regarding this event you may contact me directly on 269-8637. Thank you.

Sincerely,
John J. Capobianco
Director of Education
and Trade Relations

The American Civil Liberties Union (ACLU) advised UPI of a press conference in a release bearing the name of the ACLU and the National Association for Repeal of Abortion Laws. Two press contacts and their separate telephone numbers were listed. Also under the letterhead was this capsule:

*Press conference:*
Thurs., June 28, 10:30 A.M.
Wendell Willkie Hall
20 West 40th St.

The heading read:

LAWSUITS TO FORCE PUBLIC HOSPITALS TO OBEY SUPREME COURT ABORTION DECISION
National Campaign Launched by ACLU and NARAL

In rewriting this release, this would be the story received by subscribers:

NEW YORK, June 28—The American Civil Liberties Union and the National Association for Repeal of Abortion Laws today announced a national campaign aimed at forcing public hospitals to obey Supreme Court decisions legalizing abortion.

The campaign involves court actions in Massachusetts, Missouri, Minnesota, New Jersey, Ohio, Wisconsin, Texas and other states, including one where a public hospital has been ordered to provide abortion to two women by a Federal court.

"We are determined to end this flagrant abuse of the law by many public hospitals, often abetted by religious pressure groups," said Lawrence Lader, NARAL chairman. Brenda Fasteau, attorney and coordinator of ACLU's women's rights project, said the refusal to obey the Supreme Court "hits hardest at poor and minority group women who may have to travel great distances to secure a right guaranteed everywhere."

If you were an assignment editor, your job would be to decide which of these events warranted staff coverage, considering all the other news stories that are going on and the availability of your reporters or camera crews.

Four of the thirty-eight items listed in the June 28 daybook were covered by UPI reporters: the City Council meeting; the Board of Education meeting; the ACLU press conference; and the Crangle press conference. Two other items, the Legal Aid attorneys' threatened strike and the story about the ballet dancers taking sulky lessons, were rewritten from the press material.

At a TV station, each of the daybook items is looked at by the assignment editor and the news-show producers, with an eye to story and visual content. The ballet dancers and the sulky; the poetry contest winners in the park; the demonstration of a new home protection device; the retarded children going to camp, all these events offer interesting opportunities for cameramen. This is why it is so important that you incorporate in the event you are scheduling an approach that has visual appeal. You want photographers and film crews to attend.

The competition is fierce. To get mentioned in the daybook, here are the things you should do: Send in your press release, fact sheet, or letter about a week before the event, if possible. Stress the pictorial qualities, if there are any. But don't oversell, overpromise. If you bring out the camera crews and you don't deliver as promised, you won't get another chance for quite a while.

In an emergency, you can work with a shorter deadline. A telephone call can get you listed, but this is recommended only when absolutely necessary.

The release should bear your group's letterhead, printed or typed. It should include the name of a press contact, the telephone number, and the basic facts—the who, what, when, where, and why.

As of the date of this writing, the wire-service daybooks are supervised by Thomas D. Zumbo, UPI metropolitan editor, and Pierce Lembreck, AP bureau manager in New York, or John

Carroll, AP city editor in New York. They read through each piece of mail. Many releases are tossed out because they deal with matters that are too insignificant for general-circulation newspapers or TV and radio stations. The toss-outs most likely will include notices of PTA meetings, bridge parties, garden-club meetings, community cake sales or block parties.

Releases that have a wider appeal can be given to rewrite men, who will boil down the information into a few sentences or a couple of paragraphs and file the story.

The releases that make daybook material because they announce an event are placed in a special file. The file contains folders that are numbered for each day of the month. Folders for future months also are in this file. The release that goes into the daybook file bears on it, in large print put there by the wire-service editor, the date that the event will take place. The release is then inserted into the proper folder.

For the Thursday, June 28 daybook, the weeding-out process went on for days. Each mail delivery could bring in a release dealing with a June 28 event. On Wednesday, June 27, between 3:00 P.M. and 3:30 P.M., the collection for the June 28 daybook halted and one of the rewrite men who was assigned to the actual writing of the daybook—a chore, to be sure—went to the file and pulled out the June 28 folder material. Along with the press releases, there were clippings from newspapers that told of an event that would occur on June 28. Those dates, in news stories, were circled. The rewrite man organized this material in a time sequence—earliest events of the day were listed first—and then he wrote a sentence for each.

You can get listed in the daybook for the next day even though the 3:00 P.M. deadline has passed if you have an important event to announce and there is no way of knowing it in advance. You can telephone the daybook editor with this information. Or you can hand-deliver it to the bureau office and leave it for the daybook editor. Don't expect to deliver it personally. These editors are busy people. They don't need you interrupting by turning up at their desks unexpectedly.

Address your release to the daybook assignment editor. Some material is sent by telegram, but there are too many instances of late delivery; this route isn't recommended.

Remember, the daybook editor always wants to know the name of a contact person and telephone number. And if your event is postponed, you must telephone immediately and let the editor know. To fail to advise of a postponement or cancellation is to disqualify yourself from this game.

The reason is obvious. If a TV crew is assigned to your meeting and there has been a postponement, the TV station has just wasted about $500. The other reporters have wasted valuable time and taken themselves away from other stories. There will be an outcry, and the daybook editor will bear the brunt of it. And if it was your fault that the daybook editor is getting flak, you share in the trouble.

The daybook usually moves on the local wires between 5:00 P.M. and 6:00 P.M. in order to give the respective editors at the newspapers and radio and TV stations a chance to plan ahead for the next day before they leave the office.

If you have something for the daybook that is important, you can deliver it, or telephone it in, during the evening. The wire services will carry additional, late daybook listings sometime before midnight, usually around 10:30 P.M. This addendum can read like a mini-daybook. The overnight editor at the wire service will combine the addendum with the daybook material that moved between 5:00 P.M. and 6:00 P.M. and move the final integrated listing between 1:30 A.M. and 2:30 A.M. on the UPI wire and, a few hours later, on the AP wire.

Press conferences that must be scheduled virtually at a moment's notice—usually by city government officials or district attorneys—are noted as advisories on the wire. These notices may read like this on the wire:

> EDITORS: DISTRICT ATTORNEY JOHN JONES WILL HOLD A PRESS CONFERENCE TO ANNOUNCE NEW DEVELOPMENTS IN THE CO-ED MURDER CASE AT 3 P.M. IN HIS OFFICE AT THE COUNTRY COURTHOUSE, MAIN STREET, THIRD FLOOR.

Wire-service editors look for material that will have an effect on the community or simply provide some entertainment. They will carry news about scheduled events in the state capital, miles away, on the theory that their subscribers may want to schedule coverage on their own if interested.

Daybook editors receive releases from other wire-service departments, and they, in turn, pass along some releases to writers and editors in the features department, to the business news desk, or to the foreign desk.

If you notify the wire service of an event too far in advance, the release may be placed in a file folder for early checking. That is, if the scheduled event is for July 2 and the wire service was advised about it a few weeks ahead of time, the release may be placed in the June 30 or July 1 folder for later confirmation. The wire service also may file a few paragraphs about the forthcoming event on July 1 and then carry it in the July 2 daybook.

Daybook lists are being developed by more and more major wire-service bureaus. Even where they do not exist, the bureau manager will maintain a file on forthcoming events, so you can proceed in each case as if the daybook is in existence at the bureau. The same rules apply whether there is a daybook that moves on the wire or remains on the bureau chief's desk in the form of a marked-up calendar or notebook.

Another universal rule: Don't telephone the editor to ask if he is going to assign someone to cover the event. Don't try to sell the story to the editor. At best, he'll tell you that he'll try to cover it. At worst, he'll tell you to stop bothering him. The odds are against your event getting covered by a wire-service reporter.

What happens if nobody shows up at your press conference? Cover it yourself. Send in a brief account of what took place, straining to be objective, and see that the wire service gets it as soon as possible. Telephone the city desk and ask if they want to take notes on the meeting.

Your constant appearance on the daybook will, over a period of time, help establish your group in the minds of editors. As you pursue your goals, your work can take on more significance to the media and the community. This changed status will also change your status with the wire-service desk and the local media. As you build credibility and reliability, you also build the reputations of the key people in your group. This growth can evolve into a degree of celebrity that reaches a point where the media—wire services included—will seek out your key people. As interest in your group and its leaders grows, the task of dealing with media should grow easier.

## FILM FEEDS

The wire services also supply TV stations with a daily wire-fed schedule of filmed news and features that can be used in locally produced newscasts.

The originating cities for the UPI Television News (UPITN) service are New York, San Francisco, Washington, and Chicago, and the feeds have been going to stations in those cities and others, including Los Angeles, Minneapolis, and Phoenix. The feeds begin at 6:30 P.M. and last for an hour, with commentary provided where needed. The stations also receive, via Teletype, a script and an advisory service that enables the subscriber stations to prepare their own comments to accompany the film.

UPITN not only supplies the major independent stations and network-affiliated local stations in this country, it supplies such major foreign TV networks as Eurovision, Independent Television Network (ITN) in England, and networks in France, Germany, and Japan.

Reese Schonfeld, assistant general manager of UPITN, has noted that his operation is "hard news" oriented; the unit concentrates on fast-breaking news stories and major government officials making statements before the cameras or being interviewed by newsmen. UPITN also likes to include a light, bright piece each day, since such features are popular with TV news-show producers as program "kickers," or upbeat closing stories for a newscast.

To direct story ideas to UPITN, call UPI at (212) MU 2-0400, Extension 481 in New York (460 West Fifty-Fourth Street); in Washington, (202) 393-3430, Extension 70 (at 1017 New Jersey Avenue, S.E.); in Chicago, (312) 321-0553; and Los Angeles, (213) 656-4644. The best way to get action on your story request is to deal directly with the nearest regional office of UPTelevision or UPITN and the UPI Audio Network, in New York, Washington, Chicago, Los Angeles, or Boston. UPITN will look at "hand-out film," but be sure to let them know if you have sent the film elsewhere. UPITN doesn't want to be embarrassed by supplying a station with film that it already has. Still photos are of no use to UPITN.

UPITN has about 110 clients. Occasionally, UPITN will exchange some film with a station that isn't a client. UPITN also operates a film library. Footage from this library is used mostly to produce documentary films.

## AUDIO NETWORKS

UPI's Audio Network serves 700 radio stations and the UPI broadcast newswire reaches about 3300 clients. Along with TV stations, it supplies about 100 cable-TV systems. About 100 sports and news "cuts" a day are fed to UPI clients. These feeds consist of ten- to sixty-second cuts that can be inserted in local newscasts. It also sends out market, sports, and feature reports that make use of voice reports from UPI correspondents around the world.

Peter S. Willett, vice-president of broadcast services at UPI, has noted that the purpose of the audio feed is to try to take the listener into the middle of the story, with natural sound, on-the-scene reporting with "believable sound underneath." He suggests that if one of your group's spokespersons is issuing a statement, it should be pretaped and fed over a telephone. The use of alligator clips on the telephone bypasses the telephone mouthpiece—a poor microphone—and makes the cut more understandable. Those who use tape feeds often purchase a recorder-connector from the telephone company.

This practice has developed to meet the trend toward "actuality" broadcasts, where radio stations seek to air the quote right from "the horse's mouth," so to speak, rather than from an official spokesperson. This trend leads to the use of "natural sound" as well. "They don't all have to sound like they're speaking out of a studio or a board room," Willett says. He suggests recording the speaker outdoors or on the job. Speaking at a seminar sponsored by New York University's Division of Business and Management, in association with the New York Chapter, Public Relations Society of America, on April 13, 1972, Mr. Willett told the public relations professionals to have the speaker answer a question rather than read from a prepared statement. "Record the statement (in a room) while you get some raw sound from the plant, feed 'em one-two, and we'll mix it just like casting a picture. I think you can often make your material more interesting if you use a little actual sound," he said.

He also offered this advice: "If you study ratings, you know you can reach more people at the peak radio time between seven and eight in the morning than you can reach at the peak television time between seven and, say, nine at night [and] nearly all of your television producers, like everyone else, will listen to the radio in the morning when you're shaving."

Willett also explained the "overnighter" story, and the work of overnight reporter-rewrite crews at the big metropolitan daily or at the wire service who work from about midnight until 8:00 A.M. These reporters are responsible for the news reports that air during early-morning "drive time" —when many people drive to work—and the early editions of afternoon newspapers.

"It's a rather thankless job because you're always using something that somebody else has first crack at," he noted. This means the overnight desk loves to land its own stories or freshen up the older ones with some new material. And this opens up some opportunities for those who want to be heard.

Whenever a major news event occurs, the overnight news desk is prepared to telephone certain people for reaction. You might want your group or your spokesperson to be on this list. But if you get a call and are asked for reaction, it's highly unlikely that you will be ready with good material in the middle of the night. More likely, you will want a bit more time to prepare. It may be that you will have developed a proper statement in the morning, or late morning, after the overnight man has gone home.

By that time, the reaction angle to the story may have yielded to new developments in the main story or to someone else's reaction. Here is what Willett recommends: "It might be better sometimes if you hold off on your comment and about three the next morning call the overnight man and say, 'Geez, I forgot, I was supposed to get back to you guys and forgot all about it. Somebody wanted to ask me about this latest price freeze or whatever.' I suspect you'll find that story very heavily played in the morning drive time because it's the overnight man's story and that makes a difference. They're all human. And then you'll have some Av Westin [ABC's "Evening News" executive producer] or someone like that shaving in the morning and he hears it, comes running in, writes a memo, 'Why didn't we have this the day before?' That's my idea of a really practical hint."

UPI Audio Network, besides feeding "insert" material to its clients, also does its own newscasts twenty-one times a day, seven days a week. Feeds are taken from anywhere. The main control bureau is in New York, but many feeds come out of Washington, Los Angeles, and overseas capitals.

These feeds all go into the New York bureau, where UPI controls its network transmission, a twenty-four-hour leased line that provides individual "cuts" and hourly newscasts, as well as live coverage of major news stories to its 700 radio station outlets. (The TV unit serves 15 domestic stations and 100 overseas stations.)

UPI also uses interview tapes and works with public relations people and press contacts to set up interviews with newsworthy individuals. This operation has the greatest capacity for outside program content, which should encourage those who want to be heard. It is national in scope, but it works with its local news desks. When a newsside staff member at UPI goes out to cover a story that lends itself to audio pickups, that reporter carries a tape recorder and uses it. On returning to the office, the cassette is delivered or transmitted to the audio desk.

Willett suggests that stories of national interest be presented directly to UPI Audio. He notes that on a slow news day—a holiday, for example—volunteering of feature-type material is most welcome. The UPI Audio feature editor, Ed Kearins, is constantly on the lookout for interesting, well-produced stories.

Willett adds, "There's always a demand for light, bright stuff, particularly if you use sound. It's got to be more than just a fellow talking. . . . Remember, most stations are in a rock-type, or hyped-up format. They don't like lengthy talk pieces. In their news shows they move very fast, use short items—it's a very quick, slick approach and I think you have to hold single items to forty seconds at the most, and if you can, keep them to thirty seconds. It's amazing how much you can do in thirty seconds. Your chances of being used, I would say, go up 50 percent."

The daybook, again, is of great value in UPI Audio's work. Willett and his staff check the daybook closely to see what is happening in the area so that they can hitchhike coverage with the local news desk. The reporters don't mind: they get paid extra for handling an audio cut.

The AP's audio service involves a taped service for daily shows that follow a 3½-minute format. These radio feeds deal with sports, features, or women's interests and other specially gathered stories. The AP daybook also serves as a source for this service. The procedure involves calling the broadcast news desks in major cities with your suggestions and requests.

To telephone-feed a story of spot news value to UPI, New York, dial (212) TN 7-3995. A recorder handles the call. For feature material (anything that isn't a spot news story), mail the reel-to-reel or cassette tape (7½ i.p.s.), to UPI Audio Network, 220 East Forty-second Street, New York, New York 10017.

In mailing a taped interview, remember that if it is used, the interviewer (possibly you?) will be cut out so that the announcer at the station that is airing the tape can replace your interviewer. In practice, the radio listener may hear the announcer say, "We asked Joseph Jones of the Better Schools for a Better America Committee what he thought of the proposed new school construction plan and here's his reply." The taped comment follows.

There is a cautionary note for medical stories. They will be checked and double-checked by the wire services because a carelessly handled account of a new medical development can be translated into a new miracle cure. And, as Willett has pointed out, "There's no faster way to create an uproar in the country than with claims of miracle cures."

## OTHER SYNDICATES

In addition to the wire services, there are numerous syndicated news and features services that supply material to the media. The *Editor & Publisher Yearbook*, published by *Editor & Publisher*, the newspaper trade publication (850 Third Avenue, New York, New York 10022), fills more than four pages with the names, addresses, and specialties of syndicated news services. They furnish newspapers with articles on virtually every subject, including religion, household material, and cartoons.

Services such as Reuters offer their own reports. *Reuters News Report* consists of spot news and background material.

Reuters also produces the *Reuters Business Beat*, culled from financial and commodity sources. The company has a bureau in Washington as well as a features desk and a business editor.

The Chicago Tribune-New York News Syndicate also supplies its subscribers with a long list of feature articles, including business, consumer matters, finance, food, religion, and women's-interest columns that range from cooking to career subjects.

Enterprise Science News (ESN), made up of Enterprise Science Service of New York and Universal Science News of Houston, offers clients a combined news and features report dealing with science, space technology, ecology and natural sciences, oceanography, general science, defense and technology, and environmental and medical sciences. ESN articles seek to contribute to public understanding of technical subjects. More than 150 newspapers receive this material through Newspaper Enterprise Association (1200 West Third Street, Cleveland, Ohio 44113).

A nationwide Teletype network also in operation links the National Catholic News Service (NCNS) and subscriber papers. The wire service is available around the clock to the National Catholic News Service and offers national and international news to Catholic newspapers in the continental United States. The NCNS is a division of the U.S. Catholic Conference (1312 Massachusetts Avenue N.W., Washington, D.C. 20005). While the U.S. bishops own this operation, it is staffed by a lay director and professional journalists and maintains full editorial independence.

If your group's program calls for distributing press releases beyond the local community, you should be sending your releases to the newspapers, the radio and TV stations, *and* the wire services. Remember to keep the media informed of your plans, your scheduled meetings, postponed meetings, changes in programs, changes in meeting places, and new developments that bear on the issues or projects your group is dealing with. In this way, you will be functioning as a main source of information in an ongoing story. As such, you will find your relationship to media advancing in importance. Before long, if you succeed in your work, you may find the TV camera crews being dispatched to your meetings whenever the wire-service daybook shows that your group is getting together again.

# 6

# Graphics: Symbols and Posters

## IMPORTANCE OF GRAPHICS

LIKE IT OR NOT, the way a person looks can influence the way others evaluate what he says. On television, for example, no matter how profound or relevant the statement, if it comes from a source that does not look trustworthy, much of what is said will not be believed.

The look of a person can also be transferred to the look of every element of your communications effort. Sometimes a face actually becomes the message. A good example is the 1960 political campaign of the late John F. Kennedy. No one knows how many people decided he looked better than Richard Nixon. It has been widely stated that it was the way Nixon looked on television (sweaty and heavily made up) that influenced enough voters to elect Kennedy president.

Each of us is exposed to hundreds, if not thousands, of visual images each day. Not just people's faces, but signs, advertisements, and symbols of all kinds. Thus, graphics can be very important to the total image of a communications effort.

If you are not seen, you are not likely to be remembered. Unfortunately, too few communications amateurs realize this. You can often win or lose on just the visual images that you present.

With some talent and a lot of effort this aspect of a communications effort can be used effectively. However, creating a positive visual image requires considerably more *professional* help than writing a news release or backgrounder. You need an artist-designer.

Care also must be taken to avoid winding up with too slick a look. It is usually better to understate when it comes to graphics. To go for the instant communications via a symbol (like Smokey the Bear) takes a great deal of skill, not generally available to beginners. Instead, most of us are better off if we try for the simple, clear, and, above all, the memorable. The face of a candidate properly used in posters is just this kind of a memorable symbol.

There are many office-holders today who delivered only a few speeches, rarely circulated a well-thought-out or well-written campaign statement. Instead, all they did was put up some billboard posters, distribute window posters, and shake a lot of hands. At the polls voters couldn't think of what they were for or against, but they remembered the name, usually associating it with a friendly face, and voted for that candidate merely because of that association. There is no substitute for an appearance or a name that seems friendly and unthreatening. Too strong an image can often defeat a political candidate or a cause.

## SYMBOLS

The Star of David, the Cross, and every nation's flag are symbols that inspire some to love and others to hate. But once known, the symbol is associated. Depending on how you use it, a symbol can cut across nationality and language. It becomes packed with more and more meaning as it is used. To almost everyone in the Western world, the red cross is a symbol of a hospital. Whether it is painted on a roof of a building or worn on an armband, when you see a red cross you think of someone helping the injured, the sick, or the needy. But this symbol has been abused and exploited by some to hide a military target or sell a brand of adhesive bandage. Nonetheless, through promotion the symbol of the red cross has become established with something that is good and with health.

FIG. 3

Recently an article on the Dreyfus Fund, one of the most successful mutual funds in the. nation, called attention to the fact it is their symbol—a lion—that is responsible in many ways for the fund's success (see fig. 3). Research revealed that many people remembered the lion when they decided to buy a fund.

For several years Dreyfus used a live lion in TV commercials to portray the excitement and courage of their investment approach. The lion was shown bounding up a set of subway stairs onto a stone pedestal. The live action of the lion was then "frozen" to present a noble, chin-up profile. The lion on the pedestal is now the symbol of Dreyfus.

Many studies have been made on the use of symbols, but few can tell anyone how to create a symbol that will be memorable. Being memorable is only part of the job a successful symbol must handle. It also should be associated with the idea that it represents. A good symbol makes the idea obvious to the person who sees it. He doesn't have to wonder about what it is supposed to represent.

The Dreyfus lion, with the words of the TV commercial and print advertising, hopes to make it very clear "that with a lion-like ferocity" Dreyfus management will take your money and invest it. They want you to believe they will be aggressive, lionlike, in pursuing profits and lionlike in getting you what you want—money.

The swastika was used centuries ago by ancient Egyptian and Aegean designers to denote the sun. According to historians, it was actually a pre-Christian cross.

The Star of David (Magen David, Mogen David, David's Shield) was first used by Egyptian scribes but was not widely associated with Judaism until long after the death of Christ. A printers' trademark in the fifteenth and sixteenth centuries, the Star of David was widely used without any religious significance at all. King David probably never saw or used the symbol, and in no Jewish religious document is it recognized as a symbol of things Jewish, since Jews traditionally avoid any symbols of their god. But the six-pointed star was used by Hitler's Germany to "mark" Jews, and a six-pointed star appeared on the flag of resistance that was raised above the Warsaw ghetto. Only since the emergence of the Jewish state of Israel has it become the "official" Jewish symbol.

Smokey the Bear first appeared in 1945. Now almost everyone in the nation associates this symbol with fire prevention. In fact, the owner of Smokey, the U.S. Department of Agriculture, makes several hundred thousand dollars a year selling the rights for others to reproduce the symbol as part of their message (see fig. 4).

## HOW TO GET A GOOD SYMBOL

No one can guarantee that if you create a symbol it will become as widely known as the Cross or Smokey the Bear. It is probably the most difficult of all graphic problems, and we would advise you to ignore the use of symbols in your graphics unless you have the rare gift and good fortune to acquire or modify an existent symbol that immediately tells those who see it what you are all about.

The use of adaptations of the red cross by pharmaceutical

FIG. 4

manufacturers, drug stores, ambulances, hospitals, and such is an example of successful steals of a known image.

Recently one of the women's lib groups—made up of airline stewardesses—took the biologic symbol for female and redesigned it. Another steal of a recognized symbol with a minor but very effective change.

## GET AN EXPERT TO HELP

Experts in graphics are often associated with advertising agencies and design studios. Any company that creates print or TV advertising has the capability to help with the graphic side of communications.

It is best to recruit a designer at the outset of a communications campaign, since every investment you make in a serious program that involves print will in one way or another involve graphics.

Since you usually have to pay for making an impression, the organization of the graphics part of your program should get a high priority. If you don't do this, chances are you will be wasting tremendous amounts of impressions.

If you think that you have to use a symbol and must create a new one, be sure that it does not already belong to someone. Check with the Trademark Bureau at the U.S. Patent Office before investing in a campaign. For more information about copyrights, write to the Register of Copyrights there.

Also be sure you know what your symbol means to people of various backgrounds. Improper use of a religious symbol can alienate some of the people you want to attract. For example, the color green cannot be used commercially in Moslem countries, since it is reserved for religious use only.

The fact that the antiwar movement used the U.S. flag and old army uniforms to protest administration action was a self-defeating way to use these symbols. Protestors often alienated more people than they attracted, by appearing to denigrate those symbols. To most Americans the flag means goodness in action and purity of thought. When antiwar groups burned the flag, they seemingly burned the very souls of millions of people whose support they wanted and needed.

However, dramatic destruction of symbols does get attention. Ideally, the way to use symbol destruction is to develop a new one. For example, the environmentalists did not need to burn the U.S. flag to gain a symbol. They created a flag of their own with green stripes and a solid green top.

The bearded, long-haired antiestablishment forces that cite Jesus and his followers as examples of what they look like have missed an important point. When Christians first organized, every man had long hair. If Jesus had wanted to look different and anti-Roman establishment, he might have shaved his beard and worn a crew cut. Obviously he did not want to look different.

## POSTERS

Too few organizations understand and recognize the use of wall posters. Possibly the reason for this is a general lack of poster sophistication by artists in this country. This is not true in Europe where the outdoor poster (best illustrated by artists like Savignac and Picasso), usually plastered on kiosks and walls, has been a commercial success for generations.

The illicit use of posters or wall-painting as graffiti is probably more common than the legal use of signs. However, poster art is a medium that lends itself to such exploitation.

Posters come in a variety of sizes. The most common sizes are 11 by 14 inches and 22 by 28 inches, yet stickers as small as 1½ by 1½ inch can be purchased cheaply ($2–$5 for 1000) and used effectively to get attention.

To design a poster, you need the help of a good graphic artist who can put on paper the elements that help tell your story. The most successful efforts are those in which graphic elements are communicated without the need for words. The examples are few, but Picasso's doves comes to mind as one of the most successful.

## COSTS OF POSTERS

A local printer can give fairly good service for most jobs. The key is to get a competent designer to help.

Costs vary, but once you have the original artwork, a local New Jersey printer, for example, would print 10,000 posters 14 by 22 inches for $190 per thousand. The same artwork for a larger poster 17 by 26 inches would cost about $274 per thousand.

Look at the poster of "Diamond for Assembly" (see fig. 5). It has everything important for a good graphic approach to getting votes. It shows the candidate clearly happy and sincere. It gives his name and the office he seeks simply. There is no better way to reach the undecided voter than through the use of the poster.

The yoga poster and next to it the one on "Reality" (fig. 6) are other good examples of the use of posters. They don't have the simple visual appeal of Diamond's, yet in their own way they are excellent.

DIAMOND
for
ASSEMBLY

FIG. 5

"REALITY"
MEDITATION
AND
INSTRUCTION
• EXPERIENCE ENLIGHTENMENT
• HARMONIZE YOUR LIFE
• ACHIEVE YOUR GOALS
LOUISE BERLÉ (BerLAY)
TEACHES THE WISDOM
OF EAST & WEST IN
"THE NATURE OF REALITY
THE CREATIVE PRINCIPLE"
IN TWICE WEEKLY MEETINGS AT
STEINWAY CONCERT HALL
111 WEST 57th ST. - 3.d FLOOR - N.Y.C.
EVERY SUNDAY AFTERNOON 2 to 4
EVERY THURSDAY NIGHT 7 to 9
ALL WELCOME • SUGGESTED DONATION $1.50
YOGA
Classes in Exercise – Breathing, Concentration, Relaxation – Meditation – Psychic Development – Personal Guidance
Small classes / daily / morning, noon, evening
Coed / beginners, intermediate, advanced / all ages
Free Introductory Lesson · $2 per lesson / call now
Yogi Gupta Ashram
871 Seventh Ave. & 55th St. New York, N.Y. 10019
Telephone 541-8389

FIG. 6

Neither of these will interest all who see them. Yet if you are thinking about taking a yoga class and happen to see the poster, you are given enough information to contact the Yogi Gupta Ashram. The same is true for the meditation offered by Louise Berle. Those interested can get to Steinway Hall to see if they want to spend $1.50 to learn what she can do for them.

## GETTING THEM UP

Professional organizations often have contracts with building owners giving them permission to place posters. Even empty buildings or boarded-up buildings and lots are owned by someone; therefore it is usually best to get permission before placing a poster. A "Post No Bills" sign is a warning that if you put a poster up without permission, you can count on having it removed.

Outdoor signs and billboards, car cards in buses and subways can be excellent for getting your message across, but you have to be sure that the location picked has good traffic and that your message does your cause some good. Environmentalists and others have succeeded in getting many states to restrict or ban billboards on or near highways (by 1976 over 800,000 will have been removed), but there are still many locations in towns and cities where a good sign or billboard message can literally deliver your message to the entire reading population of the area.

In South Orange, New Jersey, for example, it is very difficult to go to the store, library, or post office without passing the Erie-Lackawanna railroad station. Each year, when the local United Fund Drive is in progress, the railroad cooperates in providing space for a giant United Fund poster that is tied onto a bridge over the main street. Almost everyone in the area sees this sign more than once before the campaign ends.

The costs of an effective graphics campaign can be simply the cost of a single sign, like the one used in South Orange. This includes the cost of design and creative work, printing, and the labor for installing the sign. An outdoor campaign to reach over 90 percent of all the adults in an entire county would cost thousands of dollars for painting or papering the billboard. You would also have to pay for the design.

## SUBWAY AND BUS ADVERTISING

An excellent way to get a message to the public is via transportation advertising. Most cities in the nation with public transportation have space available for nonprofit organizations and charge about $1.25 each to put up the cards.

In New York City it would cost at least $6000 a month for two cards per car in 6600 cars. You would have to supply the cards (14,000 of them).

Two cards per subway could be seen by 5 million riders in the Metropolitan New York area, each riding an average of thirty-one times a month. The average ride is about seventeen minutes—plenty of time for a rider to read your message if he wants to. Organizations like the American Cancer Society are heavy users of subway advertising in New York, yet each time they change the message they must pay for artwork.

## GETTING NATIONAL COVERAGE

The Advertising Council, an industry organization that for the past thirty years has been responsible for many notable public-service print and TV campaigns, responds to well-organized nonpolitical appeals. To warrant this organization's support, you must obtain the blessing of one or more of the nation's largest users of advertising.

Not long ago when the Minority Enterprise Small Business Investment Companies (MESBIC) was licensed by the Small Business Administration, the Advertising Council was mobilized to tell MESBIC's story to American businessmen. The board of directors of the organization had almost every top advertiser and agency in the nation as a member. There wasn't much of a problem in getting free TV and print coverage via the council.

The power of the council is formidable if your program is national in scope. Thomas Asher, writing in (*MORE*), says that the council has a monopoly of network public-service time. The council estimates that since it began thirty years ago, over $5.6 billion of free service has been given by the media for public-service messages. Thus, even though you can get a commitment for free time you have to pay for the out-of-pocket production costs to make spot announcements. This can run from a minimum of $75,000 to $200,000 *just for the cost of making and distributing spots.*

Not even the best campaign will get the help of free TV time unless the material sent to the stations looks good. It must also have the backing of important people. In 1973, Jerry Lewis, using a network of TV stations for twenty-one hours, raised in excess of $12 million for the Muscular Dystrophy Association. He paid for what he had to, but nevertheless his contacts in business and show business cannot be forgotten. What he raises provides almost the entire operating and research budget for the association's 106 clinics.

Here is the Advertising Council's statement of policy:*

1. Accept no subsidy from Government and remain independent of it.
2. Conduct campaigns of service to the nation at large, avoiding regional, sectarian, or special interest drives of all kinds.
3. Remain non-partisan and non-political.
4. Conduct the Council on a voluntary basis.
5. Accept no project that does not lend itself to the advertising method.
6. Accept no campaign with a commercial interest unless the public interest is obviously overriding.

## OPERATIONS

The keynote here is "voluntary." Advertising agencies do the creative work on Advertising Council campaigns free of charge; an executive from a national advertiser serves as the volunteer coordinator, and national media contribute vast amounts of time and space. Broad additional support is given by local media and advertisers across the country.

When a campaign is proposed to, or requested of, the council (usually by a private public-service organization or a government bureau or agency), it goes to the board of directors if the request

* For more information on how the council works, write to The Advertising Council, Inc., 825 Third Avenue, New York, New York 10017.

meets the council's criteria of acceptance. The board may accept or reject the request.

If the campaign requested is covered by an act of Congress that sets policy, no further approval is needed to make it a council project.

## USE OF PHOTOGRAPHY

Every day the *New York Times* uses sixty or so photographs. Of that number, about one-third are taken by the *Times* own staff photographers; about six come from outside professionals who were asked to take pictures as part of a *Times* assignment; fifteen are supplied by the wire services; but ten, or one-sixth, of all photographs used usually come from outside sources—handouts from public relations people or others who want to be seen as well as heard.

One of the best known suppliers of the handout photograph is Gary Wagner, International Photos, Inc., a photographer who specializes in pictures for the business community in Manhattan. Wagner commented on the use of photographs by the press to specialists in business public relations, but his words apply equally to anyone who wants to get a photograph taken for publicity purposes: "Very often the best results are not obtained when a photographer shows up at a location and starts shooting, especially when the subject is a business or industrial operation."

Here are his tips:

Make sure your people are not posed. Have the photographer shoot without upsetting the operation. There's only one thing worse than people looking at the camera and that's when they're shaking hands and looking at the camera. Instead of lining up people for a group photo so it resembles a picket fence, pick another pose. Get the people on a stairway. Use furniture to have some people seated and some standing. If outdoors, use a hill, steps, pertinent equipment. In a nutshell, use your head and imagination.

Camera angle and distance can enliven the award presentation photo. The trophy, certificate, check or plaque can loom in the immediate foreground for a more dramatic composition. Another trick: arrange beforehand, and in confidence, with the recipient's husband or wife to surprise the winner with a congratulatory kiss—right in front of the photographer's lens.

For close-ups or head shots, candid photos make the person come alive. Mood and character come through. Readers always favor a photo that shows a real person. A long lens is often useful for tight close-ups without the self-consciousness caused by the close proximity of a camera.

Available light eliminates the distraction of artificial light.

Shoot fast and often to catch those once-in-a-lifetime fleeting expressions. The position of a person's hands or fingers near a face can be expressive and add interest to a picture.

When you want a full-length photo, the picture will communicate more if you show the person in an environment related to his or her major activity.

Action in a picture—the feeling of something happening—always gets reader attention. The action can be simple—someone opening a letter or peering into a file, taking a call, penciling a report. Action begets interest. Have the subject leave the room, then open the door and come back in. Shoot as he enters. Call his name—shoot as he turns toward you.

"Frame" subjects with arches, windows, branches or other objects in the immediate foreground.

Lighting and unusual weather can work to your advantage. If there's fog, a long lens will heighten the effect. Light near sundown and sunup is often unusual, giving striking color results. Use sunlight to backlight for silhouette effects. Shoot toward the sun across water for a foreground full of silver ripples.

In sum, Wagner says, "To learn about pictures, look at pictures. Experiment by clipping pictures you like, accumulating them on a bulletin board, going back to them from time to time, and analyzing why you like them and how they were taken. It is excellent conditioning for your frame of mind when you plan your next edition, and if you will be assigning a photographer to shoot an event, you can give explicit instructions."

For a good example of the successful use of photographs look at the photograph sent out early in 1973 on the UPI wire (fig. 7). Hundreds of TV stations and thousands of newspapers all over the world subscribe to this service. The photograph was taken by a UPI photographer who was assigned to the story by

WAP 021608 2/16/73 WASHINGTON: Nine robed women, all executive board officers of the National Organization for Women conducted a "mock" session of the United States Supreme Court 2/16 to protest the urgent need to appoint women to the U.S. Supreme Court. The action took place across the street from the court building (shown in background). (UPI) rkm/fc

FIG. 7

the Washington bureau. Because of it, the entire nation was given a chance to visualize a protest of the National Organization for Women. This photograph and its caption probably violated several of Wagner's rules: It is posed; the people are looking at the camera. Yet, it is exciting, even memorable. Whoever staged it knew that there was a good chance for a wire-service pickup, and they were right.

# 7

# Handbills and Pamphlets, Newspapers, Booklets, Position Papers, White Papers, Newsletters

THE ART OF pamphleteering mastered by Tom Paine and many others is still well within the capability and budget of almost anyone who wants to share his point of view with others. Consider Ted and Nick Fox. Early in 1971, the two Laconia, New Hampshire, high-school students found that publishing and distributing a limited number of copies of their newspaper *New Times* was enough to get them nationwide attention. They did very little that was original. Yet their second edition of 500 copies caused many local citizens to choose up sides. The Fox brothers demonstrated that a simply printed newspaper is one of the most effective methods of communications.

The Fox boys came to national prominence when an article by Ted appeared on the "op ed" page of the Friday, May 7, 1971 *New York Times*. He described the origin and attempt at suppression of their *New Times*. The impact of this simple anti-establishment newspaper on Laconia is not likely to be forgotten soon.

After the initial shock of a publication that challenged the Vietnam war, supported Angela Davis, and described the action of birth-control pills, the town finally permitted continued publication.

Writing in the *Times*, Ted Fox said: "A large portion of Laconia High students do not go on to college, which means that as soon as they get out of school they will be faced with the draft. Most of those drafted will go; they won't want to go but they will because nobody has ever told them that they can get counseling. . . ."

Later he described the impact of his article on birth-control pills on two parents: "The woman told me that if she had a shotgun she would blow my head off. She said I'd better get out of the way if I saw her Cadillac coming toward me. . . . What really bothered me was that the woman and her husband hated me so. Why? Apparently because the *New Times* gave their kids the truth that they refused to give them. . . ."

The fact is that simple four- or eight-page handbills or tabloid newspapers are changing a lot of people's minds as they present information that their editors unearth. The underground newspapers are good examples of this. As with the Laconia *New Times* (total circulation was less than 1000) there is the possibility of tremendous impact. Probably greater and quicker notoriety was achieved in Laconia, New Hampshire, by the *New Times* than by any professional newspaper in the area at the time.

## WHEN TO USE HANDBILLS

Handbills, underground newspapers, and pamphlets are all excellent methods of communication if their use is understood. The keys to success are simplicity of expression, good distribution, and frequency of publication.

Perhaps one of the reasons for success with this kind of communication tool is that the text fits closely with the needs of the readers. The underground press doesn't just depend on dirty words and pornographic photos to keep its readership. Many of the articles could be reprinted in *Time* or your local newspaper. The headlines may be a bit sensational, but the text has to inform if the paper is to keep readers.

## TABLOIDS, NEWSLETTERS, NEWSPAPERS

Tabloids are useful to anyone who needs photographs as the prime medium to deliver a message. Tabloids can't be beat if you want to get a message to a lot of people with a shocking photograph plus a statement, one that probably won't be printed in any other place.

You can use newsletters or newspapers when what you have to say will be passed on to many more people than a message on radio or television. Print can be very effective in influencing behavior, perhaps because for many of us who grew up before television took over, anything printed usually took on more importance than what we heard. The very process of reducing a message to print gives it validity, especially if you can get what you printed picked up and reported in a newspaper.

To succeed in this medium you have to master the form. Good lessons can be obtained by careful study of the *New York Daily News* and the *National Enquirer*. The writers and the editors of these successful publications are also helped immeasurably by their use and layout of photographs.

Note that the sentences are short, using no more words than are absolutely necessary. No large words. Few wasted words. Sharp editing punches up every sentence. Many paragraphs, rather than many sentences in a few paragraphs. It takes great skill to write and edit this kind of message. The technique is worth trying to emulate.

## USE OF PHOTOS

A drawing or cartoon could replace a photograph, but there aren't many artists who understand the use of cartoons (see Chapter 6 for more on photographs). It may be better to use a fair photograph or none at all than to use a poor drawing that attempts to look like a cartoon.

What is said is as important as what is shown. Headlines should telegraph the message and invite readership of the article. The words should be few and to the point. Readers look to this method of expression for facts. It is better to label your opinion an "editorial" even though the entire newspaper can represent a narrow point of view.

When expressing an opinion, you should use as much supporting factual information as you have. A carefully organized rebuttal of an opponent's speech in a political campaign, printed and widely circulated as a pamphlet, can help win votes from the uncommitted if the printed message is believed.

The Fox brothers discovered that the facts on draft counseling were not available to most Laconia students, so they printed them. Often just the act of putting information in type will make the difference.

## LAYOUT

Get professional help with the graphics of anything printed, especially tabloid newspapers, newsletters, and handbills. Poor graphics will actually discourage readership. The well-put-together message is often destroyed by bad graphics. Unless you are very lucky, don't count on the printer to design your layouts. Get an artist with experience. If none is available, get something you like that someone else did and tell the printer to copy it exactly, including type faces, leading (the space between the type), and column width. Whatever you do, unless it's an emergency, ask the printer for proofs. Use the proofs to check your type and the captions for the photos. More than once a printer has used the wrong word and mixed up the photos. Proofreading is your only protection.

Good layouts are the ones that invite reading. The open page that invites you in to look over the stories is the one that will deliver readers. Good design is simple, direct, and uncomplicated. Even though it is cheaper to use two pages instead of three, six instead of eight, large type and big photos have greater impact. It usually won't pay to economize on this aspect of your communications effort.

Once you start a communications program, keep the same format. When you develop a design that you like and it seems to work well, don't change it for the sake of change. Especially if you have a title like the *New Times* or *Women's Voice*. The more you use it, the more familiar it will become and the greater your influence will be. When someone says they saw it in the *New York Times*, chances are the other person will see the front page of that paper in his mind's eye.

Color is rarely used properly in graphics. It is best to avoid the added expense unless there is no alternative. The most powerful combination still available is black type on white paper. You may be tempted to experiment with colored stock and unusual type faces, but if you want to deliver a message fast, stick to a very simple use of type and ink.

## HOW TO PRODUCE BOOKLETS, POSITION PAPERS, WHITE PAPERS

Your group may develop to a stage at which the publication of a detailed, in-depth booklet, brochure, or book is in order. These may take the form of a lengthy history, background report, survey of a problem, status report, or fact sheet. In effect, such publications are press releases because they are related to the generation of news in the media. But the specific difference between such publications and the press release is that the press release is designed to deal with an immediate situation, to spread some news or information immediately or to get a statement, usually brief, on the record.

Press conferences, since they are designed to deal at greater length with an immediate situation, sometimes can provide the basis of a booklet, position paper, or white paper. That is, the transcript of the meeting may be edited and published in one of these forms.

Let's assume that your group has been functioning for some time and has accumulated a history of sorts. At one of your meetings, you may raise the question of whether the time has come to publish a booklet that deals with your group's work. If the purpose is to recruit new members or generate support and money, perhaps you will decide that a booklet—varying in length from four or eight pages to something much thicker—can be used as a "leave-behind," or "envelope stuffer." A leave-behind is what one leaves behind after meeting with a prospect or group of prospects. When this publication is sent through the mail, it becomes a stuffer (i.e., it is stuffed into an envelope). Usually, this mailing is made in response to a request for information. With postage costs and printing charges important considerations, you must design your booklet with a thought to economy and ease of mailing. The weight of the paper and the size of the envelope determine costs. Ask the local postmaster for his suggestions.

The booklet may also be sent to the newspapers, broadcast media, magazines, and community "opinion leaders"—school officials, church and religious leaders, heads of governmental agencies, service clubs—in order to generate support. Your hope in sending the booklet to the media is that its contents will lead to stories about your group's special area of concern. The booklet should be accompanied by a letter or a press release that summarizes the material or explains its purpose.

What we are discussing here are simple booklets that contain basic information about an organization or an issue and perhaps a coupon for prospective members or contributors to fill out.

## THE POSITION PAPER

The position paper can be issued in booklet form. Its name suggests its contents: a statement that sets forth a position on an issue. It is published after an issue has developed to a point at which a clear statement is warranted so that the public and the media will have a clear idea as to where your group stands.

One or two pages can suffice, but these pages should be factual, carefully prepared, and closely checked for accuracy. Look for inconsistencies or contradictions in your material. If such errors are published, they will haunt you and make you wish you had never put it in writing.

The position paper can be Xeroxed or mimeographed and treated as a press release in form and distribution pattern if its timing is related to a newsmaking event.

## THE WHITE PAPER

The most comprehensive publishing venture that your group will probably undertake is the white paper. But it is a rare project, reserved for matters of high interest. Since it is a difficult and time-consuming project, you should realize that it may not be worth the effort if it is to deal with a subject of low, passing interest.

The white paper deals with the history of a problem, issue, or event. Its scope may embrace a major national or world issue or a purely local subject, such as a school bond referendum.

If your group is advocating passage of a bond for construction of new school facilities, the white paper will be useful. It should be, in effect, a history of the school district. It should project population trends, set forth a plan to deal with growth, and inform the public as to costs, taxes, and advantages and disadvantages.

This publication should be regarded as an "everything you want to know about the issue" venture—and more. It should answer every question. Its tone must be objective. It should include texts that are pertinent to the issue to help spread the full story before the public. If done properly, the white paper emerges with the status of an "official" document. It becomes part of your community's history as well as your organization's.

Ponder the pros and cons of a white paper very carefully before going ahead with its preparation. You may decide that a fact sheet is a better alternative. The fact sheet is a chronology of an issue in which your group is active. It can be most helpful to reporters who are covering a continuing story, since it will list key dates, names, titles, and events, as it consolidates material. From time to time, the fact sheet should be updated and reissued.

The basic tone of the fact sheet should be objective, barren of adjectives or other coloring phrases. It must be written with your opponents in mind. Ask yourself as you write it or read it, Is there any language being used here that the other side will find objectionable? Biased? Inaccurate? If you can arrive at an even-handed presentation in your fact sheet, you will have helped your group build greater credibility with media and also have helped to give the members of your group a more sharply focused sense of what the work and goals are all about.

The essential ingredient in any of the papers described here is research. Don't trust to memory. Look for corroboration in your records or elsewhere. You should understand how to organize research work and produce it.*

* There are a number of books and booklets in the library that deal with this aspect of publishing. Among the best are *The Research Paper*,

Bear in mind that in dealing with a local issue, your library cannot be expected to have much material that is directly relevant beyond a file of back issues of local newspapers. You will make use of such files, of course, and then gather additional pertinent information by interviewing those in the community who have kept records such as minutes of meetings, contracts, reports, studies, and personal correspondence.

If you need to recruit someone with research and writing experience for your project but don't know of anyone qualified, check with the libraries for names of students or free-lance writers in the area who might take on your assignment for a fee.

Consider hiring a public relations counselor or a local writer for the job if your group has a budget and can afford to pay for professional work. Look for someone who is reliable, fast as well as accurate, objective, and not overloaded with other projects. Make certain that the writer who gets the assignment understands the purpose of the work and knows exactly how much help can be expected from your group. Appoint a member to serve as liaison and work out deadlines for an outline, chapters, and so on.

Publishing your booklet, brochure, white paper, and so on usually presents a financial problem. Scout around for someone—a company, a philanthropic foundation, a national organization, a private benefactor—to underwrite the cost. Another approach is to check with the head of a department at a nearby college or university—the department being one that broadly concentrates on the area of activity that your group effort relates to—and see whether a student can prepare a paper, for credit, on the subject.

---

by Lucyle Hook and Mary Virginia Gaver (Prentice-Hall), and *A Manual for Writers*, by Kate L. Turabian (University of Chicago Press). These how-to books deal primarily with the various ways libraries can be utilized by researchers, the preparation of outlines, determining objectives, proper form and content, and typing the paper. The Hook-Gaver booklet contains this advice for writing the paper: "You should use the third person throughout except in the optional preface, where you may express indebtedness and discuss your personal interest in the subject. The first person plural (editorial we), always recognized as formal, is correctly used in discussing common knowledge ('We know that . . .') or for reminding readers of an already completed statement ('as we have already noticed . . .'). The bulk of the theme should be impersonal and without reference to the writer."

The paper may become useful to your group if it is made available to the community later on.

In any of these publishing efforts, remember that attention spans are constantly growing shorter these days. This means that the white paper is not as powerful a persuader as it was some years ago.

Today, it appears, there is a tendency on the part of the press to riffle through a white paper and look for a likely news peg. That angle becomes the lead of a news story. The news angle dominates the story and, as far as the reader is concerned, is the whole story. It may turn out that no white paper was needed; a press release could have accomplished as much.

Government bodies today will create commissions to study a problem. After a long, intensive study of all the issues involved, the commission publishes a report. The press latches on to the most spectacular pronouncement in the report—many times, the paragraph that criticizes an elected official or well-known person, since names make news. If an obvious handle is missing, the press may elect to use some interpretive comment with which to generate news interest. The press is often criticized for this tendency. The criticism frequently is from those who wouldn't have read the news article if it was handled in the same formalized style as the original report.

If a white paper is, in your opinion, misinterpreted by media, you should decide whether the misinterpretation is worth correcting. If the matter is important enough, go back to that medium and point out where and how you think the problem arose. If you are reasonable and convincing, a method can be worked out that enables your views to be brought to the public's attention again without embarrassment to either party. A letter to the editor will be published. Or an editorial will be written and published. Or a follow-up article or interview can appear that reviews the situation and seeks to set forth more clearly the views of your group. This can take the form of a story that reports on reaction to the white paper and looks ahead to the future work of your group.

Because it is so difficult to predict how your white paper will be received or reported upon, ponder very carefully the question of whether to embark on the project. If you decide that a white paper may be a form of overkill or too costly for the size of the audience or importance of the issue, you may find that a position paper or press release can actually do the job more effectively.

If more than one chapter is involved in a position paper or booklet, it may be wise to assign different chapters to different people in order to expedite production (this assumes that the work is being done "in-house," not by a writer hired for the job). Make certain that outlines of each chapter are submitted to your chief editor or project supervisor so that the details can be checked and duplication avoided. It is highly unlikely that you will want to embark on a project that will produce a slick-paper booklet filled with four-color photographs, for if that is your requirement, you should try to raise enough money to have professionals produce the booklet under your supervision. You could consider selling advertising space in the booklet to help defray the cost of production. The chapter on advertising will supply you with information on this approach.

Sometimes, the simple four- or eight-page booklet can be distributed to the community as an insert in a local newspaper. Before you start to produce this booklet, check with the newspaper's advertising manager to learn what rules you must obey. Consider, too, the circulation of the various newspapers to determine which "mix" can reach the most households. The cost for such insert handling is generally around $20 per 1000 copies, but the number of pages, their size, and the weight of the paper you are using can bring that cost up.

## PRINTING SHORTCUTS

A friendly printer can save you money and time. If he wants to, he can print your job on off-hours or at the end of someone else's run and thereby pass the savings on to you. He can tell you what size paper to use to minimize waste. If he has to cut to a size your artist specifies, it can cost twice as much as if he used leftover stock from another job. You won't know until you ask, but the word is always *ask*.

The printer can literally wreck a publication despite the best efforts of all who worked on it. Poor type, bad setting, mistakes, all can ruin your effort. Once you have given the printer the order, you often have no choice when the job is done but to accept it no matter how it looks, hoping he won't repeat the mistakes next time. Often a printer won't accept a return. He will insist you keep and pay for an order if you accepted the galleys and did not change anything when he showed you the "blueprint."

The best protection is to insist on seeing everything given a printer for a job. Don't take his word for anything. Even the best printer can make a mistake, especially in caption misplacement, spelling errors, or mixup of headlines. Your only hope is to check over carefully what you give to him and, more important, what he gives back to you. Also, never proof your own copy. Try to get someone else to read the text that you wrote. Never assume the job will be done exactly as you want it if you haven't given exact instructions to the printer.

## DISTRIBUTION

No matter how effective your printing, the key to getting seen, heard, and believed is the number of people who see and read what you said. The more important and communicative the reader, the better for you.

In properly designed communications, you are reaching people who see and talk to many other people. Barbers, beauty parlor operators, dentists, and teachers, as well as newspaper editors, are important to reach to extend the scope of your audience. These people who talk to many people are in a sense "communications amplifiers." The trick is in getting them to help you with your message.

Obviously, if you recruit all the beauty shop operators, barbers, and medical people in your town as active and committed members of your group, you won't need much outside help. But you may find that beauty shops will put up a poster or let you leave a copy of your newspaper in their place of business.

The only way you can actually count on delivery of a printed message is to hand it out yourself, get others to do it for you, and mail it to those people you cannot see. The postal service, despite all the problems it has, still can be counted on to deliver a message if you pay the postage.

Getting correct and valuable mailing lists is a science all its own. The experts on this aspect of distribution are few and not generally available.

Senator George McGovern surprised a large number of people in the spring of 1972 with the extent of his organization, which raised $28 million. Not a small part in financing his efforts was played by the use of computer print-outs for mail solicitations and volunteers to man the candidate's local offices. The mailing lists were obtained from a variety of sources.

Mailing lists are extremely valuable. It was reported in a recent issue of (*MORE*) that *Moneysworth*, a publication started by Ralph Ginzburg, makes over $3.5 million a year from "renting" its list of its 500,000 subscribers.

Two of the best known sources for national mailing lists are Dunhill International List Co., Inc. (444 Park Avenue South, New York, New York 10016), and Alan Drey Co., Inc. (420 Lexington Avenue, New York, New York 10017).

For local lists, try to get help from various local publications. With a little luck and some consideration it is possible to get lists of voters, church members, Rotary and Lions clubs members, PTA members, and many others. You should not overlook official and semi-official sources. You can even get the names of everyone married in a town, all who were buried, and everyone who was born by asking for it at the right place, usually the town hall.

Your distribution technique can be simple handouts at the local supermarket or mailings. Don't underestimate the impact of a newsletter, pamphlet, or newspaper that somehow gets into publication as an added insert.

When *Ms.* magazine was starting, the pilot publication was inserted into every issue of *New York Magazine*. The 500,000 copies of an established weekly publication were used to deliver an actual copy of a new publication. The device was successful.

## USING HANDBILLS FOR RECRUITMENT

Too often the authors of handbills don't think about the use of their publication for helping them with recruiting and for fund-raising. Handbills work well as mass appeals for workers and funds. Remember, the same person who reads a message appeal-

Vol. 4, No. 2

# The Spokeswoman

An independent monthly newsletter of women's news

August 15, 1973

IN THIS ISSUE



## Griffiths Hearings Reveal Widespread Economic Discrimination

Hearings before the Joint Economic Committee of Congress, chaired by Representative Martha Griffiths (D-Mich.), have produced a flood of evidence on women's second-class economic citizenship. Highlighting the testimony are revelations that the Federal Government is doing a poor job of enforcing anti-discrimination legislation. Specific charges against the Government include the following:

*Less than one-half of the back pay found due in violation of the Equal Pay Act has ever been paid.

*The Equal Employment Opportunities Commission (EEOC) has a backlog of some 65,000 cases and is acting on less than a quarter of that number per year.

*Government agencies holding anti-bias enforcement responsibilities do not themselves adhere to EEOC guidelines. For example, the Office of Federal Contract Compliance has no women in professional positions in any of its field offices.

*Although the federal Work Incentive (WIN) Program is specifically designed to provide job training for welfare recipients, only 60% of those enrolled in the program are women, although women comprise 87% of the people with dependent children receiving welfare.

*Women represent only 25.9% of persons enrolled in the Job Corps, although they constitute 45% of the unemployed in the eligible age group.

Government officials conceded many of these and other charges. EEOC Chairman William H. Brown agreed with a charge by economist Barbara Bergman that not one of the nation's 500 largest corporations was in compliance with anti-discrimination laws. Assistant Secretary of Labor Bernard De Lury conceded that only 48% of Equal Pay Act settlements were actually collected, but failed to explain why. Former head of the Department of Labor's Women's Bureau Elizabeth Duncan Koontz cited the Department's failure to live up to EEOC standards and the low enrollment of women in federally funded training programs. The Federal Reserve Board was also cited for failure to use its influence to equalize access to credit. Representative Griffiths commented caustically that "the Fed apparently is responsible only to God. I have always been surprised they don't stockpile their own nuclear weapons."

In other testimony, top Nixon Administration economists went beyond statements made in the Administration's Annual Economic Report and said that pure discrimination reduces the average earnings of women to 80 or 90% of what men make for the same work. The figures, which were submitted by Herbert Stein, Chairman of the President's Council of Economic Advisors and Council member Marina Whitman, were attacked by other witnesses as too low. Economist Barbara Bergman charged that of seven recent studies done on the subject, only one showed a differential as low as 20%; that was the one the Council quoted. Ms. Bergman also challenged the Council's argument that the relatively high unemployment rate for women is due to the fact that women move in and out of the labor force because of family responsibilities. She countered that every woman who leaves

(cont. on page 2)

The Spokeswoman is an independent monthly newsletter published at 5464 South Shore Drive, Chicago, Illinois 60615 (Tel: 312-363-2580). Subscription price is $7 per year by individual check and $12 per year by institutional check.  Editor and publisher: Susan Davis. Managing Editor: Karen Wellisch. Advertising Manager: Joanna Martin. (For advertising information write her at 1380 Riverside Drive, Apt. 7G, N.Y., N.Y. 10033, Tel: 212-568-5007). Circulation Manager: Sandy Contreras. (For circulation problems, write her at 2806 E. 93rd St., Chicago, Ill. 60617). Second class postage paid at Chicago, Illinois. This publication is on file at the International Women's History Archive, 2325 Oak St., Berkeley, California, and is available on microfilm from Bell and Howell, Wooster, Ohio.

FIG. 8

ing for support may want to help you as a volunteer worker or may contribute some money. All too often there is no address included. A simple idea that works is to use a self-addressed printed business (postage-paid) reply envelope as part of your publication.

## NEWSLETTERS

There are thousands of newsletters. According to the *Newsletter on Newsletters*, the reasons for this proliferation of reading material are many, but most important is the fact that a well-written newsletter can be cheap to produce and easy for one or two people to get out. And depending on how well it's written and how carefully it is distributed, the impact can be considerable.

A good case in point is *The Spokeswoman*. This twelve-page, 8½-by-11-inch monthly newsletter now has a circulation of several thousand, after three years of publication. Cost for one year is $7 per subscription for individuals and $12 for institutions. Created in Chicago in 1971 by Miriam Desmond, Susan Davis, and three others, this excellent independent publication for women produced an income of $33,000 the first year of operation. A profit of $3000 was realized and paid to the publisher as her salary, after paying $5200 for printing, $5700 for promotion, and $6500 for salaries plus several thousand dollars for travel, office expenses, postage, and the like.

Each issue covers women's news from several angles and also contains several want-ads for women—some from national companies like CBS; Pfizer, Inc.; and GTE-Sylvania. A typical issue will have short articles on women's-rights organizations like National Organization for Women (NOW) and a summary of articles on books, films, and periodicals that deal with women's rights. Free space is given for announcements from feminist organizations.

With permission, the front page of a recent issue is reprinted here as figure 8 (for information, subscriptions, etc., write *The Spokeswoman*, 5464 South Shore Drive, Chicago, Illinois 60615).

The newsletter's greatest problem is probably that most often one or two people have to put it out, and few newsletters can boast that they are in the black very much of the time. There are notable exceptions. *Moneysworth*, created and published by Ralph Ginzburg, has a circulation of over 500,000. *Kiplinger's Newsletter* now goes to over a million, contrasted to *Business & Society*, a newsletter offered as a bi-weekly report on business and social responsibility. Now in its fifth year, circulation is less than 1000. An annual subscription to *Business & Society* costs $75, yet daily newspapers and magazines will quote *Business & Society* far more often than *Moneysworth*. The reason is that there are many publications that purport to tell readers how to save money or find good products, but almost none that will perform an annual social audit on the top companies in the United States. That's what *Business & Society*, and no one else, does regularly.

In order to put out a successful newsletter, you should study the need for this medium of communications. Do you have enough important material to offer twelve, twenty-six, or fifty-two times a year? Do you know how to write and can you get help in writing? Have you access to money to put it out regularly? Will your subscribers pay their way?

Once you decide to go, be sure of your lists. Even though you will have to pay for postage both ways if you use first-class mail for your newsletter, it is an effective way to check a list for accuracy. If you want to sell subscriptions try to get a list of another organization that has already been able to sustain itself for some time (see Chapter 15 for more information on piggyback mailings, swapping lists, etc.).

# 8

# News Releases and Fact Sheets

THE NEWS OR PRESS RELEASE, fact sheet, and editorial query are the mainstays of almost every publicity effort. No newspaper or news service could run without the receipt of news releases. They are the editor's contact with the outside world. He recognizes that for the most part they represent one-sided, subjective points of view. But every editor needs them.

Every day, before assignments are made to newsmen by their editors, the morning mail is opened. In it are the news releases, letters, and, on occasion, an anonymous "tip." The greatest user by far of news releases is the U.S. government; second is private industry. This is not surprising, since almost every one of literally thousands of government agencies has a vested interest in being in the news. They know that sending out a news release is the simplest and most direct way of getting a story into print. One of the few people who accompanies President Nixon on every trip, from Camp David to Peking, besides his secret service bodyguards, is his press secretary.

A trained eye looking over the front page of any morning newspaper can pick out the stories that originated in the office of a publicity specialist and probably got into print through the news release route. The very first thing many people read on the front page is the weather report. It is sent over the wire as a news release from the National Weather Service, part of the U.S. Department of Commerce.

News on the condition of a famous person who is hospitalized originates from a news release issued periodically by the hospital's information officer. The latest player hired by the hometown baseball or football team is announced in a release from the owner's office by his press representative. Famous actors and actresses announce their marital plans through their press agents.

It is difficult to be certain, but it is a fair "guesstimate" that on some days 50–75 percent of all news used in newspapers originated from press releases from a paid or volunteer news or publicity director of a government agency, business, congressman, or organization that wanted to be heard.

At the end of this chapter are some samples of news releases and fact sheets along with the story that eventually was used. You will notice how simple the releases are. This is probably the hardest kind of writing: simple, persuasive, and easy to read. But taking the time to write a good release is worth it. One single-page release to a wire service (see Chapter 5) that is used is often all that is needed to alert the entire nation to your story.

## FACT SHEETS

A fact sheet is different from a news release in format. It is often the preferred form when you don't have the time or available talent to create a strong narrative release but you do know your facts. The fact-sheet format makes it easy to organize your information. The simplest example is an announcement of an event that you want covered by the press. A release isn't really needed in most instances.

Here is a fact sheet used to get a major story in the *New York Times* for a private community-supported mental health agency in New Jersey. The fact sheet retained by the reporter was quoted in the final article written after lengthy interviews with the staff of the clinic.

A letter was sent to the reporter with this fact sheet attached:

Fact Sheet

1972 Services (Estimates)

*4,170 Families
*6,537 Individuals
*31,207 Direct hours of service

PROGRAMS

75% of all direct service was in the Center—25% in schools, hospitals, health departments, public housing projects, etc.

* *School for Emotionally Disturbed-Neurologically Impaired Children*
The only one of its kind in New Jersey offered as an extension of on-going treatment services of the Center. Under the supervision of a school director, there are now 13 children in the school with a staff of 3 teachers, 3 aids, 3 special-education teachers, plus the day to day availability of a psychiatrist. Enrollment will go to 24 by 9/73.

* *Drug Abuse program*, now in its fourth year, it offers a professional staff to the community with a 24 hour a day "hot line."

* *Consultation to Day Nurseries*
Preventive services to five inner city community nurseries provide psychiatric consultation to these classes, as well as training of their teaching staff plus group therapy for parents of the school population.

* *Department of Outreach*
Our professional staff is attached to County Welfare Board, public housing projects, community nursing services, YM & YWCA, etc., to work with the lower income population of the communities we serve.

* *HAY (Help Aid Youth)*
This East Orange, New Jersey, program sponsored by the Board of Education and the Community Service Council offers intensive aid to high school students.

> * *MAYBE (Men Aid Youth By Experience)*
>
> Immediate intervention to any child in West Orange who becomes known to the Juvenile Aid Department. This project also trains police to be more sensitive to the needs of children in trouble and their families.

The reporter called the director of the clinic a few days after receiving the letter. After a few minutes a date was selected for an interview. The reporter, experienced in writing about this kind of facility, was able to determine, *from the fact sheet*, the relative value of the operation and its worth as a story.

After the visit by the reporter, a photographer was sent to the center, a few more calls were made for additional information or checking, and a lengthy article appeared. The article was fourteen inches deep and spread across five columns of a page. The photograph printed measured five by seven inches, obviously an important news break for the clinic. Here is the section of the article used by the reporter taken almost word-for-word from the fact sheet.

> The same attention to detail is shown in other projects the center has undertaken. Among them are:
>
> * A school for emotionally disturbed and neurologically impaired children, an extension of on-going treatment services at the center. There are presently 13 youngsters attending, with enrollment to be increased to 24 by the end of 1973.
>
> * A drug-abuse program, now in its fourth year, that offers a professional staff to the community and a 24-hour-a-day "hot line."
>
> * HAY (Help Aid Youth), an East Orange program jointly sponsored by the Board of Education and the Community Service Council. It offers intensive aid to high school students.
>
> * MAYBE (Men Aid Youth By Experience), a dual-purpose program that offers immediate intervention for any West Orange child who becomes known to the Juvenile Aid Department. The program also trains policemen to be sensitive to the needs of children in trouble and to their families.
>
> * Outreach Department, in which members of the professional staff are attached to the County Welfare Board, public housing projects, community nursing services and Y.M.C.A. and like organizations. The aim is to work with lower-income families in the communities.

## NEWS RELEASES

### *Getting Read*

In major cities, news or feature editors look at the day's pile of news releases very, very hurriedly. An average morning mail may literally bring in 200–300 releases. To be noticed, you have to attract the editor's attention and pique interest. Unless your release is read, understood, and creates interest, your effort to get a story into circulation is going to stop right there.

Hints to help get a news release looked at must begin with the form you use. If you don't use the proper format, there is a chance that even with a good story no one will bother to read past the first few words on the first page. Take the time to study the samples of release formats most often used. Some examples of news-release headings are reprinted here (fig. 9). Remember, they are looked at before the story itself.

Look at the Kraftco news release form. Then look at the one from the hospital. Any item on either of these pages has a good chance of being read by any editor in New York City.

Only the Kraftco release will probably get read in Akron, Ohio. The reason is obvious. Probably no one ever heard of the hospital there—that is, no one but the science-medicine writer on the Akron *Beacon Journal*. Chances are he would know the hospital to be one of the finest private nonprofit teaching hospitals in the East. But unless the release was sent to the individual editors by name, there would be small chance that it would be read by the local editors, regardless of how attractive the heading was.

Now look at the release head used by the director of pharmacy services for the hospital. There is no artwork heading. Yet *Time* magazine used this release and printed a small feature article about the talk.

If you have a decent-looking format for your release and quickly spell out what you are going to be talking about and if the headline, your name, and the name of the company, institution, or organization you represent sounds legitimate, most editors will read your release. At least they will read enough to decide what they want to do with it: read more, assign it to a reporter for a follow-up, file it for future action, or throw it away.

SCHERING CORPORATION
BLOOMFIELD, NEW JERSEY

CONTACT: Mr. Kerrigan, Ext. 283 Broadacres
Public Relations Department
Bloomfield, N. J. (201) 743-6000
New York, N. Y. (212) 964-1122

FOR IMMEDIATE RELEASE

news

KRAFT FOODS DIVISION
SEALTEST FOODS DIVISION
BREAKSTONE SUGAR CREEK FOODS DIVISION
KRA PAK DIVISION
RESEARCH AND DEVELOPMENT DIVISION

AREA CODE 212 477-9170
CABLE AMHEART NEW YORK

44 EAST 23RD STREET, NEW YORK, N. Y. 10010

FIG. 9

Most editors follow the latter course; they don't read more than the first fifty words of a release and then use it or throw it out. Over 25 percent of all news releases sent to *Advertising Age* never get past the first person who reads them. But the 70 percent that does get read all the way through at least once helps to account for a good part of what goes into this leading business publication.

Major newspapers alone receive literally thousands of news releases every day, many hand-delivered (at a cost of from $3 to $5 each). Probably only 1 percent gets read completely. With few exceptions—wedding announcements, death notices, and financial information from listed companies—almost no others ever get past the editors. Yet, day after day, news releases arrive for them to throw out.

If an editor knows that most of the releases are going to be useless, why does he read his mail at all? The fact is that he can't afford to take the chance that he will miss an important story. So he plods through his mail, looking for names of companies, institutions, and people that he trusts. When he culls a few from the pile that seem interesting, he starts his day.

## *Design of News-Release Heads*

The first hint for the design of your news-release format is to use simple elements, with or without artwork, to make the front page attractive. But no matter what the design is, the front page of a news release has to start with several important standard headings. In order of importance, they are as follows:

1. *Who is sending the release?* Be sure to state clearly the name and address of the person or organization responsible for the information that follows.

2. *Who can the editor contact for verification, more information, and the like?* Be sure the telephone number is listed with both a home and office telephone. Many stories are killed because a reporter or editor can't get a verification by telephone.

3. *Date to be used.* A good rule is for a release to be dated for use at the time the news was made. But there are important exceptions.

### *Date of Release*

You should date your news release for the hour and day that you are making the news. It is customary for news releases sent to newspapers to show an "A.M." or a "P.M." release time as well as the date, since most papers are either morning or afternoon papers. You don't have to be exact with this, but these are conventions that are widely used by reporters for general news coverage. If you are going to work with live radio or television, the exact moment that the news is made is when it will be heard or seen.

### *Release Times*

The talk that is given after 6:00 P.M. is usually released to the morning newspapers the following day. The story would show the place that the news was made, the date, and above this, to the right under "Date of Release," would go the time of day as well.

Thus, if your talk or event takes place at 8:30 P.M. on December 14, you can send out the talk a week ahead with the for-release date "A.M. of December 15."

In this way the editor who gets the material in advance can decide if he wants to assign a reporter to cover the story. He may choose to run exactly what was said in the release. He may have someone call you after the scheduled time and date of the story to make sure of the facts and to see if the talk was given as scheduled. (No editor wants to run a story on December 15 that reports a talk that was scheduled to be given on December 14 but was canceled because of the illness of a speaker.)

An editor doesn't need to know a time of release and usually won't bother to check the contents if all the news release provides is a time and place for a meeting or a position statement by an individual that has no time and place for the announcement; the release itself then becomes the vehicle for the announcement.

### *Headlines and Lead Paragraphs*

There is some debate as to whether or not the person who sends the story should also write a headline to the story. Some editors will actually run a news release exactly as they get it but will write their own headline. For them you don't need to write a head. However, you never will know who wants to write his own headline or who will accept yours. Most editors will rewrite the headline and then use most of the release.

We believe that you should send a release with a headline already on it. A well-written headline attracts attention faster than even the best first paragraph. Try to use as few words as possible to deliver the message. Writing headlines is not easy; it is a job left to specialists at most newspapers, and rarely does a reporter write his own.

It takes a lot of time to reduce a story to the few words that comprise a headline. Read the headlines of your local newspaper and then see if you want to read further—a good test of a headline, but not always fair, since some headline writers will "trick" a reader with a headline that really doesn't apply to the story. Like some of the still photographs outside a movie, they are usually exciting enough to get you to buy the ticket, but you may have trouble finding the scene as you watch the movie.

Before you start to write, think over the reason for the release and try to see it as it may appear. Always review the media before writing the release. Look over your newspapers. Count words and sentences used in a first paragraph of an important story on the front page. You will quickly see that there are very few words in a news story, most of them verbs, not many adjectives. More adjectives are used in features, but newspaper writing wants and uses short sentences.

The largest circulation newspaper in the nation, the *New York Daily News*, is an excellent primer of news writing, as is the *Wall Street Journal.** Neither wastes time with words that aren't needed. Most paragraphs have three or four sentences and most sentences consist of fifteen to twenty words.

The first paragraph must tell the editor what it is that is hap-

* *The Wall Street Journal* never uses photographs. They will run an occasional drawing done by a staff artist. Yet every day photographs of new company officers, a new building, or a piece of equipment arrive for the editors, who will throw them away, often with the thought that whoever sent it doesn't know the *Journal* and probably doesn't have a usable story anyway.

pening, where it is, and who is involved. At that point he decides whether or not to use the release. If you don't grab his interest in the headline or first sentence, chances are good that you have lost him.

You should not be content to simply dash off a few sentences and then send them to the editor. Take care that what you write follows the proper style of the medium as closely as possible, and make sure you send it to the proper person in time to arrange for coverage of the event.

Writing news releases takes a lot of practice. Writing two good pages is probably one of the most difficult aspects of publicity work. Keep trying to tighten the copy so that it "zings" with hard news that makes anyone who reads it want to know more.

## *Writing Hints for News Releases*

After you master the technique of writing good short headlines, try to keep these thoughts in mind before sending out the release:

1. Date of news
2. Date of release
3. Name of your contact with home telephone number, and alternate contact if at all possible
4. Headline—strong
5. First paragraph: what, when, who, where
6. A quote from a spokesman
7. Where to get more information; price of a booklet for sale; dates of regular meetings
8. Final summary of who you are
9. Every page numbered; "MORE" at bottom of every page
10. On the last page of the release be sure to mark it with a "that's all" signal. Use -30-, -0-, ###, or END.

## *How Many Pages*

Use as many pages as you need to tell the story. Without knowing your subject, it is difficult for anyone to know how many words you need to tell your story. Newspapers are interested in tight, simple, concise descriptions of what happened. Usually 250 words double-spaced on a page can and should cover the subject. Two or three of these pages may be needed to get your message across. Run longer and you may run the risk of making an editor feel that the story is too long for his consideration. You'll discourage him from using even the first page.

## *Lists*

The most wasteful aspect of many news releases is the improper use of lists. The lack of time spent in deciding who to send the release to is no excuse. If you are not careful in list-building, you can waste a great deal of effort and money; more important, you may miss the very person who could make use of your story. Spend as much time as possible researching the list for your releases. You may have several different mailing lists. One large newspaper, for example, can have many people whom you feel should know about your organization, yet often only a few will have the authority to decide who will cover a story and what will eventually be used.

It is very difficult to know just who will make the decision at a given newspaper or TV station unless you know the people involved very well. If you don't, the best person for you to send your news release to is the city editor if it is a hard news story and to a feature editor if you know the special subjects each editor covers. When in doubt send your news release to the editor. Send it to a specific person if you are sure the person is there and if you don't care if your story is held until that person gets it. If it is a news event, don't address the news release to a specific person, but use a title—editor, financial editor, women's editor—even if you are sure of the names of the specific persons involved.

## *Building Lists*

There are several excellent sources for lists. Your specific needs will dictate the media to be used. The local telephone book will give you names of publications, newspapers, and radio and TV stations where you live; it will not give you the names of the editors or news directors. National directories are always out of date; the best source for the specific name of a person is the paper-station itself. In New York, Chicago, Los Angeles, London, and a few other cities it is possible to subscribe to services that maintain accurate lists. Below are sources for national lists of media available in most libraries:

Newspapers (daily, sunday, weekly): *Ayer's Directory of Newspapers and Periodicals; The Working Press of the Nation,* National Research Bureau; *The Press Intelligence Directory; Editor & Publisher Yearbook.*

Magazines: *Literary Market Place*, R.W. Bowker

Radio-TV Stations: *Broadcasting Yearbook*, Washington, D.C.

Mailing Lists: *A Directory of Lists*, W. Lads, 200 Park Avenue, New York, New York 10017

*National Radio-Television News Directory*, 527 Lexington Avenue, New York, New York 10017; *Writers Handbook*, a guide to 2000 markets, 22 East Twelfth Street, Cincinnati, Ohio.

For locating newspapers, the best source is N.W. Ayer's *Directory*. This publication lists every newspaper in the nation—daily, weekly, foreign language, and even the "penny saver" shopping papers that run publicity material from local organizations.

Once you start to make up lists for your use, keep them up-to-date. A good system is to make a three-by-five-inch card for each important publication and station. On the card make a note of what you sent, to whom you sent it, and if it was used.

Soon you will develop a contact list that can be very useful. Those who use your material may be the ones to try closer contact for a big exclusive feature story. Those who consistently don't use what you send may be poor choices for you, or you may not know what they want in a story. A direct approach to an editor at a "no-use" publication may straighten you out (see page 62).

## *Deadlines*

Most newspapers want the material they intend to use well ahead of the publication hour and date. However, depending on the nature of the story, there is great flexibility. Morning newspapers want announcements for meetings at least two days ahead.

If you want the meeting covered (because you are sure that hard news will result from the event), you should send the release describing what will happen at least two or three days ahead. Invite coverage with a special "note to the editor."

Evening newspapers usually print stories about what happened from nine o'clock in the morning to about five o'clock the same day. Morning newspapers print news from the previous evening—they try not to print the same news.

If your judgment tells you that you have a good "hot" news story, you can take a release over to a paper. If absolutely necessary, you can telephone a story in.

Weekly newspapers want their story at least five days before, if possible, or on Monday for Thursday. It takes experience and judgment to learn how best to handle placement of new releases. Only by actually doing it a few times will you learn the different needs of each editor. Each person responsible for news editing has his own way of handling assignments, and no one can tell you how best to deal with all editors.

## *Whom to Contact*

The city editor of a newspaper is your best contact for almost any story, but there are important exceptions. If you know that a paper has an editor responsible for writing about the environment, and your story is about some aspect of ecology, then it may be best to send your release to this reporter. However, you take a chance if the reporter is away or on an assignment that keeps him out of his office. Therefore, unless you are able to contact the specific person, it is often best to send the release to the city editor with a note on it, "Copy sent to Mrs. Edna Smith, environment reporter." This will show the city editor that the special assignment reporter has the material, or will have it. Direct contact may help a reporter decide to ask for the assignment, or if the reporter is important enough at the paper, the release you sent may get used without any editor making a decision.

It may seem redundant, but *there is no substitute for reading the publication if you want its editor to use your material.* Only by careful review can you determine how a paper positions itself on a given subject; who it is that you must contact; and whether or not they prefer photographs, human-interest coverage, or dry, factual material. Read the publication regularly, then write the news release.

## *Mailing Services*

There are companies that specialize in handling the mechanical aspects of publicity and news-release mailings. You write the release and send whatever photographs you want to go with it, and the mailing service helps you with all the mechanical aspects of the mailings, including selection of whom to send it to.

In New York City, two of the companies having such lists of editors ready for mailing are P. R. Aids (305 East Forty-Fifth Street, New York, New York 10017) and Media Distribution Services, Inc. (260 West Forty-first Street, New York, New York 10036).

They will prepare the distribution lists, duplicate your releases and photos, and will stuff other information into the envelope as well. They will make the mailings to editors throughout the United States, Canada, and several English-speaking foreign countries as well. You will get one invoice for all the elements, a saving in time if you need mass distribution quickly and don't have the names of people or the publications you need.

## *Follow-up*

Be sure of your facts before you call an editor or a reporter to see if they received your news release. Rarely does an important story get lost. If the paper comes out and your article or announcement wasn't in it, you can assume that you did not get in for one of several reasons.

The first and most obvious reason for nonuse of a release is simply that the editor or reporter didn't think it was worth using. By the time you call him he can't use the story anyhow. You may contact an editor if he consistently is the only one in town not using what you send in. *Don't ruin your chances for getting stories used by sending out "no news" news releases.*

Second, your story may have been good, but it got there too late for consideration. *Be sure you know the timetable for every publication to which you send material.*

Third, your release was incomplete; it raised questions that the editor could not deal with quickly. *Make certain your news release covers the subject completely and then, for insurance, have someone available to respond to telephone queries from media.*

To learn about a newspaper's deadline, a call to the city desk will give you the information you need. For weekly magazines, assume a one-week deadline; for monthly magazines, it's at least one month, often two or even three months.

For radio, material can be used a few seconds after you call via a taped recording of your call. TV news requires a bit more time, but occasionally an item used on the 6:00 P.M. news was shot on film at 5:30 P.M. Audio reports from a reporter are sometimes used on television during a "breaking" story.

If you have a story that you *know* is hard news, below are some hints on how to get the maximum use of the information. Remember, be as sure as you can that your story is worth covering.

## *Getting Coverage for an Important Talk*

Your organization has succeeded in getting a nationally known authority as a featured speaker. You do not want attendance as much as you want media exposure for his talk. Contact the speaker and ask him if he will agree to a press conference.

Send a two-page release to the media with all the details three to four days before the event.

One day before the speaker is to arrive, call the editors on your list. In one minute (100 or fewer words) explain who you are and why you are calling, who is coming to town, and something about the speaker's background. Tell him you hope that he has decided to cover the event.

The specific newspaper editor or assignment desk at the radio or TV station will look at the assignment book and then tell you if your meeting is scheduled for coverage.

If your speaker has agreed to a hold press conference, explain to the editor and others you talk to that you will be holding a press conference (see Chapter 9). Ask the editor if he plans to cover it. If he has scheduled coverage of the talk, he may not want to cover a press conference, too; but if the editor knows that other media in town are going to be invited, he may decide he can't afford to miss both the press conference and the talk itself. It all depends on who the speaker is and how controversial or newsworthy the talk is likely to be. Obviously if your premeeting conversation with the speaker permits you to find out whether or not the speaker intends to say anything new about his subjects—you do this by asking him—then you may be able to tell an editor honestly that you were told by the speaker that he will say things that are going to make news.

### *Postmeeting Coverage When No Press Shows Up*

Your meeting was sensational; everyone came but the press—at least, *you* didn't see a reporter—and you know that the talk really was newsworthy.

Call the local editors and ask them if they had a reporter there. They will know and won't resent it if you explain that they missed a story and you can send over something that should interest their readers or listeners.

As soon as possible write a report of the meeting or summary of the speech. Send it to the papers as a news release, with extensive quotes from the speaker. Usually a well-organized speaker will have one or more copies of his talk (another good reason for you to have had contact with the speaker well before he arrives in town).

If you can, call the newsroom of the local radio and TV stations, identify yourself, ask for the person you have been trying to get to cover (and didn't), and explain that you have a brief story on the meeting to give, right there on the telephone. If you sound convincing enough (i.e., you seem to know what you are doing) and if the speaker or the subject interests the person on the other end of the line, then you or your story may be on the air a few minutes later. It may be repeated once, twice, or even half a dozen times during the next two or three hours. This is especially true of the radio stations that feature continuous news coverage of local and national events (see page 43 for information on dealing with radio news directors).

## *Comment on an Issue*

Someone says something that you don't agree with. You can get coverage for a rebuttal if you are organized and know what you are doing.

Be sure you know what was said. Get a copy of the statement before you take a position.

Carefully prepare a rebuttal. Be sure that it is short, very simple, and accurate. The president or another high officer of your organization should make the statement in writing. Send the statement as a letter to editors or as a reply to a radio or TV station editorial.

Distribute copies of the statement as a news release to the local press, even if it was a reply to a radio or TV editorial.

## *Use of Photos*

One picture is worth one picture unless it's very, very good (see page 120 for more information on the use of photographs). Many newspapers will not use any photographs unless submitted by their photographer or the news services to which they subscribe. There are exceptions, but they are few.

Photographs of an organization's newly elected officers, brides, important committee people, and people who were recently hired or promoted will often be accepted and used with news releases.

It is difficult to get a photograph of a meeting used even if you send it along with your story after the meeting, because it will be of a meeting that *has* occurred. The newspaper editor who wants a picture will read a premeeting release and then assign his photographer, reporter, or both to cover.

There are other exceptions: If you plan to picket an important speaker, have well-prepared signs, and if you want publicity, you can write an editor or TV news producer and tell him that you will be at a certain place with your group and will be identifiable by the big red hat you wear. Send the release and your note a day ahead. A reporter may very well come to you with your release in his hand. Before you know it, you are on film ready to tell the world why you are there (see Chapter 1 for how to do a good TV interview).

If you send a photograph of a person, be sure that it is clear and suitable for reproduction. If you lack a gummed sticker on which to write, print on the extreme edge of the photo's back the name of the person and his title. Five-by-seven-inch prints are large enough; so is a four-by-five-inch print if it is just a shot of a person. Wrap the photograph carefully with heavy backing so that it doesn't get bent. You won't get it back, so don't ask for its return.

### *Summary*

The news release and fact sheet are the workhorses of every publicity effort. To be effective, they should be short, well written, accurate, and concise. Each must have a strong news lead in the very first paragraph. To get into print, they should be sent to the right person at the correct time, in the best format. The name, title, and home telephone of the person to contact should be on the first page.

To keep good relations with the media, it is almost never advisable to call up an editor and ask if your material was used when you have failed to see it in the paper on the day, or the day after, it was scheduled for release.

It does not hurt good press relations for you to write a thank-you note once a story has appeared. Don't make it too strong; just a few words of thanks will remind the editor or reporter that some people with manners are still left.

# 9

# The News Conference

IF USED PROPERLY, the news conference is a format that can be helpful to both sides of the communications equation. This chapter will provide detailed information about when, how, and where the conference should be held.

## WHERE TO BEGIN

If your group's efforts are limited to one small area and the media that you deal with are nearby and clearly defined, the chances are that you will never have to call the press together to issue statements and answer questions. You can simply pick up the telephone and call the local editor, reporter, or radio or TV station and thereby get your story across. Or you can write a news release and put it in the mail. You can deliver the release personally, taking a few minutes to say hello to the people at the media with whom you deal, thereby quickly accomplishing all that is possible with the material you wish to disseminate.

There are times, however, when your group's story may take on a broader interest. Perhaps your story ought to be known in greater detail to the people in neighboring communities, throughout the region, or in the rest of the United States. To cast your story beyond the borders of your own community, you must consider calling a news conference. Some publicity experts call this a "press" conference, but "news" is the reason for the event—not just an occasion to meet the reporters—so calling your meeting a "news" conference can make a difference.

You meet with your associates and discuss your situation, your story, and your aims. Is it time to make your story known "outside"? What can be gained? What can be lost? Weigh the pros and cons carefully.

Consider the message you want to deliver. Is it necessary, at this point in your group's history, to meet with the media and review your work; perhaps clarify some points that have been misunderstood; redefine your purposes; announce a new program; introduce a new officer or important addition to your staff; discuss the past, present, and future; and respond to questions that have accumulated since your last meeting or that have been gleaned from inquiries made at your headquarters? Will you issue a new report or the results of a study that has just been made? Announce a decision that will be of interest to the community? Appeal for support (funds, membership, a rally or meeting)? Praise an action taken by others? Condemn something?

In each case, it should be clear to all that a simple news release cannot answer all questions and that the matter can most conveniently and effectively be dealt with at a news conference. You should be convinced that the material you are dealing with cannot simply be dealt with at a regular meeting of your group, to which you invite the press.

Remember, if you don't have a worthwhile story to tell at a news conference, the trappings of the conference itself cannot add much to your story. Do not try to whip up a story out of nothing just because someone in your organization enjoys talking to a crowd of reporters. Bear in mind that when the last question has been answered at a news conference and the reporters are on their way out, they'll talk to each other about your meeting. Often, their judgment is, "What a waste of time!" Be very tough, very realistic in your analysis when it comes to deciding if a conference is warranted. If in doubt, don't call it. Trying to "stretch" a minor bit of news at a conference can be counterproductive.

## THE PLANNING BEGINS

Once you decide to move ahead with your news conference, you can begin to put into words the key points that were covered in your earlier discussion on whether to "go" or "no-go." This will define *exactly* what will be said at the meeting.

Who will do the talking? Who should be on hand to answer questions? Will you distribute any material at the meeting? Is a press kit necessary? (The press kit is a collection of background material, texts of statements made at the conference, photographs, and any other pertinent material that can be supplied to the press in order to help the reporters prepare their stories.)

Decide where your group's story should be at the conclusion of the conference. How do you structure your presentation so as to point the way to the kind of story you are after? Bear in mind that you are not going to dictate the story to the reporters; you can only tell them what you want to tell them and they are going to write what they want—if anything—about what you have said. If you respond to their questions fully and frankly and thus develop credibility, your story should come out, generally, the way you want it to, give or take a few points, in the ensuing stories carried by the media.

You must decide who will be the principal spokesman at the meeting. Your group's president? Chairperson? Executive secretary? A committee chairperson? A combination of these people? Choose someone who is unflappable, for questions can be hostile or loaded, and you will need someone who can think quickly, speak clearly, and has a personality that, at best, is a winning one and, at worst, a neutral one. Leave your abrasive members out of this format; the wrong word can take the entire project down a path you would rather not follow. Your spokesperson should be able to move the direction of questions with some carefully thought-out responses.

If you are going to introduce a celebrity of sorts to the assembled reporters, someone who has agreed to participate in some way in your group's program, you must consult with that person's aides. The chances are they will have had some experience in handling reporters. Be certain that you do not relinquish total control to these transient aides; you can end up in a secondary role that completely obliterates your purposes. Review the structure of the conference if the transient aide has prepared it, to make sure that your organization remains in control and is visible and audible at the conference. If banners or posters are involved, decide beforehand on who will be in charge of bringing them to the meeting, how many there will be, where they will be posted, and so on. We suggest all this because your celebrity may have posters to put up that promote something other than your cause, thus diluting the impact of the meeting *you* are calling.

Once you choose your principal speaker, host, or guest speaker, decide on who will introduce that person. The "emcee," or moderator, of the press conference will be the one to open the meeting by welcoming the press and making the introductory remarks. In all of this, remember to keep it simple—no long statements. The moderator must not "tip" the story or steal the spotlight from your principal speaker. The moderator may review any ground rules for the conference.

The length of the main statement to be made at the conference will in all probability be determined by its contents. If possible, prepare a brief statement. It can be carefully prepared and delivered, word for word, by your main speaker. Comments by others on the program could follow, and then your meeting can be opened to the reporters' questions.

Your emcee should be prepared to direct the questions to the proper person if the reporter hasn't done so. He should also be ready to repeat the question in order to make certain everyone has heard it. (And also to give the respondent a bit more time to frame a reply.)

Will the meeting include the presentation of evidence to support a statement? You will also decide whether a film or slide presentation is to be given as part of the meeting. Or a flip-chart presentation? Will it be a blackboard presentation? Will you introduce a "witness" or an expert who will submit to questions from the press?

Once you set up the outline of the formal presentation, you can move on to the selection of a meeting date and place.

## LOGISTICS

You will have to pick a site before you can nail down the time and date of the conference. If your group has access to an adequate room for the number of reporters involved, you have no problem; you can move on to the next step, notification of media.

If you lack an adequate room, you will have to select a hotel meeting room, a public auditorium, theater, restaurant, storefront, private club meeting room, or an outdoor site (park area, sidewalk, building site). In some cases, the site is indicated by the nature of the news conference. For example, if you are calling a meeting in order to call attention to some deficiencies in a building project or a zoning problem, you ought to consider conducting your conference at the actual site.

Your notice to media could settle upon a time and a street corner. If a picket line is involved, perhaps it will be there while your conference is in progress. Make certain that you have obtained the proper permits, that the police are notified, and that you have their cooperation. One problem with outdoor meetings is that neighborhood partisans or youngsters drawn to the "action" try to get into the act.

If you are demonstrating for or against something in an outdoor area, you may find that your conference becomes too hectic. Try to arrange an alternate meeting place to which the group can move in case of inclement weather or heckling from bystanders.

Most news conferences are held indoors. They draw a small number of reporters, most of whom may be acquainted and may, in fact, be moving together from one such meeting to another that day.

## WHOM TO INVITE

Decide on the invitation list. You have your list of media contacts, reporters, and writers with whom you normally deal. Decide whether you want to broaden the range of your group's audience to include reporters from other areas or regional media. Make telephone calls to friends or associates in other communities to inquire about the press contacts in distant communities. In seeking to attract the attention of the distant media, you must prepare your press release or make your telephone calls with a view toward persuading an assignment editor that your group's story—perhaps unknown to him—truly relates to the interests of his audience. Sometimes this can be accomplished with a personal visit, which in effect becomes a press conference of sorts. The representatives of grape and lettuce harvesters from California attracted national attention to their causes by dealing with national media and following up in major cities across the country with "local" press conferences that generated further publicity.

## WHERE TO HOLD IT

If you must conduct the meeting in a hotel, check with the hotel managers in the community. Larger hotels have sales directors or convention managers, who specialize in handling meetings for groups of all sizes. These people will tell you what kind of room you need and will help you with your plans.

You will be expected to place a deposit. You can expect to be charged for the full day even though the actual time for the meeting is an hour or so. If you can get a half-day rate, you are already ahead. Do you want to serve coffee? Are you planning to feed the reporters, too? A breakfast or luncheon? Will there be a bar? The hotel can give you all this, of course, but we suggest, again, that you keep it simple. If your group's budget can handle a luncheon, which is most often held immediately after the press conference, scheduled for 12:30, you might follow this route if you are in a community in which not many luncheon press conferences are held. In major cities, the reporters too often are quite busy and the luncheon isn't a real inducement for attendance.

## TIMING

The meeting should be held as early in the day as possible to give the TV people enough time to do their work, process and edit the film, and work it into that night's newscast. No matter what time of day you select for your meeting, if you are dealing with half a dozen or more different news outlets, you will never be able to select a time that is perfect for all. Try to minimize disappointment by checking with your media contacts. You can call up those you especially want to be present and ask them which of several alternate dates and times would be best.

## SPECIAL NEEDS

Check with the hotel manager if you have special needs. Is an outlet needed for a slide projector, film projector, sound equipment? Will the hotel supply this equipment? Is there a screen? Microphones? Lectern? Tables? How many chairs are needed? Tape recorder? If the room is small and the audience numbers a handful of people, or even twelve to twenty-five people, there is probably no need for microphones and speakers. If the room is large and scores of reporters are expected, along with camera crews and radio equipment, plan for microphones. You can arrange to have an associate operate a tape recorder or cassette unit during the proceedings so that you can have a record of the meeting.

Find out about ice-water pitchers and glasses. The hotel should make them available. Discuss the number of tables needed at which your speakers would be seated, either alongside or behind the lectern, if a lectern is to be used.

If TV and radio attend the meeting, plan on these crews' arriving well ahead of the starting time. They may need an hour or more to set up and nearly as much time again at the end in which to remove equipment. Find out their power requirements and check with the electrician at the place you booked to make sure they won't blow all the fuses.

## PUBLICIZING THE CONFERENCE

Having selected a site and a time for the conference, decide on whether to notify the media by mail, telegram, or telephone. The most common technique is by mail, with a press release. Whichever approach is taken, be sure you include a brief description of the purpose of the conference, names and titles of those who will be there to address the reporters, the time, the date, and the place. If for some reason you cannot divulge the name of a principal speaker, use the teaser approach and promise that the reporters will have a chance to question "a leading authority on such-and-such" or whatever your speaker's claim to fame might be.

Include in your release, call, or telegram, any special instructions pertaining to the conference. That is, a release date or details on how to reach the meeting site. Include, too, the name of a contact at your organization and your telephone number. Try to arrange distribution of this release from seven to ten days before the meeting, thus giving assignment desks about a week's notice. A telephone call should be made to each media contact one or two days before the conference. This call serves to remind the media and also to build some importance to the session. If the editor says no, he can't have anyone at the meeting, don't argue. You can express your disappointment, but add that you will make sure he receives the press release that follows the meeting as quickly as possible. Assure him, in other words, that you will "cover" for him and see to it that whatever news occurs at the conference is relayed to him. You can also voice the hope that if his assignment schedule opens up, he'll be able to send someone to the meeting after all.

The press release that tells the media of your news conference should be limited to one sheet of paper, double-spaced. Keep it simple; stick to the facts:

(Date)

NOTE TO: ASSIGNMENT EDITORS

A news conference dealing with a new plan for raising and distributing funds for school districts will be held at (time) on (day and date) in the (room location and site, including address) sponsored by the (name of organization). Speakers will be (names, titles).

If there is more to the agenda, note it in the release. And list your group's press contact, by name and telephone number, as one of the signatories of the release.

## CONDUCTING THE NEWS CONFERENCE

Prepare carefully for your presentation. You may wish to read a statement. Have copies of it available for the press. Prepare a fact sheet and any other background material. Give the reporters their copies of official statements and other papers at the conclusion of the meeting.

Sometimes, a reporter with a deadline problem will ask for the press release when he arrives. What you want to guard against is giving anyone an unfair advantage. If the reporter is with a radio station or a newspaper with an early edition, he can leave with your press release before you begin the conference. This penalizes the other reporters who will not begin to file their stories until the conference ends.

When asked for a copy of the press release before the meeting, tell the reporter that the release will be available at a specific time, choosing an hour that will take you through the conference. For example, if it is 10:30 A.M. and the meeting doesn't begin until 11:00 A.M., tell the reporter that the release will be available around 11:30 or noon if that is when you think the meeting will end. If the reporter complains about missing an edition, a broadcast, or some other deadline, make the release available, but set a time for its publication. Tell the reporter that the release must be held until the conference ends. This should be acceptable to the reporter. There are times when reporters are given the press release well in advance of the meeting in order to accommodate their deadlines; the reporter shows up at the meeting anyhow in order to make sure that the story doesn't change in some way during the question-and-answer period. And if something unexpected occurs and the story must be changed, the reporter can try to catch up with the earlier story by writing "inserts," or "adds," or by "killing" the entire story and refiling it.

Bear in mind that the TV crews, if they appear, will arrive early to set up. Before the press conference begins, they may want to film your main speaker reading his prepared statement or discussing the issue with newsmen. The best arrangement, of course, is when the TV crews can keep working through the conference and wait to film the TV reporter interviewing your speaker after the meeting. The TV reporter may repeat a question or two that came up during the meeting. The TV director also may ask your speaker to pose in conversation with someone or just to look off to the side, as if in conversation, in order to film cover shots, or transitional shots, for use in the newscast.

The main thing to remember is that the TV people, important though they are to the success of your conference, should not intrude too much on the so-called pad-and-pencil press—the newspaper reporters—who are in the room. That is, don't give up so much time to the special TV requirements that the entire schedule for the meeting becomes a long stage-wait. Your speaker or moderator should intervene in order to work out a proper "schedule" for the TV crews. Avoid preferential treatment beyond the necessary accommodations that must be made to TV and radio reporters. One possible approach is to see if the TV crews will agree to film the pad-and-pencil reporters as they question the speaker.

The press release that you prepare for the conference should be in the form of a news story. It can report on the main points that were made and can be accompanied by a copy of the full presentation. Occasionally, speakers at press conferences decide they do not want to take up time discussing the background to a particular situation that has led to the press conference. They can say that the press kit contains a backgrounder.

If you can supply photographs with your press kit, they should be eight-by-ten-inch black-and-white glossies. If you are planning to distribute color illustrations of any sort, have them converted to black-and-white glossies as well. Colors do not convert faithfully in some cases, but your black-and-whites can be produced to properly register the different tones.

The press kit can be put into envelopes or can be left open and unfolded. This material should not lay around on a table before the meeting begins. It should be kept out of sight until the press conference is nearing a close. Someone previously designated should then bring out the press material for distribution.

If your presentation deals with complex matters and requires charts for clarification, then you may find it helpful to distribute the press material—or parts of it—before the meeting starts. This will help the reporters follow you more closely. This approach also can eliminate the use of slides or a blackboard.

A slide projector should be used only when absolutely necessary. Avoid them if possible. If you cannot avoid the use of a slide projector, be sure the room has the required electrical outlets, that chairs are placed so that the audience doesn't block the screen, that you know how to lower the lights in the room, that someone is assigned to handle the lights, and that your slide projector and slides are on hand, along with the operator, well before the start of the meeting. Make sure the projectionist is carefully rehearsed. Insist on a run-through to make certain his focus is right, slides are in order and right side up, and that he understands the cues. After the run-through, make sure the slides are back in order. There seems to be a rule that no slide presentation ever goes off 100 percent smoothly. Rehearsals can bring your score close to 100 percent.

If, despite your rehearsals and attention, something goes wrong with the slide presentation, your speaker mustn't feel obligated to fill in the pauses with ad libs that are supposed to amuse the audience. The speaker can easily admit to embarrassment on behalf of the projectionist and himself and let it go at that. He shouldn't scold the projectionist; he should ask the audience to be patient and the loose ends will soon be pulled together. There's no need to "perform" in this situation; it's not a night club.

Do you want the reporters to wear lapel name-tags? Do you want them to sign in at a registration desk? If the meeting is small and you know most, if not all, of the people present, name-tags and registration aren't necessary. Just get the meeting started, attend to business, and let the reporters out as soon as possible. If it's a major conference, attended by scores of reporters, it will be wise to have the reporters register, either by signing their names and affiliations on a piece of paper that is circulated when they are seated or in a looseleaf notebook that is at a registration desk. The list that you obtain in this manner will come in handy for future press releases or follow-up contact work. It also enables you to know which newspaper, magazine, or broadcasting station wasn't present; you can then have the press material delivered to the absentees.

If there is going to be a bar and an opportunity for the reporters to mingle, to socialize with your group and with each other, name-tags can be helpful. They may raise some negative feelings while being attached to jackets or dresses, but since everyone is sporting one, the negative vibrations soon vanish and the tags become useful as conversational ice-breakers in a room where not every person is known.

Gummed labels, or those affixed with safety clasps or straight pins, are the most commonly employed badges. If a large number of reporters are going to attend your press conference and stay on for a drink or a meal, have the badges made out in advance. Write the reporter's name and affiliation on the badge. Make certain names are correctly spelled. If in doubt about the correct spelling of a name, wait for that person to arrive and fill in the badge. You will keep some blanks on hand for those who arrive unexpectedly. The badges are spread on a table and arranged alphabetically, so that incoming reporters can pick them up. If there is a registration notebook or sheet of paper, leave it next to the badges and try to have someone at the table supervise this procedure and greet the guests.

If it is overcoat weather, make certain there is a checkroom near your meeting room or some spare chairs and tables on which the coats can be placed. If you can afford to cover the coatroom tips as part of your rental arrangement, fine. But if this expense is a problem, don't worry about having the reporters leave their own tips. Assume that they are reimbursed for their expenses. Make sure that the management has enough people working in the checkroom to keep the line moving swiftly after the meeting ends. Reporters like to hurry off when the meeting ends; spending time on a line in order to retrieve a coat is painful. Also try to hire a room, if you are using a hotel for your press conference, that is accessible by stairs. Elevator-waiting, like checkroom-waiting, is unpopular. If you are dealing only with a handful of reporters, consider holding the conference in your office. A few extra chairs can be brought in, and you can conduct your business effectively in that setting.

If you plan to hire a photographer to take pictures at the press conference, be prepared to spend a minimum of $50 for a dozen pictures. Your photographer will have to work fast. The pictures he takes should be delivered within hours to the key newspapers and TV stations if you are interested in getting pictures published. This can also entail hiring messengers if your volunteer staff cannot take the time to do the delivery chores.

## INSTRUCTIONS FOR YOUR SPEAKERS

Discuss in great detail with your key speaker, the questions and answers that will in all probability comprise the news conference. Deal with the dead-ends that should be avoided, the issues that would divert the course of your presentation. Discuss whether your meeting is a possible target for disruption. If so, consult with the hotel management if you are renting a hotel room for your meeting.

Before you have gone too deeply into making arrangements for your news conference, you will have reviewed all questions that can be asked. Employ your toughest devil's-advocate manner in discussing alternative responses. Choose the response that best deals with the purpose of your meeting. Try to make this preparatory session so intense, so hot, that the actual "grilling" can never approach it in harshness.

We are dealing in this section with the carefully prepared, scheduled, and controlled press conference. There can be occasions when you must call a news conference in a hurry and, while waiting for the reporters to arrive, do your planning. We will discuss this kind of situation later in this chapter.

Should your speakers use the phrase "off the record"? In general, avoid the phrase, especially if you have a roomful of newsmen around. The best way to keep something off the record is not to utter the remark in the first place.

If you come to a sensitive area during your press conference, take whatever time is needed to explain to the reporters why the area is so sensitive, why you must deal with it carefully, or why you would rather not discuss the matter at this particular time. Level with the press. Should you decide to deal with the sensitive topic, you may find it best to begin by dealing with the broad generalities and skipping over them as quickly as possible. If the reporters' questions refer to details of the subject you have quickly mentioned, you must know how far to go. Here again, level with the press. Tell the reporters that you have really said all that you are prepared to say on the subject and when the time comes that you can say more, you will be sure to do so. There are things that are best left unsaid, even at press conferences.

To avoid the use of the phrase "off the record," your speaker might say, "We're not really prepared to deal with that subject now because it's still being discussed by our executive committee." Or, "We'll have something to say on that (aspect of the discussion) on (some unspecified future date). Right now, we're in no position to say one way or another." Or, "At this point, I could get myself in a lot of trouble if I traveled down this path because, really, we're not ready to say anything that is very meaningful. It's just too soon to discuss that point."

Otherwise, everything you are telling the press should be something your group can bear to see in the public prints or hear played back on radio and television. Be discreet. Remember that there are no indiscreet questions; only indiscreet answers.

In his news conference of early 1973 in which he discussed the Vietnam ceasefire pact, Henry Kissinger, then the national security advisor to President Nixon, was asked some hard questions. What would happen if the treaty is violated? Would American soldiers again be sent to Vietnam? Mr. Kissinger's reply is a model for staying out of trouble. "I don't want to speculate on hypothetical situations that we don't expect to arise," he replied.

Earlier, he was asked if North Vietnam is considered a foreign entity in South Vietnam under the treaty terms. His reply: "This is one of the points on which the bitterest feeling rages. And which it is best not to deal with in a formal and legalistic manner." Later in the meeting, he again squelched further discussion of this issue by saying, "That is an issue which we have avoided making explicit in the agreement, and on which opinions—and in which ambiguity has its merits." Ambiguity, indeed, has its merits. If Kissinger was permitted to bring to a halt speculative, hypothetical questions of such serious import and to do so in so credible and proper a manner, you should be able to accomplish similar results with your questioners.

Along with off-the-record material, you will also have to know how to deal with unattributable material. This is information that reporters would be free to use in their stories provided they do not attribute the source of their information. Thus, you find news stories or commentary that refer to "informed sources," "reliable sources," "it is believed," "it was learned," "industry sources believe . . .," and "one theory being advanced by some. . . ." There is an almost endless range of language that goes into the masking of sources. The common denominator: No names.

Before telling a reporter that he must not use your name in connection with what you are about to tell him, make sure your disclosure is worth the masking effort. There are those who have inflated opinions of the news value of what they tell reporters. Be sensible and realistic. Will the use of your name *really* be unwise? Why? If you can justify your response to such questions, then by all means stick to your guns.

Reporters have trouble with unattributable comment or information, because they must decide how much credence to give it. There have been times in which "unattributable" information turned out to be misleading, serving the source's purposes by being unfair to someone else. Be sure that the information you want to get on the record without attribution is both accurate and fairly stated.

You need not state to the reporters that your announcements are for immediate release. Reporters assume that what they are being told at any given moment is for immediate publication. If you must impose some restrictions, make them clear every step of the way. When you send out your notice of the conference, you should point out that the story is being embargoed and must be "held for release" until such-and-such a time. Such requests however are usually not a good idea and should be avoided.

At the conference, you should explain the reason for your embargo. You will find that there is always a reporter with a deadline problem who must be given advance information. Be prepared to cooperate with him, but do not permit him to break any release dates. If you learn that the reporter to whom you gave an advance story is known to break release dates, contact that reporter again and politely review your ground rules with him. Let him know that you want the release date maintained. If he breaks the release date, you must contact all the other reporters as quickly as possible and tell them they are free to use the story at once; the release date has been broken. Another reason to avoid embargoed stories.

Contact the reporter who broke the release date. Find out what happened. If his action was deliberate or gives evidence of being deliberate, you will have to bear his action in mind the next time you have news to dispense. If the reporter goes on behaving in this manner, you can consider discussing the matter with his superior. Occasionally, the breaking of a release date turns out to be the result of a misunderstanding. This is why it is important to impress on all the hold-for-release aspect of the story.

Can you ever tell a reporter, "I don't know," when he asks a question? You should if you don't know, rather than waltz around with the question. Turn to your moderator or other associates and ask if they know. If no help is forthcoming, tell the reporter you will find out the answer as soon as possible and get back to him. Sometimes the reporter will relieve you of this responsibility by saying it's all right; he was just wondering. The important thing here is to bear in mind that you are not Henry Kissinger talking to the world, in effect, about the Vietnam ceasefire agreements. You are simply trying to impart some information to the community. Be honest. You are expected to do your homework, to try to anticipate every possible question, but you may not be able to do so for a variety of reasons.

Don't be afraid of professing ignorance. Don't be afraid of the press. Some people set off bad vibrations when dealing with reporters because they are tense, defensive, and fearful of what the reporters will do to them in print. Approach the press more openly. Remember that the reporter is trying to do his job honestly and quickly; he'll appreciate any help you can give him. He doesn't know all the answers either. It's that simple when you are dealing with a bona fide activity.

If, on the other hand, you have something to hide and you dare not talk unless a lawyer is with you or speaking for you, the best advice you can receive is that this book isn't going to help you. Listen to your lawyer. And pray that you have a good lawyer.

Not every reporter at your press conference will ask questions. Many of them take notes as the question-and-answer session proceeds and quietly try to develop questions that aren't being asked by others. After the conference ends, they approach the speaker and pop a question or two. This is a perfectly valid procedure. The reporter is trying to come up with his own angle, covering some aspect of the story that he believes has not occurred to his competition. Answer his questions. Should you sense that his questions indicate he is trying to create a story or pursue an angle that doesn't exist, discuss your misgivings with him. Make it clear that he is on a dead-end path, chasing an angle that doesn't exist, if that is actually the case.

Anything can happen during the question-and-answer period. There may be no questions. Be prepared for the long pause when you ask, "Are there any questions?" Use the time to elaborate on the main points that you are hoping to make. Then close the proceedings by announcing that you will be available for questions after the meeting or at your office later.

A flurry of shouted questions from all parts of the room may come as you ask for questions. Choose a question from among those that are being shouted. Repeat the question. Answer it. As you finish, other questions may be shouted. Repeat the process, moving from one part of the room to another. If the flurry continues, point to one of the reporters who is trying to gain your attention and ask him for his question. Try to control the proceedings by eliminating the noise level, the chaos, if it exists. Acknowledge the reporter, let him ask his question. Move from one part of the room to another until all have been heard. If you are in a large room and the acoustics are bad, repeat the question before replying. If the room is small but there is background noise, repeat the question. If you aren't sure you understand the question, don't hesitate to ask that it be repeated. Don't begin to answer a question unless you understand it. You might be thought to be dodging a question if you give an answer to a question that hasn't been asked.

What happens if your news conference is dealing with a controversial subject and a group can be expected to attempt to disrupt the meeting? If you are renting a hotel room or other public or private room, let the management know. The management has to decide if it can cope with the situation and if it wants to take the risks. You may be asked to move the meeting to another place. If the situation seems serious enough, postpone the press conference and disseminate the information by telephone to one reporter at a time, through the mail in the form of a press release, or by visiting the various newspapers and stations whose coverage you are seeking.

If someone at the news conference turns out to be there under false pretenses, is not a reporter, and is determined to disrupt the meeting, you can deal with the situation in a variety of ways. One effective way is to invite the intruder to the front of the room and tell him he has five minutes in which to be heard, after which he must remain silent so that you can continue with the scheduled program. If this doesn't work, you must ask the person to leave. Tell the intruder that he is free to call his own news conference; he cannot be permitted to break up yours. If the intruder refuses to remain silent and will not leave, send for the manager. While waiting, you will find the reporters trying to restore some order, working to get the conference under way. This may occur before the manager arrives. Tell the manager that the situation now seems to be under control, but let him know that you would appreciate it if he remains alert to what may have to be done if the intruder later interrupts the meeting again. You have come too far to call off your conference; push on with it.

## THE SPONTANEOUS NEWS CONFERENCE

Let us assume that an issue has erupted in your community and that your group is involved with the issue. Developments begin to occur. Your people are being called and asked to comment on a variety of subjects dealing with the issue. They may not be fully informed about what has taken place. In such cases, your group's leadership must confer quickly—in a body or by telephone—and schedule a press conference in order to present a cohesive viewpoint to the community. You have no time to issue press releases or book rooms. You call key reporters to your home or to your office and conduct your meeting. Use the time that it takes for the reporters to assemble to work out your approach to the issue and decide on your spokesperson. Your main concern should be to get the media representatives together with your group. This can take place on a sidewalk, in a coffee shop, in a restaurant, or in a park if the numbers aren't large. If the group you must deal with is large and time is short, consider sending your spokesperson to the local TV station or radio station for an interview, live or on tape. If the local radio station has a call-in show, perhaps you can use it to make your statement. Visit the local newspapers as soon as possible to talk to the proper reporters. These meetings aren't necessarily news conferences, but as emergency procedures they employ some of the principles of the news conference.

# 10

# Seminars

THE PRESS SEMINAR, round table, or symposium is an excellent way to get heard. The differences between a press conference and a seminar are many. The latter, when effective, is usually longer, has more speakers, and permits closer participation between the participants. A press conference is short (an hour at most) and doesn't permit extensive participation by the press, other than a few questions from the more aggressive reporters. At a seminar a reporter can often spend several hours with a single expert of his choice at breakfast or after dinner in a one-to-one exclusive interview, which permits an exchange of views.

Seminars have long been used by industry and nonprofit groups to brief reporters in depth on a single topic. They can also become an informational "backdrop" for fund-raising. Some examples are cited here.

### *American Cancer Society Annual Science Writers Seminar*

Perhaps the best known and best attended annual seminar for science writers is the one sponsored by the American Cancer Society (ACS). Each year since 1959 just before the national appeal for money, this national health organization provides the nation's science writers with an opportunity to see and hear first-hand what is going on in cancer research and treatment. The 1973 seminar attracted about sixty-eight writers from all over the country. Included among the speakers were four Nobel Prize winners. Stuart Auerbach, a science writer who attended it, quoted one of the ACS officials as saying that the seminars generate at least $12 million a year in collections.

According to Joseph Clark, director of press for the ACS, the typical seminar starts late in the afternoon on a Friday and ends the following Wednesday. Usually a warm climate is chosen for the meetings, which begin in late March of each year.

Each day of the seminar usually has two sessions, with fifty or so leading scientists presenting information on newsworthy subjects of their choice. They have prepared their papers in advance and assume that all writers present have had a chance to study them well before the sessions. Thus, both the expert and writer have to do some homework before coming to the seminar.

This is an excellent technique for presenting information to a group of reporters who are willing to invest the time and energy to study information before it is presented. It takes considerable effort to organize this type of seminar. The experts have to send all their talks to the organizer well before the meeting so that duplicates can be mailed to all who will cover.

The scientists do not read their papers but *discuss* them, each one limited to ten minutes. After all of the scientists give their talks at a session, the writers can then question them.

There's usually a twenty-four-hour interval between the presentation of the paper and the release date for publication. (Full text of all the papers are included in a bulky kit given to each writer on arrival.) Writers also have maximum opportunity to speak with the scientists informally after the sessions.

The people who cover the ACS seminars represent major newspapers, TV stations, and wire services. If they are there to get "instant" news, the reporters will send a story in by wire or telephone it to their papers or TV or radio stations.

If the writer is not there to write daily coverage of the meetings, he can use the sessions to obtain background for future articles or TV or radio programs.

The ACS spends about $25,000 on each year's seminar. It is

generally agreed by any scale of measurement that this investment is a bargain. A note to those who want to try to copy these meetings: It would be best to get a professional to help organize one.

## *Political Training Seminar*

Each year since 1968 the U.S. Chamber of Commerce, in conjunction with local chambers, has sponsored a series of three-day seminars on political-action programs for businessmen.

A recent seminar attracted two dozen business and professional people who heard a series of lectures and attended workshops on various topics related to organizing local political campaigns.

The panel members included two professionals whose knowledge was gained by actual participation in political campaigns. They were Joseph Napolitan, media director for both Hubert Humphrey and Lyndon B. Johnson; and Clifton White, who was responsible for the 1964 "Draft Goldwater" campaign and directed the successful 1970 James L. Buckley race for the U.S. Senate in New York.

Before the three days were over, those businessmen who attended heard how to organize their campaign, get money, use polls, and obtain media coverage.

If you know what you are doing, and need to train workers in your action program, the training seminar with press invited can serve to get you publicity and still help your own staff. However, it is important to make certain that you will be presenting information that, if printed, will not hurt your efforts. If the press is there as an observer, it's definitely not the time to have policy arguments within the organization, unless newspaper coverage of such differences is what you want.

## *National Program for Dermatology Seminar*

You don't have to have a special meeting for a seminar. Often, you can take advantage of a gathering of experts and simply tack onto the front, middle, or end of the regular program your own seminar. The press will be there covering the meeting and will be grateful for news opportunities that are not a part of the regular program.

In 1971, the National Program for Dermatology was able to get sixteen writers and editors to spend a full day with top dermatologists from all over the country. The purpose of the meeting (held in Chicago at the same time as the annual meeting of the American Academy of Dermatology) was to talk about some of the major issues in dermatology as related to the public's need for information.

Here is the program:

*Morning Program*

9:00 Welcome
J. Graham Smith, Jr., M.D., Moderator
Professor and Chairman, Department of Dermatology
Medical College of Georgia

9:05 Dermatology for 1970s and beyond—Dermatology patients do get well!
Clarence Livingood, M.D.
Chairman, Department of Dermatology
Henry Ford Hospital

9:15 Questions and answers

9:30 Can sunburn be prevented? Do we have to get wrinkles?
Fred Urbach, M.D.
Professor and Chairman, Department of Dermatology
Temple University

9:40 Antihypertensives, antidiabetics, tranquilizers and other drugs that enhance sun damage to the skin.
John Epstein, M.D.
Associate Clinical Professor, Department of Dermatology
University of California, San Francisco

9:50 New topical treatment for precancerous skin lesions.
W. Mage Honeycutt, M.D.
Associate Professor, Department of Dermatology
University of Arkansas

10:00 Evaluation of methods for treating skin cancer.
John Knox, M.D.
Professor and Chairman, Department of Dermatology
Baylor University

10:10 Control of skin color.
Thomas B. Fitzpatrick, M.D.
Professor and Chairman, Department of Dermatology
Harvard University

10:20 Round table discussion with questions and answers

11:10 Acne—modern management.
John Strauss, M.D.
Professor, Department of Dermatology
Boston University

11:20 Psoriasis—new drugs—risks vs. benefits.
Eugene Farber, M.D.
Professor and Chairman, Department of Dermatology
Stanford University

11:30 Round table discussion with questions and answers

12:00 Lunch.

At the lunch every writer was able to sit where he wanted. The members of the panel tried to sit with the writers and give each about two more hours to share opinions and discuss mutually interesting subjects.

*Afternoon Program*

2:00 Allergy and the skin.
Rudolf L. Baer, M.D.
Professor and Chairman, Department of Dermatology
New York University

2:10 Poison ivy.
William Epstein, M.D.
Professor and Acting Chairman, Department of Dermatology
University of California, San Francisco

2:20 Occupational skin disease.
Donald Birmingham, M.D.
Professor of Dermatology
Wayne State University

2:30 Insects and repellents.
Howard Maibach, M.D.
Associate Professor, Department of Dermatology
University of California, San Francisco

2:40 Round table discussion with questions and answers.

3:10 Baldness—is it just due to heredity?
Edward Krull, M.D.
Henry Ford Hospital

3:20 Sweating.
Richard L. Dobson, M.D.
Professor of Dermatology
University of Oregon

3:30 Questions and answers
3:50 Prostaglandins and the Skin.
Harvey Blank, M.D.
Professor and Chairman, Department of Dermatology
University of Miami
4:00 Questions and answers
4:20 Can anyone else besides a physican treat skin disease?
David G. Welton, M.D.
Clinical Instructor, Division of Dermatology
Duke University Medical Center
4:30 National Program for Dermatology
Philip Anderson, M.D.
Associate Professor and Chairman, Department of Dermatology
Associate Dean
University of Missouri
4:40 Questions and answers

The following publications sent reporters to cover the sessions (most stayed all day): AP, *Chicago Tribune, Chicago Daily News, Chicago Today, Dermatology News, JAMA Medical News, Medical World News, Minneapolis Star, Science Year Book, Skin & Allergy News, Today's Health, Vogue, Wall Street Journal.*

Articles that originated from the seminar ran the following day in Chicago daily newspapers and, up to a year later, in *Vogue.*

The *Wall Street Journal*'s science writer spent another two weeks or so working up a long story that finally appeared more than a month after the seminar and ran in over a million copies of the nation's only national daily newspaper.

## ANCILLARY USE OF SEMINARS

Once a seminar has been organized, there are several ways to get other coverage of the event. For example, in Chicago, once it was decided to have the seminar, it was then easy to book some of the participants on local television. An announcement about the meeting of dermatologists was sent to all stations a week before, and two of the top stations in Chicago booked members of the panels to be guests on interview programs.

One of the best ways to get coverage for a seminar is to feature a leading figure in a field as chairman. Not long ago, Matthew B. Rosenhaus, head of the J. B. Williams Company, the makers of Geritol, co-chairmaned a conference on health care for the aging. At no time during the conference was any mention made of the company's tonic for tired blood. However, the article by Barbara Yuncker, science writer for the *New York Post*, noted that Matthew B. Rosenhaus, head of the company that makes the tonic, was co-chairman of the one-day seminar with Mrs. Aldous Huxley. She reported that the seminar was organized by the newly created Huxley Institute for Biosocial Research.

You may feel that this commercial connection would preclude coverage. This was not the case. Similar meetings organized by private and nonprofit organizations almost always will get covered if they get top speakers and know how to alert the press. The important factor is never to hide the commercial if there is one.

The Huxley Institute was able to get hundreds of invited guests to spend a day to hear many notable people including Dr. Roger O. Egeberg, special health advisor to President Nixon and former chief health official in the Department of Health, Education, and Welfare; and Dr. Heinz Lehmann, a Canadian psychiatrist, who spoke about the need for a "euphoria pill" to keep old people happy. That was one of the stories that got nationwide coverage for the meeting. Other speakers who attracted coverage were a former president of the American Medical Association, Dr. Walter C. Bornemeier, and Dr. Chauncey D. Leake, past president of the American Association for the Advancement of Science.

## HINTS ON ORGANIZING A SEMINAR FOR PRESS COVERAGE

### *Selection of Topic*

You can decide to have a seminar anytime you feel that there is a topic worthy of interest for your purposes. But you will get media coverage only if you can find a topic that is of sufficient interest to warrant general coverage and can provide speakers who will attract the invited press.

The time and place for a seminar is also of importance; however, the ACS has demonstrated that if the topic and speakers are right, reporters will spend several days at a place no one would ordinarily think of as worthy of press coverage.

Once you select a topic that you think is "hot" enough to interest the press, try it on for size with a few reporters. If you are ready for a major seminar, you should know a few reporters to call. Tell them the title of your seminar, mention a few of the "names" you intend to ask, and see if the reporters think it is of sufficient interest to ask their editors for the time to cover it. Try mentioning different "names" to help gauge reaction.

It is always embarrassing to spend money and time for an event that is poorly covered if coverage was the reason for the event. A good way to prevent a wasted event is to pretest the idea. Send out the invitations well in advance and wait for replies. An experienced organizer knows when to cancel a seminar if not enough people say they will cover it.

If you do have a meeting and your turnout is very small, change the format (see page 185 for meeting-room setup) from one where a large audience was to hear speakers, to workshops where a few reporters can spend more time talking over the topic with your panel. In many instances they will prefer a small turnout to the mass scene of press you had hoped for. Often a single wire-service reporter covering your meeting can get you more national attention than ten reporters from local media.

### *Getting the Speakers*

After you select the topic the best decision and most important one you will probably have to make is selection of the speakers. If you can, choose a chairman, moderator, or leader who is so well known and respected that his influence can aid in getting speakers. Not long ago a panel was organized in New York for a one-day program. The chairman was a young expert in his field. He was not as well known as many of the people he invited, but each of the experts who eventually came did so because they were flattered that the Young Turk invited them. One or two members of the panel said yes probably because they were afraid not to come.

If you can't pick a well-known chairman to do the inviting, then get someone who really knows the subject and can also run a meeting.

## *Details to Consider*

Once you have decided on the chairman and who else will be on the panel, be sure to organize all the details of your meeting. Assign dates for follow-up on the invitations, know where everyone is from, get telephone numbers, and make sure you get a recent biography and photograph from each panel member. You will need these for your publicity and follow-up.

You have to decide if you will pay the speakers for their presentation before you do any asking. It is customary to pay all expenses, but paying a speaker for his time depends on whom you invite.

Usually an honorarium of $100 is the minimum for any well-known person. Speakers are accustomed to being paid for their talks and will tell you what they charge. You can expect to pay anything from a few hundred dollars to $2000 for a nationally known authority. Agents for speakers are listed in most telephone books under "Lecture Bureaus."

Always confirm all details of the arrangements in writing with the speaker or his agent. Be sure to follow up a few days before your program, to remind a speaker of the time, place, and date. If you are paying for someone through a lecture bureau, you get a contract and you won't get disappointed. If you invite a celebrity to attend a meeting and are not going to pay him, it is prudent to plan for his not showing up. Thus, you will always have at least one or two alternates ready and willing to substitute in the event you lose a speaker.

## *Setting Up the Seminar*

Countless expensive meetings that offered excellent programs primarily organized for publicity coverage failed because the organizers did not know how to run a meeting. Here are some hints on the details that can make or break a seminar.

The physical setup of the meeting is often the reason for poor results even though many reporters actually attend. Before starting, think about the needs of those you invite. Good coverage results from a variety of factors: selection of a good and timely topic, well-informed and recognized authorities in the field as speakers, and an atmosphere that lends itself to an exciting interchange between the audience and the speakers. Seminars should not be crowd scenes with speakers jammed together or too many reporters.

Be sure you have a good, solid news-making reason for a seminar. Don't have one just to take up time unless you are willing to run the risk of antagonizing reporters.

Pick a time and place where you know the top reporters will attend. Places remote from the big cities are not going to get a turnout unless you have a tremendously interesting panel. The large cities will get the best coverage. Washington, New York, and Chicago, in that order, will get the best coverage for a press seminar.

Make sure your setup has a comfortable place for the seminar and a place for reporters to meet with the panel on a one-to-one basis as well. If it's a hot or cold room or one with poor ventilation or bad lighting, you may lose good coverage.

Follow up carefully.

## *The Place*

Pick a place that is accessible to the people you want to cover your meeting. In a major city the best place may be in the heart of the business district at a well-known hotel. Or, if possible, a neutral place, such as a local college or private club.

In New York City the world famous New York Academy of Sciences will often sponsor a conference. To find out if they will sponsor one for you, simply write a letter to the executive director asking for his consideration. List your subject and the reasons for the seminar. The requirements imposed by the Academy are simple: any member can suggest a subject for a conference, but the executive committee must agree that it is worth having. The actual costs of the conference may or may not be contributed via a grant to the academy.

If you don't want to use a hotel, every city has public halls that can house seminars. Some universities, and even churches and high schools, will rent out magnificent facilities to organizations that can demonstrate that they are acting in the public interest and are not for profit.

### *Whom to Invite from the Press*

Chances are that if you don't know whom to invite to cover the conference you should seriously consider not having it. The reason for what sounds like a snide remark is simply that it will probably be a waste of time, effort, and money to have a seminar just for the sake of the sponsor or the speakers unless there is a good, solid news-making reason for it.

The best examples of successful seminars are such because those who attended came there to learn from eyeball-to-eyeball contact and got it. Almost everyone who goes to the ACS seminars has one or two major stories guaranteed. Some actually will get the idea and make contacts sufficiently worthwhile to aid them in writing a book, film, or TV program. That's why they go.

Press representatives or others who you want to attend should be invited by printed invitation or by letter. Spell out the program in detail, with background for each subject, and list the speaker selected to cover it.

A great deal of research should go into making up the press lists. Know who you want and what they are interested in before sending out invitations. Also make sure your subject hasn't recently been covered in depth by someone else.

### *Setting Up the Room*

If you expect a large audience—100 or more—then you will have to have a podium and probably a public-address system. Plan for an audience seated about ten feet from the speaker. Many speakers use film or slides (be sure to check with them well before the meeting on their needs for audio-visual equipment; many will assume that you will have a 16-mm sound movie projector or a 35-mm slide projector standing by for their use). If they are planning to use a film, you will have to arrange for a place that can be darkened and where the screen and audience are sufficiently separated to permit comfortable viewing.

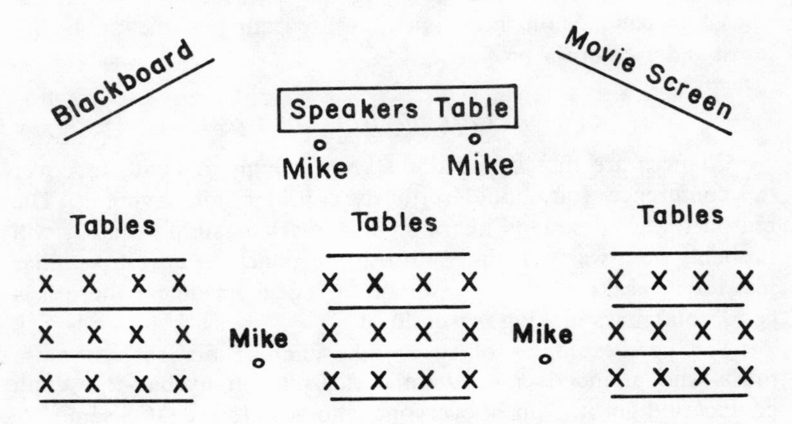


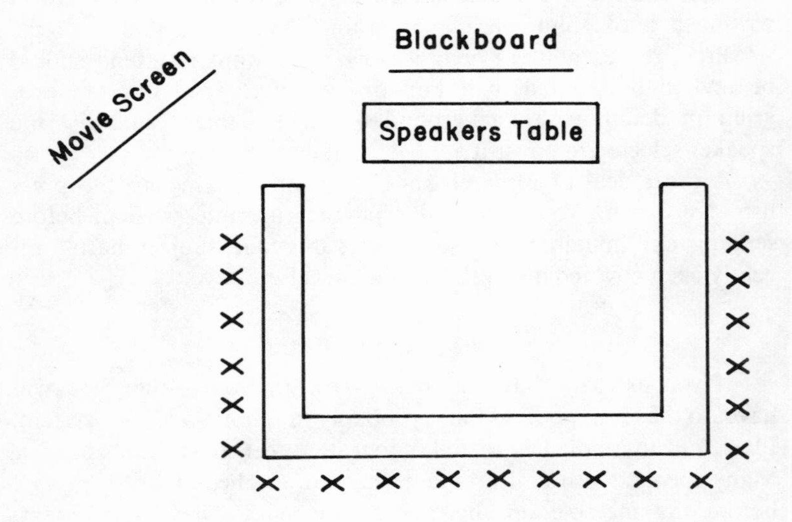


ROOM SETUP NO. 1 FOR 30–50 REPORTERS

ROOM SETUP NO. 2 FOR 15–20 REPORTERS

FIG. 10

The best setup for meetings in which you want audience participation is classroom style. The speaker should be able to stand or be seated at a table, have easy access to a blackboard, and be able to face the reporters, who should be seated at tables in front of the speaker. If at all possible, avoid the use of a public-address system. For small audiences, they are usually far more trouble than they are worth.

For large audiences you need the very best system and should get outside expert help to check the units supplied. A poorly functioning sound system will ruin even the best-planned presentation by an outstanding panel of speakers.

Here are some suggestions for room setup (see fig. 10). An experienced hotel banquet manager will know just how to help you if you tell him how many people will be speaking at any one time and how many you will have in the audience.

It is generally best to let the audience as well as the speakers sit at tables. Chances are that if a reporter has to sit for several hours on an uncomfortable seat without a desk, he won't write very interesting copy.

## *Facilities Needed*

Depending on the length of a meeting and the place, it is always good to offer the press use of certain equipment and facilities. For example, if you plan a meeting that will result in important announcements that need to be communicated to radio, television, and newspapers for same-day release and you invited daily newspaper reporters, you should provide telephones and typewriters.

If your seminar is really a backgrounder-type meeting that doesn't present hard news but offers information in depth (the Science Writers meeting for the National Program for Dermatology is an example), then you don't have to provide telephones or typewriters, but you could have a tape recording made for use by any who request it. It is always advisable to have pads, pencils, and occasionally extension cords and spare cassettes for those reporters who use tape recorders.

Coffee breaks and meals can be provided, depending on the place and your resources. Reporters will not be offended if they are told that a meeting will break at 12:30 to resume at 2:00 if you don't want or can't afford to give them lunch. They will also expect to pay for their own rooms and meals for meetings that take them out of their home cities. Tell them in advance what you will pay for and what they will be responsible for to avoid any misunderstanding.

You will not lose coverage if you don't pay for reporters. You can't assume that if you pay for everything you will get coverage. The days when articles were guaranteed just because the sponsor of a press event paid for lush accommodations are over. *If the event is worth coverage you will get it.* There are exceptions, but for the most part all you should pay for is coffee and perhaps a luncheon or modest cocktail party.

## COPIES OF TALKS

Today most representatives of the press expect that the organizers of seminars will have thought ahead and asked each speaker to come to the meeting with copies of his talk. They know this is not always possible, but nonetheless they expect it. A well-organized chairman anticipates requests for copies of each speaker's remarks. If possible you should try to have a copy machine nearby for immediate press copies of a talk. This is essential when the speaker has only one copy and won't let you keep it.

If possible, also make arrangements to tape-record the entire meeting. Professional recording experts should be used whenever possible. It costs between $150 and $300 per day to tape-record a small meeting (5–8 speakers with questions and answers). It is best to ask that it be recorded on tape at 3¾ i.p.s., a good speed for recording speakers. (Playback units are readily available.)

You can record on cassettes for a lot less if you do it yourself, but chances are very good that your recordings won't be useful when you really need them.

If you have audio recordings (or have a stenotypist covering the meetings) then you can have the entire session transcribed. Word-by-word transcripts are then made available to all who request them.

You can always have a cassette recording made from a reel-to-reel audio tape by the professional who made the original tape. Costs vary depending on where you are, but $5–$20 per hour for a cassette from an audio tape is the rate in New York and other major cities. Often a local radio station will make custom recordings and can "dub" a cassette from a 3¾ i.p.s. reel-to-reel tape.

TV taping is a new way of recording a meeting but entirely feasible if you can afford the equipment and the costs of the video tape. Many rental places will provide instructions, a TV camera, tape unit, and all the auxiliary equipment needed for TV taping in black and white or even color. Costs vary, but in large cities you should be able to get all the equipment you need to make black-and-white TV tape for about $150 per day plus $40 per half hour for the tape.

The TV tape from these systems are not high quality but have been used on commercial and public TV stations. They are ideal for organizations with many branches who may want to share the costs to produce a complete video and audio record of an important seminar.

It is also generally a good idea to have a photographer present to take candid shots of the seminar. Some members of the press may ask for prints afterward, knowing that they are available.

## FOLLOW-UP

After the seminar you should make certain that all who were invited but did not attend have access to some of the information presented. After all, if they were important enough to ask, they are important enough to try and get to cover the session even though they missed it. The audio tapes, transcripts, or copies of the talks can often get you a story despite the fact that the reporter never was there.

Those who did attend may appreciate a note thanking them for their interest and telling them that there are transcripts, tapes, and photographs available. A reporter will be grateful if your transcript is made available to help him over a rough spot—you may save a story otherwise lost, just because you have the complete record of what was said and made it available.

## BY-PRODUCTS OF SEMINARS

The carefully organized seminar can become a future source of valuable material. For example, a one-day seminar on infectious mononucleosis sponsored by a pharmaceutical company in New York recently became the basis of a book when a major publisher read the transcript and recognized that the material presented was worthy of publication. The sponsoring company did guarantee to buy a certain number of copies, but if the material had not been first-rate, no recognized publisher would have agreed to the book. Once in print, many who ordinarily may not know about the subject will be able to get up-to-date information. The book itself can then be useful for libraries and other professional audiences.

Audio tapes can be edited, so that a three-day series of talks may be boiled down to three hours of highlights or selected talks reproduced in their entirety and offered for sale or loan for $9–$15 a session. The American Association for the Advancement of Science now has available audio cassettes recorded at their annual meetings.

Soon video cassettes will be used by many who formerly chose to make films to provide information in an exciting new format.

The maxim to follow is: record all that you can at the sessions; you never know what you will be able to do with a complete sound, or even picture, record of the seminar.

# 11

# Surveys

## USE OF SURVEYS

POLITICIANS HAVE BEEN using public opinion surveys to guide their campaigns for many years. However, it was John F. Kennedy who, with pollster Louis Harris, forever changed the political campaign's techniques for the use of public opinion surveys. An excellent description of how the Kennedy strategists used surveys is in *The Making of the President 1960*, by Theodore White.

The average individual interested in organizing for action can use surveys for a variety of purposes. If carefully prepared and executed, surveys can show if there are others who agree with a particular point of view—and just who doesn't agree. A well-prepared and carefully executed survey can show how strongly both sides feel about their views.

Surveys, especially in political campaigns, are very useful in the initial organizing phase of an effort to show potential financial backers the strength of a candidate. Then each time a survey is repeated showing added strength, additional appeals for money can be mounted using the survey as evidence of the popularity. Surveys are also useful by the opposition, who can publicize the lack of support for a candidate, thereby discouraging contributions and public identification by would-be supporters and weakening a campaign.

Industry uses market research in many ways, and some lessons can be learned from what is done to evaluate the probable success for a product.

In introducing a new product marketers often will survey panels of consumers to determine which flavor most like, the impact of a new package design, or various prices that people may be willing to pay for it. However, despite the best talent available and even sufficient funds, market or political surveys are not infallible. In recent times the disaster at the marketplace of the Edsel is frequently cited as an example of the fallibility of market research. A reason now given for this disaster was that the researchers measured a buying "feeling" of car-buyers long before the Edsel was available (many said that they would buy the expensive medium-size Edsel at the time of the survey). But by the time the car was ready (almost three years later), many of the same people who indicated they would buy such a car had just changed their minds. The market research just didn't keep pace with attitudes at the marketplace.

In politics, survey results often will convince the "undecided" voter that he should support a candidate—the "bandwagon" effect. Much controversy has been caused by the fact many people admit they are influenced by a survey that shows their candidate is either very strong or very weak. Some who were undecided may vote for the man with the most support, since they like to be associated with a winner, or they may vote for the underdog just because they feel sorry for him. President Nixon was the winner picked by computers a few minutes after the polls closed in the 1972 election. No one knows how many people who supported Senator McGovern in the Western states decided not to vote at all when they heard the forecast of the overwhelming Nixon victory. Also no one knows how many Nixon voters in the same area stayed home and didn't vote, because they felt he didn't need their help.

If you are going to use surveys to raise considerable amounts of money with fairly sophisticated contributors, it is best to get the very best talent available, preferably a survey firm that specializes in public opinion with a reputation beyond question. A good place to get help with finding such experts is often your local college or university; the head of the department of sociology, political science, or psychology will often be able to direct you to a firm that can help you.

## WHAT DO YOU WANT TO KNOW

Probably the most important first questions you should ask before starting out on a survey are simply, What is it I need to know? and What will I do with the information? Once you have formulated the questions, getting answers is not difficult. Remember, you can't use surveys to completely substitute for all actual human decisions. For example, no matter how many people say they will buy a certain new product in panel interviews *before the product is marketed*, the final proof (or "survey" if you wish to call it that) is the sales of the product once it is marketed.

You can't use surveys to find out whether or not you will get elected *before* you decide to run. You can use them to find out what people think of the man now in office, whom you will have to beat, and to find out if people ever heard of you. Only after you enter the race and are approaching the actual day of voting will they be accurate enough to tell you your chances of winning.

You can use public opinion surveys to find out how many people know the facts about an issue. For example, not long ago a prominent industrialist was widely quoted as saying that 219 factories in this country were forced to close because of pressures by environmentalists. This was simply not true. But it took a survey by the *New York Times* to find out how many plants actually did close because of pollution problems. The *Times* used its nationwide survey not just to refute the position that the anti-pollution drive means disaster to business but to discover what really happens when businessmen are forced to control pollution. The *Times* asked the federal and state governments to tell them exactly how many plants were closed because management decided it was easier to go out of business than conform to new antipollution laws. The answer after a nationwide survey was not 219, but 8.

## FRAMING THE QUESTIONS

The questions should be simple, easy to understand, and of course useful to you in moving toward what you decide is the purpose of the survey. It is expensive and a waste of time to construct an intricate study of a subject with answers that will never be useful.

Once you have the list of questions you want answered, review them again and again to make sure you really need to know the answers.

Remember, you need to know what you need to know before you start asking questions.

## GETTING THE SAMPLE

Survey experts spend a great deal of time formulating the questions they will ask, often testing the questions to make sure that they are easily understood before administering the final questionnaire. The people who conduct the interviews can get $5–$50 for every completed interview. Then the results are tabulated and a report prepared by the survey experts. Thus, it can be very costly if the questions are poor, resulting in an unusable completed survey.

At the end of each year *Good Housekeeping* magazine reports on the Ten Most Admired Women. The employees of *Good Housekeeping* and other Hearst magazines are asked to nominate five women in the world they would name as "most admired."

By this method, some 150 names are placed in nomination—the top 30 are then submitted to a panel of 1000 *Good Housekeeping* readers for ranking in order of preference.

In 1972 the panel selected Mrs. Nixon as the most admired with a three-way tie for tenth place (Senator Margaret Chase Smith; Representative Shirley Chisholm; and columnist, TV personality, and psychologist, Dr. Joyce Brothers).

It doesn't take an expert to recognize that the preparation of the sample is the key to the results of any survey. *Good Housekeeping* readers are probably not representative of the entire U.S. population; nevertheless, each year, soon after the results are published in December the entire country will know or think they know the names of the ten most admired women.

It doesn't make much difference to *Good Housekeeping* whether or not the sample was fair; they are using the results for an article and promotion of the December issue of their magazine.

But if you are going to do a survey of public opinion, make certain that your sample is a fair one and representative of the audience you feel you have to reach.

If you are interested in knowing how your neighbors feel about a local issue, it makes sense to ask only people in town who are eligible voters. To get a representative sample of public opinion in a town of 10,000 registered voters, interviewing less than 100 people is often all that is needed if you pick the people carefully and ask the right questions. Probability sampling is the technique most often used to assure accuracy in a survey. The method of random selection is used to assure that the group selected for the interview represents all the people.

For example, to find out how many people want a traffic light at a certain location you can try to stop every tenth car that goes through the intersection on weekdays at various times. After stopping 100 cars you should have your sample. But if those you polled were not registered voters in the town, you would not be able to assume that you have strength to organize an effort among voters to support a petition that would influence the state highway department.

## MARGIN FOR ERROR

Here is a table published by a research organization that shows the margin of error that you could expect if you question 100–1500 people on an issue

Thus, if you asked 750 people whether or not they support your position on an issue and 40 percent said they did, then your margin for error is 4 percent. That means that the margin for error is 36 percent to 44 percent. Even if your sample was of 7500 or more people, you wouldn't be off more than 4 percent. Therefore, a survey need not be of a large number of people to be accurate.

| Closest Percent | Closest Number of Persons Polled | | | | | | |
|---|---|---|---|---|---|---|---|
| | 1,500 | 1,000 | 750 | 600 | 400 | 200 | 100 |
| 10% | 2% | 2% | 3% | 3% | 4% | 5% | 7% |
| 20 | 2 | 3 | 4 | 4 | 5 | 7 | 9 |
| 30 | 3 | 4 | 4 | 4 | 6 | 8 | 10 |
| 40 | 3 | 4 | 4 | 5 | 6 | 8 | 11 |
| 50 | 3 | 4 | 4 | 5 | 6 | 8 | 11 |
| 60 | 3 | 4 | 4 | 5 | 6 | 8 | 11 |
| 70 | 3 | 4 | 4 | 4 | 6 | 8 | 10 |
| 80 | 2 | 3 | 4 | 4 | 5 | 7 | 9 |
| 90 | 2 | 2 | 3 | 3 | 4 | 5 | 7 |

## USING THE RIGHT KIND OF SAMPLE

You do not have to get a probability sample every time to end up with a survey that you can promote to support your point of view. In fact, often if you just ask a few of the "right" people your results will be just as useful.

Late in 1972 a group of sixty environmentalists in fourteen states calling themselves the National Intervenors released a study. Copies were distributed to major media. They used a sample of only thirty—but each person polled was an expert in nuclear safety. All were asked to answer questions on the safety of nuclear power plants. The *Times* carried a complete report on the survey and quoted the results at length, using information for the study and adding facts from other sources. The result, which questions whether or not there are now adequate safety provisions, was a major story in one of the most influential newspapers in the nation. Released in Washington and New York at the time Congress was considering new legislation on nuclear power regulations, the story and the survey it reported undoubtedly resulted in a considerable delay in authorizing new nuclear power plants.

## MERCHANDISING THE RESULTS

The results from surveys, if properly released, can add a considerable amount of excitement to any story. It matters a lot to the average reporter if you are able to show outside support for your views in an independent survey. All the better if you can show that the study was done by a recognized expert, but this is not as important as the study design.

Most reporters know the difference between a real probability sample and a study done with a random sample. Don't try to fool anyone with results from a weak study that shows how right you are. This usually backfires, ending up with a story on how your organization is trying to fool the public with phony research reports.

However, if you have a study that you feel is strong and defensible, use the results in every possible way. Start with a news release. Then, if needed, also prepare a background article based on the subject surveyed. If your study is sufficiently complicated, and at the same time really newsworthy, you may use it as the sole reason for a press conference or even the basis for organizing a seminar.

At the proper time, you can then introduce the authors of the report and have them answer questions on the study design. Let them interpret the results. It can mean a lot to have an outside research expert explain that your program has broad-based support. This is especially useful if the expert will face TV cameras and reporters with the data in his hand. But don't count on it. In fact many leading researchers will insist that you sign a contract that prohibits use of their name in any publicity unless they have prior approval of how you will use the data.

## A FINAL WORD

The selection of the expert and then use of a survey of public opinion can be an important decision for any who want to know where their cause may or may not succeed. However, it is almost impossible to find out with surveys how people will react to something they don't know very much about. Also you have to be extremely careful of how the questions were asked and how the results were interpreted. Often once a survey is completed indicating clear results, many people will simply not believe or want to believe them. Also, if a survey shows equivocal results, it is easy to push an acceptable answer further than the results would allow.

Finally, there is much to be said for good survey work, but often taking risks in spite of negative results is what it takes to succeed. In this book, Chapter 18 offers specific examples of how various individuals succeeded in establishing their views. Few relied upon surveys at the outset of their work to give them an answer to the question, How many others will share my belief and work with me?

Walter Lippmann's book *Public Opinion* (paperback, Free Press) is an excellent place to start a study of the subject.

# 12

# Dealing with the Law

"Congress shall make no law respecting an establishment of religion, or prohibiting the free exercise thereof; or abridging the freedom of speech, or of the press; or the right of the people peaceably to assemble, and to petition the Government for a redress of grievances."

First Amendment, U.S. Constitution.

A TEACHER PLANS AN outing that will involve her class of twenty youngsters. She decides to take them to a small model farm some distance from her school. Near the farm, there is a large, lovely park, an ideal place for a picnic lunch.

This very pastoral plan nevertheless presents logistical problems. The teacher, experienced in such matters, knows that in addition to getting approvals from her supervisors and parents and arranging for transportation to and from the area, she must also check with the police department. Why the police?

The police will assist in making the outing a success. They will reassure her that she isn't innocently leading her children into a trouble spot. They will arrange to have extra protection, if necessary, in or near the park during the picnic. Perhaps other groups are planning outings at the park for that day. Perhaps the park has been a gathering place for neighborhood "toughs" or vagrants and other undesirables. The teacher, then, is taking the proper precautions in consulting with the police. The police can advise the teacher about the park facilities, such as water spouts, rest-room facilities, and food vendors. They will advise the teacher as to the best routes to travel to reach the park. Parking instructions, if a bus is involved, can be detailed.

So we find that while we all enjoy the right to assemble peaceably, we also must plan ahead for the assembly itself. And such planning frequently involves consulting the police department. Any plan that will move people from one point to another should be reviewed by an officer of the law.

You may learn from the police that a permit will be needed in order to use a facility or conduct a program. Let the police in on your plan. You may learn that other governmental units—the park department, sanitation department, highway department, traffic bureau—must also be consulted about some aspect of your plan.

## THE SIDEWALK MARCH

If you plan a march to protest something, to raise public awareness about an issue or to generate public support for a matter in which your group is interested, you will do yourself a favor by contacting the local police station.

A spontaneous demonstration spells trouble—a possible riot or minor disorder—and no police officer likes to be taken by surprise. There has been so much of this in the past ten years that guidelines can be set forth. One such set of guidelines was issued in booklet form by the New York Civil Liberties Union (NYCLU), *Demonstration Guidelines for New York City*; it serves as a valuable guide for group activity. We know, for example, that a nonviolent group of people marching on a public street to call attention to an issue may not be penalized "if they stay on the sidewalk." This is because a sidewalk march is not a parade and no permit is required.

The Supreme Court of the United States holds that marching on the sidewalk of a public street is a protected privilege. The march can extend for many blocks. There can be shouting, singing, rhythmic chants, and cheers. When cross streets are reached, traffic may be delayed by the marchers. It is best that the march line be monitored by a squad of the organization's own marshals, who can keep things moving along and avoid confrontations with nonparticipants who are using the same sidewalks.

There can be incidents during a march of this sort: a pedestrian takes offense at the noise or the delays that occur because of the procession. Such irritations can easily escalate into a variety of disorderly conduct charges, failing to move when ordered to do so by a policeman, resisting arrest, and so on. The marshals must be briefed on how to head off such potential clashes. Police can usually do this, or an attorney expert in civil rights law.

Such marches do not require a permit, but it is still a good idea to let the police know of your planned route. They can advise you of what you ought to do to avoid legal complications, what you should instruct your marchers to avoid doing, and what streets to take.

## PARADES

Marchers who use the roadway are required to obtain a permit or else be deemed in violation of parade ordinances or traffic regulations. If you had planned to conduct a peaceful march along the main street of your town and the local police denied you a permit, you can be arrested if you proceed with the plan. You have brewed yourself some extra trouble and now you are mobilizing people to help raise bail money or pay court costs. Your original purpose has been lost in the legal shuffle; your group's energies are now being diverted. What have you gained, besides adding another footnote in a civil rights report? "For First Amendment purposes," states the NYCLU, "try to stay out of the roadway or get a parade permit from the Police Department."

It is a good idea to instruct parade marshals to take careful notes if a flareup occurs during a parade or sidewalk procession. While one group of marshals deals with the flareup and tries to restore order, perhaps assisting the police, another group of marshals can be jotting down notes about the flurry, getting names of witnesses if personal injury has occurred, noting times, names, distances, dialogue, and such. This material may never be used, but if it is needed, it will be needed badly.

You ought to be able to have a lawyer, or a group of lawyers, along in the role of nonparticipating observers. The presence of such persons should be made known to the police well in advance of the event. The police may elect to deal with this group in setting up procedures for the march. Another good idea is to have a photographer along, one who is accustomed to working fast in noisy, possibly confused situations.

## THE HECKLERS

Your march will attract its share of hecklers. Tell your marchers to maintain their humor and to answer jeers with smiles. Turn aside the barbs with silence. If the heckling builds to an ominous level and threatens the safety of your marchers, the police will move in and tell you to shorten your program or adjourn it immediately. *Heed their advice.* Not to do so is to risk the consequences of violence. You will face great difficulty in reasserting your group's peaceful intent later on if a violent episode has marred your earlier program, regardless of where the blame is centered.

A few isolated shouts or threats from a heckler are not to be interpreted as cause for alarm. One or two hecklers should be ignored. They'll tire or strain their vocal chords and give up and go away.

If a heckler seems to be articulate, intelligent, and sincerely motivated, you might consider inviting this person to step up to the speaker's rostrum and address your audience. Make it clear that the invitation is for a limited time—five or ten minutes—and then you will expect the person to step down and remain silent. If you follow this approach, ask your audience to listen politely to the unscheduled speaker. In small, relatively informal situations that do not center around an issue of high emotional content or immediacy, this approach can be a benefit in building good will and understanding for your cause.

## THE MEETING BEGINS

If you advise the police that you plan to have the sidewalk parade wend its way to a specific building in town, where you will conduct a program of speeches or entertainment, the police may set up wooden barricades at a point that is some distance from your destination. They may ask you to change your plan. Perhaps they have found, through experience, that large crowds are better handled at the location they have chosen. Your first choice of a rally site may present the police with unacceptable traffic and security problems.

Should you feel that the area to which the authorities are relegating your rally will somehow reduce its effectiveness or curtail the size of the audience, then speak up politely and respectfully. Perhaps a compromise can be worked out.

If the police are insistent, do it their way. If you can't bring yourself to agree, then consider doing something else instead of the march and rally. If you elect to disregard the wooden barriers and hold to your original plan, you risk arrest on a variety of charges. Again, while you might counter with a charge of unreasonable restrictions on your right to assemble peaceably, you are diluting the energies and finances of your group in order to fight a legal battle that probably didn't have to be fought.

In arranging the program that will take place at the end of your march, sidewalk procession, or parade, bear in mind that speakers do not need permits. In some jurisdictions, there remain on the books ordinances that require permits for speech-making. Similar ordinances have been held to be unconstitutional. Nevertheless, the question keeps coming up, usually from hecklers in the crowd.

Many experts on such meetings recommend that a space be kept open between the speaker's stand and the audience in order to permit pedestrians to move through the area. While this advice can be disputed—the coming and going in front of the speaker's stand can be a distraction—it seems wise to maintain a pedestrian corridor somewhere around the speaker's area in order to avoid obstructing traffic.

Another wise thing to do is to have an American flag on hand. You will show your respect for the flag and the country and also have a silent reminder that it symbolizes your right to hold the meeting. The flag should be displayed to the left of the audience as one faces the speaker. It is on the speaker's right as he faces the audience. If the flag is displayed in some other part of the meeting area, not on the platform, it should be to the right of the audience as it faces the speaker.

Do not use the flag to decorate the speaker's platform. Use bunting instead. If you drape bunting on the platform, remember that the blue is at the top. If you show a group of flags, the American flag should be in the center and at the highest point in the grouping.

## PICKETING

The picket-line format calls for a procession that walks in an oval pattern on the sidewalk in front of a building or designated area. The pickets may carry signs and shout slogans.

Let the police know about your plan to set up a picket line. They will offer advice and help you decide on the number of people who should be on hand, the duration of the picketing, and what to expect. The police will be on hand, of course, to keep a watchful eye on things. Traditionally, pickets keep marching. They don't have to keep walking, however. Remember the Quakers and their "silent vigil" near the White House during the Vietnam war? They actually constituted a picket line, but because they stood in one place, for hours on end, the format was known as a "silent vigil," another form of protest.

Some believe that if the pickets stand still, they are obstructing sidewalk traffic. But the obstructing goes on whether they move or stand still. A reason for walking is that it attracts more attention when the picket line is animated. It also gives the pickets a greater sense of participation and accomplishment.

Review with the police your picket schedules. Make sure there are litter baskets. Let the police know the names of the picket-line captains so that if any questions arise, they can deal with someone who is in a position to make decisions.

If a passerby stops to ask what the picketing is all about, the picket can take the time to explain things. The picket should step from the line while doing this and let the rest of the group keep marching around. Sometimes, the picket starts making a speech to the passerby and a small crowd collects. One doesn't need a permit to make a speech, remember, so the picket is within his rights. But if an officer comes up and says that this cluster is blocking pedestrian traffic, it makes good sense to break it up. The officer realizes that the crowd could grow larger and build into something that his small force cannot control easily. His request is aimed at forestalling the possibility of a larger hassle. Cooperate with him. A picket who refuses to move on when ordered to do so may be arrested.

Remember, you do not need a permit to conduct a picket line. Nevertheless, it is wise to check with the police. They will tell you what you should know about such public displays and tell you not to attach your signs to sticks. You probably will have to hang your signs around the pickets' collars, dangling from cords, or have them held aloft by hand. This is because picket sign sticks can become weapons.

## DISTRIBUTING LEAFLETS

You can distribute leaflets dealing with political or social matters, but not commercial advertising, while marching in public. If you are handing out the former types of leaflets to passersby, you cannot be constitutionally convicted for littering or for other public health violations. (See Chapter 7 for more on leaflets.) But if you start throwing leaflets around, letting them scatter to the winds, you are asking for a citation.

If you hope to raise funds by selling bumper stickers, buttons, or literature about your group, you do not need a peddler's license. Again, check with the police. Tell them what you intend to sell and what the money will be used for. If your fund-raising is noncommercial, you'll be protected. You can also set up a card table on the sidewalk and use it to display your buttons and literature or collect signatures on petitions. The table must be off to a side, not obstructing traffic. Don't line the sidewalk with such tables; use them sparingly.

The use of loudspeakers, microphones, sound trucks, or other sound equipment in connection with your program requires a permit. Check with the police. The permit may come with certain restrictions on it, such as limits on the hours of use. If the permit is denied, find out what the reason is. If you think it's an arbitrary ruling or that similar requests from other groups were approved, then consult a lawyer. You probably will have to get a court order.

Check with the police about distributing leaflets. Bear in mind that leaflets vary in purpose. Some advertise a business or service and constitute commercial and business advertising. The leaflets that we are interested in involve political and community matters and are noncommercial.

Ordinances that apply to commercial advertising prohibitions do not apply to the distribution of newspapers or noncommercial matter. Those who wish to speak, write, print, or circulate information or opinion are free to do so by means of handbills, circulars, cards, booklets, and placards.

## PRIVATE AND PUBLIC SITES

The preceding material deals with public demonstrations in public places. The rules are different for demonstrations in private places.

For nonschool groups, schoolground demonstrations should never be attempted without consultation with the police. There are many statutes that pertain to conduct in and around school buildings; they apply to gatherings and to the distribution of materials. Here again, the police can be helpful in suggesting alternate sites for your demonstration.

School groups, of course, are governed by school rules and whatever grievance procedures exist. Negotiations take place between student-group leaders and school authorities, who, in turn, can consult with the police and other authorities.

If the school policy makes provision for outside groups to rent the auditorium or other rooms for meetings, then you can gain access in this way. Public meetings in school auditoriums, cafeterias, or gymnasiums can be scheduled by bona fide groups without too much difficulty. But these same groups would have trouble if they tried to conduct a meeting in front of the school during school hours.

Foreign embassies, consulates, and legations are often difficult to approach with a demonstration or picket line. The police will corral the crowd, by means of wooden barriers, into an area some distance from the building itself. They are acting, in effect, as agents of the State Department and trying to protect the embassy staff from the disruptive force of a demonstration at the gates. Your group should meet this police policy without argument. You might try to arrange for one or two of your numbers to pay a prearranged visit to the embassy while the demonstration is taking place nearby. Accompanied by the police, your group can deliver a prepared statement or petition if the diplomats at the building are amenable to your visit. Upon departing, the demonstration can disband.

Gatherings in parks are covered by police and park department regulations, city ordinances, and even local traditions. Apply well in advance of your meeting date for the required permits. If you are turned down and decide to go ahead with your meeting, you will probably be arrested. But the record will show that you sought permission, which should help ease your punishment in court.

You may be within your rights in distributing leaflets in subway cars and stations and on buses, but there may be a local system of permits covering this activity. The idea is to discourage this activity in such crowded and litter-prone areas. In view of the problems involved, it is best to stay outside of subway and bus stations when handing out leaflets.

If your community has a large cultural center, a complex of buildings, or public airline, rail, or bus terminals, it is advisable to obtain permission to hold a rally at such sites. Bear in mind that these buildings usually have their own special security police. You will have to deal with them as well as the regular police.

Public-building managers have their own rules about demonstrations, meetings, rallies, speeches, and leafleteering, and you can be ejected unceremoniously, possibly arrested, if you choose to ignore them.

Private landowners and building supervisors try to keep demonstrators off their property one way or another. This includes shopping centers, private office buildings, housing projects, industrial parks, and factories. But there remain some areas in these places that you can reasonably request permission to enter.

To hand out leaflets at a shopping center, you must obtain permission from the management. The same applies to meetings, rallies, setting up petition-signing tables, and the sale of buttons. If permission is denied, look elsewhere. It isn't wise to seek out the owner of one of the stores in the shopping center in the hope that he will invite your group in. The possibility is that if he were to do so, he would be in violation of a clause in his lease. He might be willing to take some of your posters or leaflets and set them on a counter in his store.

Some shopping centers with vast parking lots find that some parts of their lots serve virtually as public thoroughfares. It is possible that the shopping center managers will permit you to set up in a corner of a parking lot, some distance from the store entrances.

A large housing project may be a likely site for a meeting. Perhaps an issue has arisen that your group wants to discuss with the tenants at a public meeting. Consult the project manager. He has his own security problems and a special police unit on the premises, and he may prefer to have you hold your meeting elsewhere. If "elsewhere" means that you will be effectively foreclosed from meeting with a fair representation of tenants, you might want to pursue the point. You can argue that your meeting is in the best interests of the tenants and that he should allow you to use a meeting room, a parking area, or courtyard. If permission is still denied, then you will have to hold your meetings elsewhere. The alternative is counterproductive.

Should you be arrested while you engage in any of the activities discussed in this chapter, bear one rule in mind: Keep your mouth shut and listen a lot.

If you sit down or go limp while you are being arrested, you can be charged with resisting arrest. If one of your associates is being arrested and you butt in with some words of wisdom, you can be charged with interference with an arrest. This is why you and your associates should strive to keep cool and quiet. Remember such things as badge numbers, police-car numbers, names, times, and dates if you think the situation is important enough. Write down this information as soon as you can. Do not trust to memory; if you are going into court, this information may be useful.

If you need help in such situations, it's a good idea to check with the civil liberties group in your area.* And remember, a good way to stay out of trouble is to check with the local police *in advance*. You might be surprised at the spirit of cooperation that will be shown when you give them a chance to help your group schedule its meetings.

* The American Civil Liberties Union, 156 Fifth Avenue, New York, New York 10017 can send you the address of the chapter office nearest you.

# 13

# Local Government

IF YOU LIVE in a town, village, or small city, you will have numerous opportunities to become involved in local issues if you care to do so.

You will recognize, of course, that any solution to an issue is in the hands of local government. The local government includes the elected officials—mayor, supervisor, town clerk, town board members (or selectmen, aldermen, councilmen), and justices of the peace. It may involve a town attorney's office, or other units such as the highway department and its superintendent, the sanitation department, the fire department, the police department, building inspector's office, zoning and planning boards, architectural review boards, and tax assessor's office.

Even before your group begins issuing news releases and otherwise utilizing local media as you apply the suggestions contained in these pages, you ought to arrange for a meeting with the local powers that be. You also will want to consult an independent and objective local group, the League of Women Voters, which may have rather complete files on local ordinances, zoning decisions, pending legislation, and background on local governmental agencies and controversies. Consultation with this group, in which you confine yourself to gathering information, can be productive.

Another source of background information is the local newspaper's library, or morgue.

Is it the mayor you must talk to? The building inspector? Call up and state the reason for requesting the meeting. Be very specific. You seek a new traffic light at a busy intersection? You think the new apartment complex in a neighboring community is going to harm your community? You want a tougher antipollution ordinance? The bus company's safety standards need updating? Don't ramble. Get to the point. State what you expect the meeting to accomplish. Do you want the elected official to lead the fight? To support your group with a statement? Appoint a committee to study the problem? Have the town board pass a resolution? Draw up new legislation? If legislation is involved, the mayor may refer you to the town attorney or invite that official to the meeting. The town official can be better prepared to discuss the situation if advised in advance of your proposal.

We assume that your cause is nonpolitical, that your group's membership crosses party lines and you do not approach the problem as a political faction. Instead, you are a representative, nonpolitical group that supports a point of view. If your activities have a political tint to them, the place to begin your effort is in the local political party's committee. The party leader, or district leader, in your community will guide your program.

Perhaps you want the mayor to publicly oppose the erection of a gasoline storage tank that you think is too close to a shopping center or of a natural-gas pumping station that is too close to an apartment-house complex.

When you meet with the elected official, remember that in his mind there may be a number of considerations that you may not be aware of. Perhaps the attorney who represents the out-of-state natural-gas company is well connected in local politics, and the town official dares not oppose him. There can be any number of subtle pressures at work on the official, all pushing him in a direction opposite to yours. And here you come, with your point of view, to put him on the spot.

The meeting is held, and you are all very polite; you try to be very specific about what you'd like to see happen. The town officer may want to be vague or speak in abstract terms; he may want to consult with others, to explore the pros and cons. This is very often the scenario of such meetings. Being noncommittal in the early stages of a controversial public matter is one stance that successful politicians have mastered. They like to wait to see which way the wind blows before hoisting sail.

You will want to have the wind blow your way. Your next move is determined by the meeting's outcome. Is the mayor going to appoint a committee or recommend to the town board that a committee be appointed to study the matter and report back? Make sure your group is going to be represented on the committee and that the committee is not unfairly balanced. If you are told a resolution will be presented to the board or that a new ordinance will be drawn up try to help in drawing up the resolution or the ordinance. And try to pin down the date it will be ready. A public hearing may be involved, and you will want to make sure there is enough time to fulfill the legal requirements and generate public support through the use of media.

You will then keep in touch with the official's office, furnish whatever new information you can develop, and otherwise maintain a sense of urgency. If the meeting ends with a vague hope that things will work out for the best, you can interpret this to mean that you haven't won over a supporter. You'll have to press harder. You can plan your media campaign, utilizing the material in this book. News releases. Meetings. Interviews. Fund-raising. Posters. Petitions. Cable television. Radio shows. Editorials. Letters to the editor. Telephone calls. Buttons and bumper stickers.

This same multimedia activity should take place if the meeting ends with a commitment in your favor from the elected official. You will then be taking pressure off the mayor's office as you strive to present the issue as one that has won wide popular support.

Either way, your course of action is in the best tradition of grass-roots involvement with community matters. In 1972, the U.S. Chamber of Commerce reminded the businessmen who constitute its membership, in a "Washington Report," as follows: "Tell your congressman how you feel about the issues which affect your business. It's a small price to pay considering what keeping quiet can cost you."

The article, while concerned with the national election, nevertheless translates easily into local concerns. Chamber president

William S. Lowe suggested that the members follow these instructions:

"1. Distribute information about candidates to your employees and shareholders.

"2. Conduct a registration and get-out-the-vote campaign among your employees.

"3. Show the motivational slide presentation, 'It's Up to You in '72,' to your associates and employees.

"4. Encourage your employees to support candidates financially.

"5. Distribute 'Probable Close House and Senate Races' to your associates so they will know where their help is most needed.

"But most of all—get personally involved yourself."

This is all excellent advice, and you will note that local members have access to slide presentations and booklets that are prepared by the national office of the organization. Independent local groups that form around a single local issue must start from scratch.

Remember that personal action in a community is an essential part of our country's dynamics. It is on the local level that such involvement can be the most meaningful and rewarding for you.

If you have ever taken part in a local zoning fight in which, against seemingly overwhelming odds, you have blocked a carefully choreographed plan to rezone residential property for a commercial use that you and your neighbors know will depress the area, you must know the exhilaration that comes with seeing that governments can and do heed the voice of the people. Elected officials don't "get away with murder." They do what they think they can get away with, at worst; with what the constituency lets them get away with. Generally, they will respond to a determined campaign by the voters. Not always, but often enough to make life interesting.

Elected officials prefer to move slowly. Letters referring a problem to a county agency or a state agency seem to take an inordinate amount of time to draw a reply. You must prod continually. Pick up the telephone and pursue the matter, even if it means telephoning the individual at the county or state level who appears to be the bottleneck. "The squeaking wheel gets the grease" is an old and corny expression. But it continues to be true.

Another approach to local action is to have your civic association or your group invite the key elected official or department head to a public meeting. These officials, being in politics, will be unable to resist putting in an appearance and, they hope, scoring points before a roomful of voters. Give them as much advance notice as possible so that if they have another engagement, they can rearrange their schedule. It isn't fair to call a few days before the meeting, extend your invitation, and then, if you are turned down, crow to the audience that the mayor "wouldn't show up."

Invite the local media to cover your meeting. If reporters cannot attend, cover the meeting yourself. Take notes on what is said, or tape the proceedings and make the tape available to the media. If you have a photographer, make sure the pictures are developed and printed immediately and delivered to the newspaper and the local TV channel, if you have one.

After the speech-making, there is a question-and-answer period. Make your points politely, concisely, and clearly. A lot of local lobbying goes on at such meetings. During the next election campaign, the politician will be back to remind you of what was done for your organization. And the chances are that if you were helped, you will campaign and vote for that official. That's the payoff.

If the concern of your group is a very local issue, a neighborhood problem, more or less, you can still contact civic associations in other parts of town and ask them to support your project. Your angle is that what is good for one part of the town is good for the whole town, and if that other group ever needs support, you'll be in its corner, too. The support you seek may take the form of a letter to the elected official, to the newspaper, or to the proper government department; the adoption of a resolution expressing support that will be read at the next town board meeting and made part of the minutes. It can be in the form of fund-raising, leaflet distribution, petition signing, or assistance in arranging a communitywide public meeting. You should publicize this support in news releases.

At times, it is helpful to organize new committees to help give your group additional clout. Let's suppose that your group is interested in having a new town library built in the center of town rather than on some empty land in the outskirts, far from the town's population center. Your group has advanced to a point where it has a name: Friends of a Central Library, or something like that. You are issuing news releases regularly, holding meetings, preparing fact sheets, distributing reprints of news articles and other leaflets, circulating petitions, and so on.

To generate more strength, you should prevail upon other sectors of the community to form separate organizations that will also support the central library building plan. Perhaps it is a North End Residents for a Central Library Committee, Business and Professional People for a Central Library, or War Veterans for a Central Library. All of these groups are bona fide committees that can circulate leaflets, raise funds, issue news releases, and help to develop more support for the project. If you are able to create this network, appoint a liaison officer to coordinate efforts and keep one another apprised of what is going on. You don't want overlapping press releases or contradictory statements to go out.

Your group should know that the town offices can make available a wide assortment of documents. Zoning ordinances, requests for variances, rulings on such requests, maps, assessments, property records, all are matters of public record. There are minutes of meetings that are available to you, although these minutes are usually quite sketchy.

It is a good idea to take copious notes at meetings of the town board, zoning board, or any other town agency's meeting at which your project is discussed. See whether you can jot down the names and addresses of all speakers, as well as the main thrust of their statements. If a speaker's name isn't given or escapes you, leave a blank and use an impromptu shorthand to identify the speaker: "sun glasses" or "checked jacket." After the meeting, try to get the name. If you suspect that the speaker will leave before the meeting ends, try to get the name during a break in the proceedings. Or check with the clerk who is taking notes for the board. If there is a newspaper reporter present, the reporter's notes may help fill a gap in your own notes; sometimes, your notes can help fill a gap in the reporter's. Have the notes typed up as soon as possible after the meeting. The purpose of all this is to build a complete record of who said what, when, where, and why, in case such material becomes relevant. Don't depend on the official minutes of a town proceeding to be full and complete. If the meeting isn't written up in the local newspaper, bring your notes to the newspaper office. Even if the editors don't base a news article on your notes, they may find them useful in developing an editorial, or in providing background for the reporter who is assigned to the story.

Many town officials still object to the presence of tape recorders at public meetings. If permission to record the meeting is denied, you must decide whether to fight the ruling—take the case to court—or attend the meeting and take notes with pad and pen. The old way is perfectly adequate for most of these meetings. Battling for the right to tape the meeting can prove wasteful of your group's time and resources.

Make sure you understand the responsibilities of the various town departments. If someone is putting up a structure without a building permit, don't call the police. Check with the building inspector. The zoning board, for example, is charged with supervising the zoning ordinances, considering requests for variances, and acting upon them. If a request is granted, the applicant's site plan may then move to the planning board for approval. A public hearing must be held. Speakers at the public hearing may persuade the board to reject the plan. There are times when approval is granted despite opposition that is expressed in overwhelming numerical force at the meeting. Residents have gone to court to seek injunctions in such cases. This phase of a community battle is best left to the attorneys that your group hires to carry the fight into the courts. The news that you are going into court warrants a press release, of course, but then there is little to do in terms of general publicity. The courts will take it from there. The ruling is something you will want to publicize. If it goes against you, interpret it to the newspaper and be prepared to state whether an appeal will be made. If it goes in your favor, be prepared with a statement that assesses the meaning of this triumph.

There are times when the mayor or town supervisor seems to be unusually insistent on doing things without regard for your group's opinion. Opportunities to meet are rejected. Compromise is out of the question. There will be no referendum despite your appeals, petitions, news releases to media, and meetings. At this point, you should consider making the issue political. If it's an election year, a primary challenge, or an independent candidate's challenge to the incumbent, can work wonders. But there is one vital proviso:

Your group's candidate must be someone of substance, of impeccable standing in the community. Your group must be willing and able to ring doorbells and pursue votes as intensively as the incumbent will. One of the great disadvantages the insurgent faction must confront is that many of its best workers are usually too busy during working hours. They must earn a living first and then devote spare time to the local election. The incumbent administration can put in many more hours getting around to the voters, planning, and speaking at meetings or in one-to-one sidewalk encounters.

Before you embark on this path, read up on the election laws so that you will meet all legal requirements. There are rules about resident and voter signatures on petitions, deadlines for filing papers, and so on. If you make one mistake, the office holders can challenge your petitions, and you can be knocked out of the race.

Of course, you will have to schedule a barrage of news releases that keep the community informed of your candidate's progress.

School matters traditionally take up much of the spare time of a community's most "involved" and public-spirited residents. The perennial struggle centers around money. Many school districts are divided on how much money should be spent on public schools, mainly because public funds are in such short supply. Parents of younger children generally go along with support for the new school budget, which is usually higher than the present one; older residents, with children out of school, generally align themselves with the budget-cutters. Educators, like others in our society, never have enough money for the schools. And there you have the basic ingredients for annual battles.

Committees are formed to help pass the budget. Those who oppose the budget don't form committees that explicitly call for less money; they set up a committee that carries a more subtle name, or they form no committees and simply sit back to await voting day.

Committee work will involve the development of telephone lists and telephone callers, usually based on school lists and voter registration lists. Leaflets are circulated; letters are written to the newspapers; news releases spew forth. The media barrage is put into effect. Public meetings are held. If there is any secret to success in such campaigns, it is in full preparation.

Instead of waiting for the budget to be made public and then leaping into action, those who support the budget year after year should be recruited well in advance of the new budget. They should know which issues to play up. Those who oppose budgets year after year usually function on a more spontaneous basis. The opposition usually waits for the new budget to appear and then spots some expenditures that can be attacked.

If the vote is scheduled to take place close to April 15, income tax time, the antibudget bloc will have an advantage (assuming the budget calls for a significant tax boost).

Even long, careful, in-depth preparation and mobilization cannot insure passage of the budget. *Ad hoc*, last-minute campaigns to knock down a school budget still succeed a good part of the time, especially where the tax hike is greater than the last one.

# 14

# How to Deal with State and Federal Governments

ONCE YOU BEGIN organizing for action, sooner or later you will come in contact with the bureaucracy of your state and, possibly, the federal government.

One of the best ways to get heard is to gain the support of one or more of the members of your state legislature. After you start with the support of a state senator or assemblyman and as you gather strength and take your case to Washington to seek help from a congressman, your task becomes easier.

If you aren't shy, you can try to start at the top. See either or both of the senators from your state. A representative and one or two senators on your side and you have what you need to press for political action on Capitol Hill.

When it comes to being heard, to dealing with the media, the power of a political office is helpful. This is another good reason for knowing politicians. It's simply a matter of logistics. Every news-gathering organization has reporters assigned to cover state and federal legislative bodies. These reporters are expected to know what is going on and are required to file stories regularly about important or interesting developments. To handle this assignment, they depend on insiders who have access to news stories before they break. You will find that if you get to know local, state, or congressional reporters, you will also meet more important newsmen and politicians, provided you work at it.

The legislator, together with the reporters who cover the Capitol and the entire structure of state or federal government can quickly take a rather obscure issue and make it prominent.

## SHORTCUTS

There are some shortcuts to getting heard in your state capitol. Here is an action program in outline form: it should be relatively easy to modify it to fit your specific needs: (1) Be sure you know what it is that you need to accomplish at the state level. (2) Study the elements of your campaign to determine what will be needed to get what you want. In the recent past, it was local organizations that pushed through abortion-reform legislation, no-fault insurance, clean-water and clean-air laws. All eventually had to confront federal action to sustain their victories. For some, the battle to sustain a position apparently will go on for years and years. Opponents of some of these laws will do all they can to push for repeal.

Abortion reform is an excellent example. The first year after New York State passed a liberalized abortion law—largely through the efforts of women—a new effort was organized and the legislature repealed the law. Only a veto by Governor Nelson Rockefeller kept the liberal abortion law on the books. The U.S. Supreme Court later ruled that abortion was in fact a right of women, and states were then obliged to change their laws to permit women residents to decide whether or not they wanted to continue a pregnancy. Yet, the forces opposed to abortion are effective and only New York, Hawaii, Washington, and Alaska continue to make abortions available to any significant number of women.

There is no doubt that until all states enact repeal laws of their own, many physicians will refuse to handle abortion cases for fear of prosecution. The American Medical Association's legal counsel advises doctors to "move with caution . . . it all depends on how local officials choose to apply the [Supreme Court] decision to their own laws."

On the national scene, there is growing support for the effort of antiabortion forces to enact a constitutional amendment that would ban abortion. An amendment would overrule the Supreme Court and make abortion illegal again. Clearly, those who fought for abortion reform legislation and thought they had won still have a long way to go. And those who resisted and thought they had lost also have a long way to go.

## LOCAL ACTION

To gain support at the level of state government, you must find out the names of your state representatives. This is easily done at any library. Once you know the names and the correct address, plan to contact the legislator when he is at home.

Personal problems—a job, Social Security matters, pension questions, military matters, a welfare claim—are the usual things that are presented. The lawmaker and his staff will help if it is humanly possible. Calls will be made in your behalf.

But regardless of the subject, when you decide you want to talk to your state legislator or congressman, try to arrange the first meeting at his home or office or at the office or home of a common friend. The first visit is very important, and you mustn't jeopardize your effort by making an ill-conceived, poorly documented presentation.

Learn his voting record and plan what you want to say. Get your facts together. Know exactly what you want the lawmaker to do or refrain from doing. If you want him to support legislation that is coming up for a vote, be sure you have studied the law in question and can explain your position on it. You won't be taken seriously if all you do is state that you are for or against a piece of legislation and don't have a cogent case to support your stand.

Many lawmakers can't, or don't, spend very much time studying every piece of legislation that is introduced. Often they rely on those who are partisans to "educate" them on a particular bill.

Once you have made a study of the pending legislation, you will probably know a lot about those who oppose your viewpoint. You may even know more about a bill than the person you are trying to influence. But that lawmaker is not likely to vote your way unless there is a benefit—or at least no danger of political injury—in so doing. We aren't suggesting bribery. Absolutely, unequivocally no. It is a very serious offense to bribe or to offer a bribe to an elected official. But no law is enacted or defeated without a carefully planned course of action by those who believe they will be aided, or harmed, by it.

Before you go traipsing off to Washington to see your congressman or senator, try to arrange for a meeting in his home office. But if you are determined to see the capital, it is essential that you first make an appointment. Call the office. The National Newspaper Association (NNA) compiles and distributes a listing called *Press Assistants and Appointment Secretaries to Members of the United States Senate and House of Representatives.* It costs $1. The NNA is at 491 National Press Building, Washington, D.C. 20004. This list provides the names of key aides—administrative assistants, appointments secretaries, executive assistants, receptionists, secretaries—and their telephone numbers.

You may end up talking to the legislative aide or the administrative assistant. Try to get past the legislative aide to the administrative assistant or appointments secretary. The legislative aide, concerned with broad strategy matters, may want to put you off if it seems that you have a bone to pick. Make it clear that you are determined to have a face-to-face meeting with your congressman and that you want an appointment.

For any number of reasons, you may find it necessary to meet first with the legislative aide. Perhaps you want to get a feeling about the lawmaker's position before you have your face-to-face meeting. You may then schedule a meeting with the aide and hold in abeyance your meeting with the congressman. Call a week or two in advance to set up your appointment. And a day before you are to leave, call again to double-check. Sometimes, schedules change and meetings must be postponed. Don't go without an appointment. And don't go with a busload of people if you can avoid it. One or two representative voters from back home, perhaps armed with a petition, are enough. If you arrive in a crowd and think you will storm the office, think again. If the congressman is in there, he can get away through a back door. The best days to try for an appointment in Washington are Mondays and Fridays, when the lawmaker—if he stays in Washington—will be more apt to have more time. Those days are used for clearing up accumulated work. Tuesdays, Wednesdays, and Thursdays are when Congress is in session; Congressmen have less time to spend in their offices on those days.

Sometimes you read about busloads of voters descending on Capitol Hill to lobby every congressman and senator in sight. The fact is that if you don't vote in the district, the congressman you lobby isn't really going to be very interested. They can be charming and polite, but once you have left, they don't give you a second thought.

Remember that congressmen and senators will make the effort to see you. They want to talk to as many of their constituents as they can on the theory that if they give you five minutes, they may have you for a supporter forever.

After you call to arrange for an appointment and you finally agree on a time and date, it is a good idea to write a letter of confirmation. And don't forget: Call again to confirm before you leave for the appointment.

If you want to inundate a lawmaker with letters, the most effective approach is to tell your group to go home and write personal letters, each telling the lawmaker something in an individual way, avoiding the carbon-copy stigma. This individualized approach works. It is better than a petition. Congressional aides have trouble responding to petitions. If there are thousands, or even hundreds, of signatures, they aren't about to write to everyone. Often, petitions are tossed out after they are read. Telegrams can be as useless or as useful as letters, depending on what you are writing about. Sometimes, very influential groups embark on letter-writing campaigns. These letters get the same reception as those from "unknowns." If the letters are individualized and well thought out, they will be taken more seriously than those that are mass-produced and carelessly written. Congressmen try to see representative batches of their mail, and they also make an effort to sign their names to letters that have been prepared by their aides, even if they haven't read the letter that triggered the response.

The mail that pours into the offices of congressmen, senators, and state legislators is opened by members of the staff, including secretaries, aides, and interns. If the letter deals with a major issue, one that is before the public and is being debated widely, a form letter will be sent back. Many lawmakers make use of automatic letter-writing machines that give the finished letter an individual look.

If you write about an obscure subject, one that isn't widely or readily recognized, the staff will be requested to research the subject, check into legislation, if any, that pertains to the subject. Calls will go out to congressional research offices for background material. Letters about obscure issues get attention; the public servant doesn't want to betray a lack of awareness or information to a constituent.

Normally, "canned" or "inspired" mail that arrives in a tidy bundle, amounting anywhere from a few dozen pieces to hundreds of pieces, isn't going to get much attention. Especially if the letters say the same thing and have no individuality. But if one morning 500 letters arrive at a congressman's office, he'll pay attention. Even if they're mimeographed. The sheer number will give him pause; he knows that when 500 constituents take the trouble to write, he can't ignore them. Bulk mail of this sort means, be careful; don't be hasty; think about your reply.

As soon as you can, follow up your visit with a letter that thanks the lawmaker for the time and attention he gave you and that restates your position. Let him know, again, that you are not alone in your belief.

This letter, followed a few days later by a position paper (see Chapter 7) that describes the extent of the organization you represent, will add weight to your visit.

## THE LOCAL EQUATION

On the local level, you may be a registered Republican, and your congressman or state representative, a Democrat. If your town is run by Democrats, talk to these officials about your issue and the legislation you have in mind.

These people can pick up the telephone and talk to people in the state capitol and arrange a meeting or serve as liaison. If you all belong to the same political party, your task may be easier. You may be able to enlist the support of the local party chairman or the executive committee, including elected officials and important businessmen and professional men in your community. A message from any part of this combination is an important message from home for a lawmaker. Work on the local level, on the local elected officials, and seek their intervention if you believe—or discover—that your cause has become enmeshed with partisan politics.

It is not unusual for a state legislator in the minority party to contact a colleague who sits on the majority side and ask that a bill be introduced. The theory is that with majority party sponsorship, the bill will have easier sailing. Bills that are introduced in this way are not major pieces of legislation usually; more likely, they are bills that either party could handle, but one party can move more rapidly. In return for the favor, the minority party lawmaker will vote for a bill that the other lawmaker favors.

Usually, your representative is a lawyer. And the lawyer may have a practice or belong to a law firm back home. To help advance your cause, enlist the support of important people in the community—bankers, builders, heads of big companies that play a role in the economy of the community. These people have additional clout with lawmakers for a variety of reasons.

A word of caution: If you become involved in an action that a public utility opposes, you will become involved in a difficult battle. You can win, but you will know that you have been in a fight. Rather than attack a utility or any large corporate body head-on and immediately, you will do well to take your case to the public first, through the media. Try to build support from the grass roots. If you succeed in doing this, your elected representatives will find it easier to heed your calls for help. If you are up against a big-time opponent, move too rapidly, and ignore the need to build a foundation of strong support (an organization), you will be brushed aside. This is what this book is all about.

## HEARINGS

When the legislature plans hearings, be sure to offer yourself as an expert for or against the proposed legislation that you are involved with. The sponsors and opponents of the measure are known to your representative. If you need help in gaining access to either side, the chances are your own representative knows them. A call or letter will be all that is usually needed for you to get an appointment to testify.

If you don't have a paid lobbyist (and most people don't), the most meaningful action you can take is a carefully planned program that offers support to the side you agree with. Often local issues are passed by very close margins. A well-planned and carefully supervised program of telephone calls, letter-writing, and news releases can make a difference. If an uncommitted lawmaker receives twenty or thirty telephone calls from constituents, a similar number of letters, and perhaps a few telegrams asking him to vote for a particular bill (which he doesn't really know much about) and if there are none asking him to vote the other way, the odds are that he will vote your way.

If he gets a lot of pressure from people he doesn't know who live outside his district, he is likely to think he is being pushed too hard. He then will be inclined to vote the other way, resenting the outside pressure. It is important that you protect your chances of success by not applying pressure to the wrong person or the right pressure at the wrong time. Get close to the dynamics of the legislative fight as it unfolds and you will be able to avoid those pitfalls.

## LOBBYISTS

There is no question that when it comes to getting state or federal legislation enacted the work of professional lobbyists is often the most important factor.

Using lobbyists is a part of—if not a way of—government. It is completely legal. It is not only the side of reaction and conservatism that wins via the efforts of lobbyists: in many instances the lobbyists recruited and paid for by liberal causes are responsible for the passage or defeat of legislation their client wants enacted or defeated.

The recent case of how paid, highly skilled lobbyists for the tobacco interests were defeated by a man with no money is not to be forgotten (see page 284).

An excellent example of how lobbyists are able to keep consumerist legislation from being passed can be seen in what has happened in New York State with no-fault auto insurance. In 1972, despite the efforts of Governor Rockefeller, the insurance industry, the Nixon administration, and every consumer-interest organization in New York State, the legislature refused to pass a no-fault law. Here is how the N.Y. State Trial Lawyers Association with a membership of 3000 defeated the no-fault bill in 1972. Three hundred members went to Albany just before the vote was to be taken. They had done their homework. They knew each legislator well, either as a fellow attorney or as a result of intensive local action in his home district. The pressure they put on these legislators was enormous. In every way, they outflanked the governor and all who wanted no-fault insurance.

Rockefeller recognized the strength of the opposition when he told the legislature during a rare appearance before the vote, "There are lawyers who benefit from preservation of the status quo in automobile insurance. There are also many lawyers in the Legislature. But I don't believe that a Legislature that had introduced some of the most progressive social legislation in the nation would deny New Yorkers the savings and the advantages of no-fault insurance."

He was mistaken. Consumer advocate and paid Albany lobbyist Eileen Hoats, with great support throughout, was outgunned by the well-organized trial lawyers. One element of their campaign was to send each legislator a letter with the threat, "If you don't support the Laverne resolution [which would water down no-fault] I will send wires and letters to 10,000 former clients to defeat your re-election."

That kind of pressure organized by a small number of people was enough to defeat a law with enormously broad-based popular support.

A year later, the legislature passed a no-fault insurance law which took effect February 1, 1974.

## THE DAYTON STORY

For several years thirty business leaders and local newspaper editors in Dayton, Ohio, have met each Saturday morning to talk over problems of mutual interest. One point that the business and press agreed on about four years ago was the need to help sustain the inner city. Against enormous pressures, this small group managed to get legislative support for subsidized suburban housing as well as inner-city construction of living units for low- and middle-income families. Traditionally, only the decaying cities have offered housing for the disadvantaged in this country. The suburbs, ideal in many ways for low-income housing, have been able to keep them out via carefully organized lobbies in the local legislatures.

It may be that Dayton's experiment in "scatterization" of low-income housing will not succeed, but the lobbying efforts of a very few businessmen were enough to get their regional planning office and the U.S. Department of Housing and Urban Development together long enough to put through legislation in Dayton to build some 800 suburban low- or middle-income housing units. A significant start in what is a most sensitive area.

## FINDING A LOBBYIST

Whether or not you want to hire a professional for state or Washington representation of your interests, it is important that you get the right man or woman, one who will be effective and who has a good chance of succeeding in your cause. Before you start out to find a professional lobbyist, be sure you have a realistic view of the problems your cause faces. Know what you can afford and who else you can recruit to join with you.

Because someone is available for a fee and says he is a lobbyist doesn't mean you should go ahead and retain him without checking. There are many ways to find an effective paid lobbyist. You can check with your elected representative. You will have, one hopes, learned to know and respect him or at least some others in the state or federal legislature. They are often the best source of information about lobbyists, since they see them all the time.

The local or state office of the League of Women Voters usually has information on who is and who isn't an effective lobbyist for causes that interest the league. Your local newspaper's statehouse or Washington correspondent will often be able to direct you to a law firm and/or lobbyist he knows is reputable and has a reasonable chance of succeeding in your interest.

The lobbyist you finally select will tell you how he is to be paid, how much, and just what he expects you to do. Often a successful lobbyist will not let you near the legislators except as a last resort, choosing to work quietly on a one-to-one basis doing his job in his own way. Or he may invite you to appear with as many others as you can, tell you to charter a bus, what to print on signs, and even act as your stage manager for a mass-picketing program.

Major businesses often have access to lobbyists. If you feel your cause is shared by a sizable corporation, visit with the president or legal counsel of a company and ask if there is a way for you to join forces with the paid lobbyist in the company's employ.

Many citizens organizations now have lobbyists on retainer. They have to be registered in the statehouse and in Washington; there are lists of who they are, who pays them, and what they are doing. A careful review of these names should lead you to someone to talk to.

When you find a lobbyist, you have to place yourself in his hands just as you would any professional. But you also have the right to ask questions and to get itemized reports of his activities —and you can always fire a lobbyist if you feel he is not doing his job. If you do make a mistake, the sooner you get out of the agreement, the better it is for you and the people you represent. If you decide to terminate a relationship, make sure those people your lobbyist was calling on in your behalf are notified. This makes for a difficult situation but is important if your man continues to make calls even though he no longer represents you—another very important reason that you have a carefully studied contract with a lobbyist spelling out what you pay him, how long in advance you must notify him of a decision to terminate the relationship, and so on.

## BASIC RULES FOR DEALING WITH LEGISLATORS

Here are some basic rules:

1. Use facts, not opinion. If you are asking him to vote for or against a bill or to support your position with a committee, organize your information so he can understand it.

2. Know what the legislator has to deal with. Your representative may not support your position because of local conditions. You may have to work with someone elected by others—even

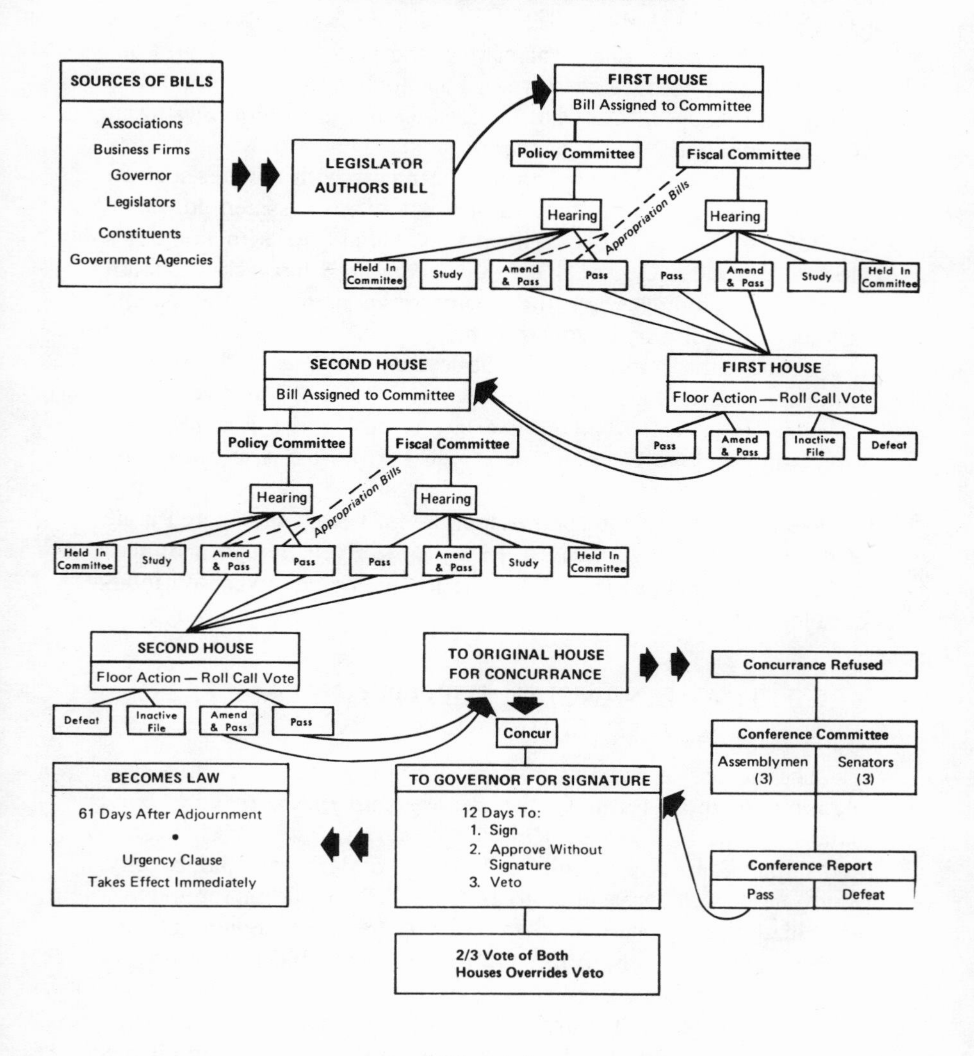
LEGISLATIVE PROCESS
SOURCES OF BILLS
Associations
Business Firms
Governor
Legislators
Constituents
Government Agencies
LEGISLATOR AUTHORS BILL
FIRST HOUSE
Bill Assigned to Committee
Policy Committee
Fiscal Committee
Hearing
Hearing
Appropriation Bills
Held In Committee
Study
Amend & Pass
Pass
Pass
Amend & Pass
Study
Held In Committee
FIRST HOUSE
Floor Action — Roll Call Vote
Pass
Amend & Pass
Inactive File
Defeat
SECOND HOUSE
Bill Assigned to Committee
Policy Committee
Fiscal Committee
Hearing
Hearing
Appropriation Bills
Held In Committee
Study
Amend & Pass
Pass
Pass
Amend & Pass
Study
Held In Committee
SECOND HOUSE
Floor Action — Roll Call Vote
Defeat
Inactive File
Amend & Pass
Pass
TO ORIGINAL HOUSE FOR CONCURRANCE
Concurrance Refused
Concur
Conference Committee
Assemblymen (3)
Senators (3)
BECOMES LAW
61 Days After Adjournment
Urgency Clause Takes Effect Immediately
TO GOVERNOR FOR SIGNATURE
12 Days To:
1. Sign
2. Approve Without Signature
3. Veto
Conference Report
Pass
Defeat
2/3 Vote of Both Houses Overrides Veto

FIG. II

from other states. If you want action, the fact that you didn't vote for someone doesn't mean you can't help him in many ways, chiefly by paying for help he asks you for.

3. Know all sides of the issue, especially the ones with the muscle. Tell your legislator all the facts, and give him some background on the behind-the-scenes action as well. The more he knows, with specific names of people, the better he can help you.

4. Keep in contact even when you don't need his help. Write him regularly supporting what he does. Don't go to him only when you need his help. An organization called New Priorities in New York makes monthly luncheon appointments with congressmen in Washington. Nine or ten times a year a few businessmen go to the Capitol and just talk over things they believe in with congressmen they admire. Out of these luncheons often have come action programs, including ways the businessmen can help the people they identify with stay in government.

5. Know the committees in the legislature. The work on legislation is done in the committee rooms. You will have very little luck if all you do is wait until a law is put up for a vote. Your work will be done by that time if you know what you are doing.

We reprint here with permission, a chart from the March issue of the *California Pharmacist* (see fig. 11). Even though it applies to California, it should be invaluable to anyone who wants to influence legislation in any state.

## GETTING FINANCIAL SUPPORT FROM STATE AND FEDERAL SOURCES

The secret of staying alive as an organization is not only maintaining the interest of the membership but a realistic bank balance as well. A key skill in today's survival is that of "grantsmanship." There are literally millions of dollars paid out by city, state, and federal treasuries to organizations working for individual citizens' own interests. The trick is to learn how to get the money. This skill is hard to acquire and invaluable to any organization that has access to it.

There are some basics. To get money from government you have to be tax exempt; thus, you can't do it as a private citizen.

Each state has a different definition of a nonprofit organization; check with an attorney to find out what is required. A printed list of qualifications is available from any secretary of state's office. Once you have nonprofit status, a whole new world can open up to you.

A privately supported community psychiatric clinic with nonprofit status can get money from many sources unavailable to organizations that have not acquired this status. For example, foundations, various charitable organizations, women's clubs looking for a cause, and private individuals will contribute money to a clinic with the nonprofit recognition. One reason, and the most important, is that any contribution is deductible from state and federal income tax. The other is that to stay tax-free the foundations and organizations that contribute have to show that they are in fact giving help to nonprofit organizations. One sort of takes care of the other.

## GETTING LEGAL HELP

Here is a message concerning legal help from the Natural Resources Defense Council, Inc. newsletter (Vol. 1, Issue 4):

> Many non-profit organizations do not know where to turn when looking for help with legal matters. There is a source of aid and support in the New York-New Jersey-Connecticut Metropolitan area which should be more fully utilized. The Council of New York Law Associates provides volunteer legal assistance to nonprofit organizations engaged in *pro bono publico* programs. The majority of the Council's 1,500 members are associates in Wall Street or Park Avenue firms who have used and developed their expertise in projects ranging from legislative drafting to full scale litigation. Attorneys in the Council take on *pro bono* projects and cases on a part-time basis. There are similar Councils in other parts of the country and information on them can be obtained through the New York Council.
>
> In addition, many attorneys in the Council are interested in full time employment with non-profit and public interest groups both in New York and across the country. The Council runs a free placement service and is very interested in hearing from groups looking for full-time attorneys.

For further information on all aspects of the program, contact Susan Belgard, Director, Public Service Placement Bureau, Room 510, 36 West 44th Street, New York, New York 10036 (212 972-9370).

Before you apply for tax-exempt status, be sure you know the rules. You will need an attorney and a tax expert to help you keep in line once you do get it. It pays to follow all the rules, since once you lose tax-exempt status, it becomes very difficult for an organization to regain it.

Know your rights, and be persistent. Find out what money is available, get the application forms, and study them to see how best to apply. It may be that you will need to join in with another organization to qualify for funding.

You may have to make a change in your plans just to be able to apply for outside money. By hiring certain kinds of skilled people and offering services that may not have been part of the original plan, you may be able to get substantial help from sources previously unavailable.

A good example of this is how a private nonprofit clinic in Northern New Jersey got state funding. For years it provided psychiatric services to children and their parents in the community. The financing was mainly from an individual and appropriations from neighboring towns served. The state and occasionally a foundation or two also provided some grants. When the clinic's building became too small, the board decided that a new structure was needed; it could also accommodate new services. After a great deal of study, it was decided not only to offer those services previously available but to add a new capability—a school for emotionally disturbed children. This decision cost the organization a great deal of money in construction of the new facility, but it is now one of the few privately supported schools of its kind in the state. It receives several thousand dollars a year for each child enrolled in the special school. Other funds are now also coming to the center for training grants and the like—all because the director of the clinic, a professional administrator, knows how to go about getting funding.

The federal government is now exploring ways to help individual citizens take action. An excellent guide to this new policy is available from the U.S. Environmental Protection Agency, Washington, D.C. 20460, under the title *Citizens Suits Under the Clean Air Act.* It details just how a citizen can get court action.

Recently the FCC has been talking about setting up an "Office of Public Counsel," which will act as attorney for private citizens or groups of citizens who want action. Without an attorney highly skilled in broadcast law, a private citizen would not be able to do much about a station that he felt should be denied license renewal. The proposed FCC counsel would take on such suits, his fee coming from the government.

## INFORMATION OFFICES

Recently the Office of Management and Budget estimated that the Nixon administration spends $116 million a year on public relations activities. This includes salaries for 5000 or more "information specialists" for many government agencies. Some are very well paid, a very few with salaries of $40,000 annually. Many are extremely competent and skilled workmen. Almost to a man, they will answer questions from the public with courtesy and dispatch.

If, for example, you are interested in environmental-action programs, the various governmental agencies with an interest in such activities include the Department of Commerce, the Department of the Interior, and the Department of Health, Education, and Welfare (see Appendix III for a complete list). Each has an information office that can explain to any writer or caller just how his department operates. Questions he can answer include, Is there money for citizens groups? How can we get funding for our program? Who do we see?

You may be surprised to learn that you can approach the great federal bureaucracy with a proposal for action that may be entirely supported by federal funds.

The many conferences held all over the country where citizens groups and government meet to discuss matters of mutual interest are often organized by a private organization and then paid for by a federal or state agency.

## ENVIRONMENTAL DEFENSE FUND

About five years ago in Washington an organization called the Environmental Defense Fund (EDF) was established (see page 318).* It now has over 25,000 members, each of whom pay ten dollars a year for professional help in watching what the government is doing to the environment. The organization has offices in Washington; Berkeley, California; and Setauket, Long Island. It has had great success in fighting the U.S. Corps of Engineers, whose annual budget is well over $1.6 billion.

EDF, using paid and volunteer help, has been the single most effective force in protecting various communities against corps actions that they believe to be ecologically unsound.

The legal umbrella for their action is Section 102 of the National Environmental Policy Act, passed in 1969. This law requires all federal agencies to prove that any planned action is ecologically sound.

Using Section 102, a local citizens group in Tennessee formed the Committee for Leaving the Environment of America Natural (CLEAN). This committee got help from the EDF and was successful in stopping a federal water-authority program in Tennessee that took ten years to plan and would eventually have cost billions to execute. The authority planned to open up a 235-mile waterway across several Southern states. The environmentalists mobilized by CLEAN used court action to stop the program by filing a statement and paying $12 in fees to a federal court. This takes a knowledge of the law.

A mod attorney in San Francisco, J. Anthony Klein, and two friends under the banner of Public Advocates, Inc. have successfully received payment from the federal government as attorneys in action against the government. The California action they initiated was reported in late 1972. It concerned a federal judge who ordered that the California Highway Commission pay lawyers' fees for action against the commission.

What they did proves that if you believe that your rights are being denied because you can't afford proper legal counsel in

* The address of the Washington office is 1712 N Street N.W., Washington 20036. Telephone: (202) 833-1484.

action against state or federal government, you should get an attorney. With his knowledge, he can file a motion for payment of legal fees to help you get the action you believe is needed.

The great bureaucracy of government is a working tool for all who learn to use it. The fact is that there are many ways you can get fair and just treatment from the bureaucracy. But you will have to get inside the system to use it and keep at it to succeed.

Any elected representative can get you help. Often a visit to his office in your home town, or if need be in the state or federal capitol, will be needed.

With the right kind of contacts and properly organized program, almost anyone can get financial support.

In their book *Making Activism Work*, William Meyers and Park Rinard describe how a few activists have succeeded against enormous odds. They cite examples of successful citizens programs in many areas of activity, including education, health, housing, transportation, law and justice, foreign policy, and media.

Their chapter on how to raise funds is especially useful. They write, "The *sine qua non* of fund-raising is the determination to get money. If you believe sufficiently in your cause, there should be no difficulty in asking for the contribution without apology and on a substantial scale commensurate with what the prospective donor can afford."

## ORGANIZING AN INITIATIVE

Donald K. Ross, in *A Public Citizen's Action Manual* (Grossman, 1973), explains how you can, without lobbyists or friends in the legislature, get a state law passed.

According to Ross, about fifteen states give citizens the right to frame a law, organize support for it, and get it on the ballot with or without the help of the legislature.

To get a law on the ballot, sufficient numbers of signers of petitions are required; from 6 percent to 10 percent, depending on the state, of those who voted in the last election must sign petitions.

Ross warns that organizing a successful campaign to get an initiative enacted into a law is a job for experts, persons who are well organized, well financed, and, most important, willing to work long, hard hours. He counsels, "Either the proposition must be so popular that people flock to support it or the citizens' group must have a strong organization capable of spreading the word of the petition and capturing support. The less glamorous the initiative measure, the more necessary it is to have a strong organization."

It was a citizens' initiative that was responsible for banning the Olympic games from Colorado.

## CITIZENS' SUITS UNDER THE CLEAN AIR ACT

Under Section 304 of the Clean Air Act amendments passed in 1970, citizens can bring suit in federal courts against a polluter or governmental agency, including the Environmental Protection Agency itself, for failure to live up to the clean-air laws.

There are very rigid rules and they must be followed carefully to accomplish this. Be careful that you know exactly what papers to file. A small, almost meaningless, omission may sink a suit before you have had time to gather your forces together. It is best to get help from an organization like the Conservation Society or the Friends of the Earth, Inc. before starting out on any citizens' suit. Ask for help in locating a local lawyer who knows all the rules. See Appendix III "Groups that Can Help" for a listing.

The National Resources Defense Council, a public-interest law firm at 36 West Forty-fourth Street, New York, New York 10036, will be able to advise you which attorneys in your area specialize in environmental law.

The booklet *Don't Leave It to the Experts,* published by the Environmental Protection Agency, Office of Public Affairs, Washington, D.C. 20460, is available free and explains just how individual citizens and interested groups can get action when it comes to enforcement of pollution control legislation.

# 15

# Finding Others Who Believe as You Do

YOU CAN'T DO it all alone unless you have an ability possessed by very few. You will need all the help you can get to succeed. Therefore, it pays to study those who have succeeded, with special attention directed at the understanding of the small details that really do make the difference between success—national or international awareness and acceptance—or failure; otherwise, no one, not even the people closest to you, will become believers in your cause.

## MARJORIE GUTHRIE AND CCHD

When you first meet her, Marjorie Guthrie does not appear to be very well organized. Aside from the fact that she has extraordinary grace in movement (she was a leading dancer and dance teacher), she doesn't impress you with any special talent. Yet it is this slight, pretty woman who may be the force behind a cure for Huntington's disease (HD), an always fatal disease.

It was this slowly paralyzing neurologic condition that killed her husband, gifted songwriter and performer, Woody Guthrie. If she is successful in her efforts she may save Arlo (*Alices's Restaurant*), Joady, or Nora Guthrie, her children, who have about a 50–50 chance of suffering the same fate as Woody.

Obviously Marjorie has a great incentive. But many of us have firsthand experience with physical or social illness that needs attention and don't try to take time to effect change. Marjorie Guthrie proves that it is possible for a single person to organize a formidable effort, one that may change the lives of countless thousands of people—many yet to be.

Even though it is very difficult for an individual to do much when it comes to effecting real social change, it is possible. It is extraordinarily difficult for most of us to accomplish in a lifetime what Marjorie has done in a few years, but it is not impossible.

It was not impossible for Ralph Nader to cause the giant auto makers of the world to change the design of their products.

It was not impossible for John Gardner to organize Common Cause.

It was not impossible for Basil O'Connor to create the March of Dimes, an effort that eventually produced more than one vaccine for polio.

It was one man, John Banzhaf, who alone, with no outside help or money, organized the effort that ended with cigarette commercials off television and warning statements about the dangers of cigarettes on every package.

All these people were able to do what they did with a gift for understanding people and a knack for utilizing media. They were able to get money, followers, and finally power. They were able to effect change largely because they were able to exploit the media.

Despite the fact that they were successful, probably the only thing these people have in common is an unbelievable inner drive that keeps them going when ordinary people would be discouraged and quit. Probably the single most important rule to follow if you want to organize a group and change something that you feel needs changing is, stick to it. Sticking to it is not easy. In fact almost no one except an unbelievably motivated person can do what a Nader, Banzhaf, O'Connor, or Guthrie did.

Not long ago the force behind Common Cause, John W. Gardner, wrote to his members his answer to the question, How does Common Cause function? Here is a very brief summary of his eight basic rules:

1. To succeed the effort must be full-time and continuing.

2. Limit the number of targets. Hit them hard.

3. Get professional help. Gardner writes that "a weakness of citizen action is the disinclination to get a professional grasp on the processes of government." We can tell you that unless you act professionally or get someone who can advise you on what the rules are, the establishment will not ever take you seriously. In fact, you will probably never really cause change. You may get heard, but you won't do more than make noise.*

4. Form alliances with others who will work with you. "The potential force of such collaboration is impressive; given an appropriate issue, it is possible to gather into one room on a week's notice a dozen people from organizations representing tens of millions of Americans." (Only a Gardner could do this easily.)

5. Know and understand the use of communications. "Effective communications is the most powerful single weapon of the public interest lobby."

6. Treat membership as a group of dedicated workers, not as a bloc of voters or a special interest group.

7. Always try to find allies within the organization you want to change. The most effective and believable force for change may very well be one of the people you oppose but finally convince that you are right.

8. Organize for action. Study, discussion, and ego trips for leaders do not make for social change. You must go outside and enter the lists. You must elect the man who will speak out, vote, and take your position to others.

Marjorie Guthrie has used the Gardner rules with some of her own to organize a nationwide effort, to find, first, a test for the disease that killed Woody and, then, she hopes, a cure.

The disease was named after a New York doctor, George Huntington, who first described it about a century ago. It doesn't affect very many people: perhaps as few as 100,000 people have it.

* Many believe that Ralph Nader has caused more social change in this country than all other social activists put together. He was recently cited by Harvard as one of a very few graduates who they believed would be long remembered for what he accomplished to make the country a stronger and better place to live.

All will die from degeneration of cells in their brain as long as fifteen years after it is diagnosed. Half of all the people with a parent who died of the disease will get it. Woody's mother had it, but he himself had a 50–50 chance of avoiding it.

What Marjorie does is helped immeasurably by the fact that Woody and now Arlo Guthrie are internationally known. Not many people could run the concerts organized by Marjorie without her contacts in show business. But she never quits working to help the almost 3000 families in the United States that she has found who have a known history of HD.

Her vehicle for action is the Committee to Combat Huntington's Disease (CCHD). It was started in 1967 with only Marjorie. Now there are thirty-two chapters, with more every year. Hundreds of thousands of dollars have been spent to date by the committee to support research in HD.

Marjorie, as the force behind CCHD, has a very simple way of getting action. She isolates the problem, takes hold of it, and doesn't let go until she is satisfied that she should.

She will badger, charm, and eventually overwhelm a physician she feels would be a key worker on a test for the disease. Her efforts involve a never-ending battle with those who forget or get tired of hearing what she says. But she keeps at it until they give in.

She will attend medical meetings to get physicians interested in the disease, because early diagnosis is terribly important, even though no treatment has yet been developed that is successful. She sets up a table near the door or in the exhibit area and collars all who come near to hear her message.

Each year she takes several trips across the country to deliver her message: "We must first find a test to diagnose and then we will find a drug to control the disease. Perhaps we can push the onset back ten or more years. At least it will permit those who are doomed to get it some additional time without disability."

Her efforts are well described in detail via many articles available from the Committee to Combat Huntington's Disease, 200 West Fifty-seventh Street, New York, New York 10019.

An obvious comment on the rare success of the Guthrie approach is that only a person so motivated can organize such an effort. Of course, this is true. Yet someone got to Jerry Lewis, who raises over $12 million via a national Muscular Dystrophy Association telethon. This money represents almost the entire annual budget of the association.

It is almost impossible to provide specific help for abstract ideas in organizing for action. By citing examples of how others worked to get people together to help them, perhaps we will provide you with ideas that only you can evaluate.

## HOW TO RECRUIT

You have to have some help, even if it is minimal, to run an effective campaign. Yet one, two, or three people properly organized and financed can really shake up the establishment and get heard. Ralph Nader worked for several years all alone, without even a secretary. John Banzhaf was a law student with no money at all, yet using his recently acquired knowledge of law, he was able to get free time for anticigarette commercials on network television. An estimated $70 million of free time was being given by the TV networks because of Banzhaf's efforts when the cigarette ban went into effect.

Obviously, the reason for recruitment is to provide bodies to do the work and money to carry it on. To accomplish real change, you need a leader. Someone who will be visible, articulate, and unfailing in availability. For most organizations the lack, or poor selection, of a leader is the single most common reason for failure. Effective leadership is the single most important ingredient in a successful campaign for social change.

It is always effective leadership that will move the idea from obscurity to national prominence. Without it there will not be a program that succeeds.

It takes a commitment to lead, and without a leader who has it, there is almost no chance that the goals of a campaign will be met. Leaders and membership alike are attracted to a cause for one basic reason: they, or someone close to them, have been affected by the problem. Most important is that the individual will in some way get personal satisfaction from the effort or money contributed.

To Marjorie Guthrie, helping those who suffer from HD directly relates to helping her three children. To some, the power they hold is enough to keep them involved. Some just need continual exposure in the press to feed their egos. Others sincerely stay at work because they have an inner need to do it.

Early in 1973 the *New York Times* reported how Hana Ginzbarg of Houston, Texas, almost single-handedly was able to prevent a subsidiary of Humble Oil and Refining Company from rechanneling a river she felt would cause widespread and unwanted ecologic damage.

Martin Waldron, writing in the *Times*, said, "Hana Ginzbarg has won her fight. For almost three years the middle-aged Houston housewife has been the driving force in a movement to save a short wilderness river from being turned into a storm sewer. . . . After months of dogged effort, 2000 letters, and nobody knows how many speeches, Armand Bayou will remain a wild river."

The keys to Mrs. Ginzbarg's success are similar to those used by many who want to get heard. Mostly she utilized the media to get followers. According to the *Times*, she organized canoe trips down the river to show off its beauty; the resulting TV and newspaper publicity attracted conservationists who, in turn, offered her access to their newsletters. Once she was able to talk directly to others interested in conservation she made the most of the opportunity. The use of existing media like newsletters can save a lot of money for anyone interested in getting heard.

The editorials in the newsletters were sent to weekly newspapers. The fact that a conservation organization printed an editorial probably had a greater impact on an editor than if Mrs. Ginzbarg had sent it in on her own.

Armed with hard information on the ecologic effects of the proposed sewer, she made an appearance before the local town council and convinced the authorities that they should not permit the construction asked for by the builders.

Before she was finished Hana Ginzbarg had contacted every available local and federal organization with any interest or responsibility at all related to the environment. She found an audience at the National Oceanic and Atmospheric Administration, the Department of Housing and Urban Development, the U.S. Corps of Engineers, the American Society of Civil Engineers of Houston, and the Texas Parks and Wildlife Department.

The latest development in her year-long battle is the fact that the city of Pasadena recently borrowed $1.25 million to match a grant from Office of Housing and Urban Development (HUD) to purchase almost 1000 acres along the river that Mrs. Ginzbarg wants to save. At the time of the article, she was also trying to raise an additional $800,000 to purchase another 450 acres.

Writing for the op-ed page in the *New York Times* on August 26, 1972, Midge Kovacs, coordinator of the Image of Women Committee for the New York chapter of the National Organization for Women, spoke of tremendous problems caused by stereotyped images of women carried via the media. Television, radio, films, newspapers, and even women's magazines, according to Midge Kovacs, are "limiting and demeaning and keep us from experiencing our true possibilities."

It will take leaders like Midge Kovacs to get visibility, and using the circulation of a major newspaper to gather a constituency is a very smart move.

The fact is that almost every newspaper in the nation is fertile ground for planting news about the struggle for equal opportunity for women.

The antiwar campaign of a solitary forty-year-old dance teacher, Louise Nruyn, received national attention in the press and on television when she walked from her home in Newton, Massachusetts, to Washington, D.C. This mother of a Quaker family of five was quoted as saying, "I had to do what I could as an individual because of the deep frustration for not having a group outlet for outrage at what we are doing in Indochina."

How many other women or men took this walking protest as an example is impossible to know, but it was effective in getting, at least for a few weeks, local and national publicity for one person's antiwar feelings.

Remember Superman? Do you remember the name of the town where he and Lois Lane worked for the newspaper? It was Metropolis. A real superman of a real Metropolis in Illinois used the legend to get his ailing city into better shape. The method was simple and very effective.

Bob Westerfield, former football star and a Metropolis resident, organized an effort to get his town back on the map by attracting attention. Westerfield and his chamber of commerce had nothing to do with naming the place, but he thought that the fact that the comic-strip character worked in a Metropolis was a good way to focus attention on his city of less than 7000.

In January of 1972 Westerfield was able to get his story of the fictional Superman's city's award to the city's own Superman to a wire-service reporter (see page 87 on wire-service offices). Maybe the story happened to hit on a man who was a Clark Kent fan, but when UPI got the story, they used it. The article about a real Metropolis ran in many newspapers across the nation. Soon came TV interviews and then more stories in newspapers. The result of the publicity was spectacular. Six months after the first story appeared, because of the resulting national publicity, plans were made for a 1000-acre, $50-million Superman Land industrial park to be built in Metropolis.

This is an example, farfetched but within the realm of the possible, of how publicity—even about a seemingly corny idea—can be used to get a point across and attract enough attention to recruit others who will support an effort in which only a few originally believed.

To succeed as a leader, charisma is needed. According to the *American Heritage Dictionary*, charisma is a "rare quality . . . attributed . . . to persons who have demonstrated an exceptional ability for . . . securing the devotion of large numbers of people."

Chances are that the leader you pick will not necessarily have charisma, but effective use of the media will soon give him some sort of an aura that looks a lot like it.

What is needed by leadership is the ability to capture the imagination. Often the immediate event will make for leadership. There is no question that Harry Truman was not a great man physically or intellectually, but the decisions that he made resulted in a mantle of greatness, since any nation in trouble needs to believe that its leader is truly superhuman.

## VOLUNTEER ACTION

If you are interested in volunteer programs, you can obtain a monthly publication, *Voluntary Action News*, from the National Center for Voluntary Action (NCVA), 1735 I Street N.W., Washington, D.C. 20006

The NCVA is a nongovernmental, nonprofit organization that

promotes and supports volunteers and voluntary efforts in the United States. Its work includes assisting communities in developing local voluntary action centers, providing data on voluntary efforts through its clearinghouse, and sponsoring the annual National Volunteer Award.

Check your telephone book. Your county may have a volunteer service bureau already set up. This office attempts to assign volunteer workers to the various organizations and programs that can best make use of their services.

## HOLD THE PHONE

During the 1972 presidential election campaign, the Republican National Committee organized a program that entailed telephoning every person who had contributed money to the GOP during the preceding four years. In studying the outline of the manner in which the GOP telephone program was conducted, the reader should pick up some important points to remember in case a telephone "tree" is part of the reader's activity.

About twenty-one persons were hired to make the telephone calls from a rented office in Washington, D.C. Long-distance telephone lines were leased, along with computer terminals and computer-typing machines. The computers were useful because the scale of the project was enormous, but for local campaigns, it should not be necessary to use so much hardware.

The GOP workers were given cards on which were printed names of contributors, their addresses, telephone numbers, and amounts contributed since 1968. Each worker read from a script that was placed before him. The script went like this:

> "Hello, Mr. [contributor's name]. This is [your name] calling from the Republican National Committee in Washington. Mr. Jeremiah Milbank, the chairman of the Finance Committee, asked me to call you and thank you for your contributions to the party in the past.
>
> "We wondered, with this being a presidential campaign year, if perhaps we might be able to count on your support of the party once again and help reelect the President. [Pause]
>
> "We'd be happy to send out a contribution card and envelope

if that would make it easier for you. I wonder if, perhaps, you could tell me what your gift will be so we can plan ahead here at headquarters.

"We'll send the card right out, and we'd appreciate your sending it right back in. Thank you."

The foregoing script can be modified, of course, for any situation, but notice how concise it is. It gets to the point after a brief introduction that is designed to create a mood of importance, which says, in effect, this is not just another telephone call.

The pause is to give the party on the other end of the line a chance to respond. The campaign workers who made the telephone calls were instructed to avoid getting involved in discussions of campaign issues or personalities. If a contributor wanted to discuss an issue or a personality, the caller was told to say, "I understand your position on the subject," and then move the subject back to the script. Another tip: Allow six rings on the telephone for contributors under $25 and nine rings for those who gave more than that amount the last time. How this formula was worked out was not explained.

Newsmen who inquired about the GOP telephone project were told by one caller that they each made about sixty calls a day. The pay was said to be $3.50 an hour. Callers were required to produce $100 an hour in contributions or lose their jobs. And they were instructed to get a $20 contributor to pledge $30 or $40—in other words, to avoid the same sum, if possible.

After each call, the card would be placed on one of two piles: the cards of those who agreed to contribute and the cards of those who said, "Maybe." Those who said no did not receive follow-up letters.

Names, addresses, and amounts pledged were then put on a computer tape, which was then placed in a machine. An envelope was inserted in the same machine, and a button was pushed. The machine typed an address on the envelope. The tape then was placed in another machine that typed the follow-up letter, mentioning the contributor by name. The letter was designed to resemble a secretary's personally typed letter, even to the initials of the writer, in this case, Mr. Milbank, and his secretary's lower-case initials in the lower left-hand corner.

The letter to a pledgee began:

"[Name of telephone caller], a member of my staff, has just told me of your intention to contribute $25 in support of the reelection of President Nixon and I am happy to extend my personal thanks for your wonderful cooperation and assistance."

The "maybe" respondent got this letter:

"Thank you for the time you gave [name of telephone caller], a member of my staff." The letter then went on to ask the reader to "join with your fellow Republicans to help provide the vital financial support required by our party as we prepare for the critical elections of 1972." The closing line asked for the "order" with this line: "May I ask you to send your contribution to us today?"

A real fountain pen, with real ink, signed Mr. Milbank's name after the letter was aligned mechanically under the pen and a button was pushed to activate the signature-writing machine. For those who pledged more than $1,000, Mr. Milbank signed his name to the letter personally.

The next step was to mail the letter. It went out within twenty-four hours of the telephone conversation. The letter was accompanied by the detached part of the computer card that the telephone caller used for the call, together with a postage-paid return envelope. Donors of between $100 and $499 were dubbed "Republican Campaigners." The designation "Republican Victory Associates" went to those who contributed from $500 to $999. For $1000 and more, the donor was given the title "RN Associate."

To quote a Democratic politician, Jess Unruh of California, "Money is the mother's milk of politics."

## LIST OF MEDIA

Here is a list of media opportunities to use primarily to get followers. The idea is to get heard in such a way that you will attract attention that you can use to get others to join with you.

### *Newspapers*

*News releases* to newspapers for every story can be useful in getting supporters if you add such a paragraph as this: "According to Mrs. Smith, anyone interested in working with [organization's name] should contact her at her office, 134 Main Street." (See page 148 for information on how to write news releases.)

*Letters to the editor* often will not only get publicity but also give the signer the chance to tell others how to get into contact. Always sign the letter with the address where you want to get mail; never use your home address when dealing with controversy unless you are willing to have crank calls and possibly worse (see Chapters 3 and 17).

*Interviews with reporters* should always end with an appeal for support and a listing of the address where you can be found.

*Advertisements* in the public-notices section of daily newspapers are cheap and an excellent source of sympathetic help. Use them for notices of meetings, requests for literature, and emergency sources of funds. There is no better buy in a newspaper than the public-notices section. Also, very few other regular sections get as much readership.

Using display advertisements is also a sensible choice to get recruits and money if you have the funds and know how to write and lay them out. Most appeals in print are window dressing and rarely will raise enough money to pay for themselves, but they do provide the organization with a public way of talking to its members and prospective members. It is occasionally worthwhile to use paid newspaper advertisements to communicate with members, but it is expensive compared to use of the mail or telephones.

## *Radio and Television*

Interviews on radio are difficult to use for the solicitation of members and support, since there is no simple visual way you can get your address or telephone number to the listening audience unless your host will agree to it. Therefore, before you go on the air, ask the program producer if you will be permitted a commercial in addition to the interview. If he agrees, be sure to give a telephone number or address more than once, slowly, and then do it again if possible.

TV stations will expect you to arrive with at least one visual if they are planning to interview you. One of them should be the name of the organization and the address you are using for public contact. The information should be on two or three lines in a horizontal format (see page 12 for examples).

## *Directories*

An excellent place to look for organizations that may be able to help you is the classified telephone book. Under headings like Churches, Women's Clubs, Associations, and Service Organizations, you will find a telephone number and address of an office with one or many people who may be ready to help you achieve the goals of what you believe to be worth your effort and that of others.

In addition to local organizations there are several national organizations that can often lend a hand. If the effort is legally registered as nonprofit, then a foundation may be able to help support your effort.

*The Directory of Foundations*, by Marianna O. Lewis (Columbia University Press) is in most public libraries.

# 16

# Advertising

## WHY TO USE ADVERTISING

THERE IS NO question that many people interested in getting heard discover paid advertising too late, if at all. For some mysterious reason, many who want social change will not face the fact that paid advertising is an essential part of the communications "mix."

In essence, you can't depend on free access to the media if you want 100 percent control of your message. For example, you can send a well-written, carefully researched news release to the media. The release can embody every salient point you wish to make. Your contact there responds to the release, calls you to check on some facts, and then proceeds to print or air what he believes is a fair, nonprejudicial version of what your release contained and what you told him on the telephone or during an interview. All this points to a great news break for you and your cause.

The article appears, or the program airs. You find that your entire effort has been wasted. The date of the big rally is wrong; so is the name of the organization! Worse, you were not quoted entirely accurately, and it reads as though you are some sort of a nut who wants to change things just for the sake of change.

Your cause has been hurt. The publicity may even ruin your hopes for a large turnout at the rally or fund-raising affair. And that was the reason you sent out the news release in the first place. The question now becomes, What can we do to salvage what seemed like a great opportunity for your group.

This sounds like an extreme example of mismanagement of promotion, but unfortunately, it happens, in varying degrees, all the time. And it really is no one's fault. Everyone thought he was doing a proper job. Therefore, the lesson to be learned is that if what you have to say is critical and the exact words are important, *the only way you can be sure that it will be printed the way you want it printed is to buy space or air time for your message: You must advertise.*

## HOW TO GET THE AD TOGETHER

Paid advertising is often the very best way to communicate with your audience, those who are important to the success of your venture. It also can help build morale within your organization. Seeing "your very own ad" come to life on a page is one way to add an official sanction of sorts to the effort. After all, the reasoning goes, if this group has the money and cohesiveness to put an ad together, it must be a serious group. That is why you should know and understand how to use advertising.

If possible, try to get the help of a professional. You may be able to get an advertising agency to act as your representative. The *Standard Directory of Advertising Agencies* (also known as the *Agency Red Book*) published by National Register Publishing Co., New York, contains listings of bona fide agencies in every state. It should be available in your library. If not, try the advertising department of a company located in your community. The telephone directory also will list area advertising agencies. The chamber of commerce also can help direct you to advertising companies or professionals in the area.

People who have an excellent understanding of how to use advertising often are found in the advertising department of a major retailing establishment. These people know how to place messages that get action. They know if their message failed the very next day, when no one comes into the store to buy the advertised item. Conversely, they can judge success when sales respond to the ad that they created and placed.

Another method of finding an ad agency to help you is to watch local television or check through the newspapers for announcements that you consider to be tasteful and persuasive. Call up the station or the newspaper advertising department and ask for the name of the agency that created the ad you admired. It will then be easy to contact the agency or individual involved.

When you get together with your agency or advertising consultant, be frank. Explain your point of view. Disclose your finances. Ask for a free and open discussion of what the cost will be. If you are fortunate, you will make your selection fairly quickly. You may have a few prospects to talk to, but your meetings will help narrow the field. You may be lucky enough to meet someone who is willing to help you for free or who would not want anything more in the way of compensation than earned commissions from the media. The commission is available only to recognized advertising agencies.

Newspapers, TV stations, radio stations, and other media that depend on advertising revenue for their existence publish rates that include a 15 percent commission, payable to recognized agencies. If an organization places the ad or the TV commercial directly (without the intervention of an agency), the published rate will be paid. Thus, agencies can often do work for a client only for the commissions obtained from the media. Usually, the amount doesn't really cover their expenses—especially if the budget is low—so they charge additional fees for copywriting, art work, and the production of the advertisement or commercial. Check with the agency about what you will be expected to pay for.

There is no guarantee that your project will interest a professional advertising agency. An advertiser with a regular advertising budget can ask a number of agencies to meet and prepare "presentations," or material that gives the would-be client an idea of the work it can expect from each agency. The advertiser selects the one he likes best. If you don't have much money, you probably will have to take what you can get in the way of professional help. But be careful: a poorly conceived and badly placed ad campaign can ruin everything for you. Don't let any advertising professional "snow" you with fancy words. If you don't like his work or don't understand why a particular ad is being prepared, the chances are good that the intended audience won't understand either. Advertising is an art, not a science. If something about the art or the copy strikes you as wrong, challenge the people at the agency. Question, even argue, if necessary. Don't buy what you don't really like or don't think will work. But if the advertising people are convincing and their record of success impressive, you can sublimate your own taste and go along with their decision.

## MEDIA SELECTION

A poorly placed campaign—one that appears in the "wrong" publication or the wrong medium—is almost as costly and frequently as fatal to a cause (or a product) as a poorly written ad. It is vital that you select the media as carefully as you settled on your message.

One of the most popular places for ads that deal with public-interest topics is the week-in-review section of the Sunday *New York Times.* This section also is being used by industry as well as private groups to reach an audience of "opinion-shapers." The *Times* also allocates a part of its daily op-ed page for ads by major corporations that seek to reach public opinion in order to present a point of view that is far removed from the sale of a particular product.

A full-page ad in the Sunday week-in-review section of the *Times* will probably cost about $11,500, based on a one-time rate (discounts apply for multiple insertions). This Sunday edition has a circulation of about 1.6 million. The number of people who see the message could well be two or even three times the number of copies sold, since there are usually multiple readers for every copy.

A full-page ad in the daily *Times*, again on a one-time "open" rate, is about $9,700. A total of 860,000 copies are printed daily. Of course, you can buy less than a full page. There are many different sizes of ads, including classified, or public-notice, ads. Your agency will work out the best size. If you don't have an agency, ask the people at the newspaper what the different sizes cost and then decide among you which you think will do the best job for your cause.

But the question is not only money. The question also is, do you have enough to say in an ad? Is there just as much of a chance that you will get what you want by spending less in another medium or using the money for something other than advertising?

An expert in communications should be able to help select the right medium for a given message once he knows what you want to say, to whom you want to say it, and what you want the prospect to do once he has read the message.

This is where the coupon comes in. Your coupon will ask for money from the prospect, or it will ask that he return it in order to receive additional information. The coupon provides you with a nucleus of a mailing list. It should include your group's name and perhaps the name of your group's president, executive director, or secretary. Include an address. Include ample space on which the prospect can print his name, street address, town, and zip code. The coupon should include some recapitulation of what its purpose is. Make certain it includes all the vital information and is clear and accurate. Don't try to get fancy with your coupon. We have seen a coupon printed white-on-black. Prospects had to fill in the coupon with white ink if they wanted to respond. Be practical.

Ralph Nader, having progressed to the status of a nationally known consumerist, has organized a fund-raising campaign to help finance his activities. He uses large-space newspaper ads as well as direct mail to get people to send him money.

Common Cause, the so-called People's Lobby founded by John Gardner, former undersecretary of health, education, and welfare, uses paid space—with coupons—in newspapers for the same reason. His organization is funded entirely from dues ($15 per year) and at last report, he had attracted 215,000 members who are scattered across the country in 435 congressional districts.

The questions you should ask professionals about media are complex, but for a start, you should include these:

1. Does the newspaper (or magazine or radio, or TV station) really reach the audience that we want to reach? Most of the media worth considering should have some surveys on file that will furnish you with a good idea of their readers, listeners, or viewers, broken down by age, education, income, and so on.

2. Is the cost per person (or the cost per thousand) worth the investment? If the cost per thousand readers or viewers is high, you may find it cheaper to try something else, such as telephone calls, direct mail, leaflets, or posters.

3. Ask for proof that your prospect is in the medium's audience. If you are going to pay for the space, the newspaper should have evidence to show who reads it.

4. What kind of space or time should you buy? Is it best to buy a small display ad every week in the Sunday newspaper, in the local daily, or in the local weekly? In all three? In two of the three? The local weekly newspaper may reach fewer (or more) readers than you really want to reach. The same may be true for the other media. The only way to learn is to test responses. This is a costly method, but it is a useful discipline for those who want to be heard. The most sophisticated advertisers employ this technique by carefully structuring their ads, the placement, and measuring response from each of the different versions that run.

5. When should you advertise? Only by discussing your proposed message with an expert will you be able to arrive at an answer. And only by understanding your message will an expert be able to advise you on when to place it.

## APPROVAL OF YOUR MESSAGE

It is the right of the owners of media to accept or reject advertising. In May 1973, the U.S. Supreme Court ruled that radio and TV stations have an absolute right to refuse to sell time for advertisements that deal with controversial public issues or even political campaigns. Therefore, no matter how strongly you may feel about using an advertising campaign and no matter how much money you have to pay for the space or time, you may not get heard through the advertising route if the managements at the media don't want their readers or audiences to be exposed to your message. The chapters on media in this book, of course, offer advice on how to be heard in nonpaid appearances in, or on, media.

Not long ago, the Planned Parenthood Association was denied permission to advertise its services in New York. Today, this organization and others can buy space, not only for ads about service for contraception but also for those about abortion clinics. There undoubtedly remain newspapers within a hundred-mile radius of New York City whose managements would never accept these ads.

If you want to argue with a publisher about his refusal to

run your ad, it is good to consult an attorney. Remember, the newspaper or station can always refuse to carry your message even if your lawyer says that it is not harmful in any way.

## WHAT TO SAY

There is no easy way to help you decide the contents of your paid message. Obviously, if you are running an ad in order to get someone elected, your message should feature the candidate's name, the office being contested, and at least one fundamental reason why a voter should support your favorite. If the ballot is complicated, an illustration showing your candidate's name on the ballot can be of help.

But more than that, comments on local issues, position statements on the current office holder, and pledges "if elected," all depend on the local situation. Some professional campaign managers can promise that their client will win election if all that is done is to run ads bearing the candidate's name and the office that is up for grabs. Nothing more and nothing less. Repetition of this simple message can, in some cases, do the job.

Assuming that your situation is somewhat different and that you must first determine what message your ads should carry, bear in mind that it is very often useful to survey the constituency (see Chapter 11 on surveys). What are the voters concerned about? What do they consider the issues to be? What do they dislike about the candidates? How do they feel about the issues? Are there enough voters out there who support your candidate's positions to make a difference?

Sometimes, even a factor as elementary as the weather can be used in a campaign. In a New York City mayoralty campaign not long ago, Mayor John Lindsay was faulted for a bungled snow-removal job in the borough of Queens. His opponents discovered this resentment from local surveys, and the issue snowballed into major proportions.

You can also employ public opinion surveys to provide you with some clues as to what issues to feature, but you must be very careful that you don't take survey results too seriously. Many things can go wrong with even the finest survey. Remember, the public is fickle. It often forgets an issue after the surveys are made. A time lag of a few weeks can nullify some situations that your carefully prepared survey has developed. Many voters change their minds during the course of a campaign, sometimes during those moments just before they vote. Don't take the results of a survey as gospel, for they can be very wrong.

If you are made uneasy by the results of your survey, question them. Get outside interpretations. Repeat the survey by asking the same questions in different ways. Don't be led down a path you don't like just because a survey pointed the way. If you're really uncertain about which course to take, try some test ads, each pursuing a different theme. Use coupons in each. The one that pulls the best response will help you decide which alternative to stress.

Again, we point out that the use of advertising tests are best left to the professionals, but you can be so bold as to try your own simple tests. You can overcome your lack of experience with an understanding of this chapter's contents and the chapter on surveys.

Here is one approach to a test-ad campaign: You pay for a quarter-page ad one week and a one-eighth page ad the following week. They are the same in every way but size. If the response is the same, then obviously you can buy twice as many of the smaller units for the same price. Even if you get only 70 percent as many responses from the smaller one, you may decide that you are better off using it.

Also, try skipping a week. Place the ad every other week for a spell, and see if the response holds up.

Test the "pull" of different headlines. Try using a photograph instead of all copy or all copy instead of a photograph. Try a line drawing instead of a photograph if you can afford these different tests. Study the test results; it's a lot of fun and well worth the effort, because you are testing your judgment of human nature, in effect, and learning something with every test. (The common denominator in all these exercises is that you learn how much you *don't* know about human nature.) Testing can't make a poorly conceived campaign succeed, but it can make a moderately well done campaign come alive. There has to be something to test, and you have to have the stamina—and the funds—to do it.

Another variable in testing is the page it appears on. Does response go up or down if the ad appears in the sports section? In the women's pages? Business section? Near the TV listing?

## BUDGETING

Paid advertising needs careful budgeting to succeed. Even a well-conceived program will be useless if you pay no attention to the important elements in it. Work on the strategy of media selection, pacing and timing, and appeals for funds.

If your purpose in running an advertising campaign is to raise money, be sure you plan for enough advertising to make it pay off. Don't count on getting all you need for your next ads from your first ad. It doesn't work that way. Repetition is a vital part of a successful campaign. If possible, spread your budget to allow for testing or repeats of your fund appeal.

We have heard of advertisers who use ads just to keep a very few "fat cat" contributors happy, since the ads feature the names of those people. These are ego trips that cannot be minimized, but they should be avoided if at all possible. Buying large ads is a costly undertaking, so you should use them after carefully pondering the pros and cons. Too many large-space appeals for money can create a backlash in which the public gets the notion that your organization is endowed with all kinds of money and, therefore, doesn't need additional help.

The elements you pay for in the average advertising campaign include copy, design, typography, and any use of photographs or drawings. Color is rarely justified, yet there are some instances where color can make a difference. The use of color is an extra expense.

Once you evolve an ad that works for you, think twice before you change it. Money and effort may be wasted just because the person paying for the ad gets bored with it. There is no excuse for changing an ad that is still drawing a response. You should resist all pressures to create a new campaign unless the alternative one is, on its surface, superior. Change for the sake of change isn't enough. Be wary, for it may be that the agency wants to try out a new idea and doesn't really care that the old one is still working and is better.

Extra mileage from a newspaper campaign can be obtained by buying reprints of the ad and using them as mailing pieces or blowing it up and converting it into a poster. Use up your ads before you give them up.

# 17

# Letters and Telegrams

ACCORDING TO A recent book by Kalman Siegel, letters editor of the *New York Times*, over 8 million people write letters to American newspapers each year. The *Times* averages 40,000 of this total but prints only 2800, or 7 out of every 100 received.

Even with these impossible odds, there is no question that a published letter to the editor of the *Times* can evoke thought, comment, and even response from many parts of the country and, occasionally, from foreign lands. Few newspapers in this country have a comparable impact. Perhaps this is the reason that senators, Supreme Court justices, and even presidents and vice-presidents have taken to writing letters to the *Times* as a means of being heard.

Editors of all newspapers, as well as magazines, both consumer- and business-oriented, use the letters section to keep readers up-to-date on controversy that they do not want to comment on themselves. They sort of let the readers "fight it out" in the letters column. This is why anyone who wants to be heard should consider the letters-to-the-editor route. This section of a publication often provides a forum for brief reports or for information that would not be accepted as an article by the same publication.

The *New England Journal of Medicine* and *Science* are two of the most respected professional weekly publications in the world.

Both print letters that often question scientific accomplishments. However, each week a few letters are printed from readers who may be calling for support on a specific issue or castigating a public person in the hope that the target will read the letter or be told about it and perhaps respond.

## NEWSPAPERS

Siegel offers these hints to those who want to get letters printed in the *Times*: Be brief. Write clearly. Peg your letter to a news event. Don't be vituperative. Keep issue-oriented. And when you criticize, be sure to offer constructive comments of your own.

He also warns, in his book *Talking Back to the New York Times* (Quadrangle, New York, 1972) that those who wish to see their letters in print should avoid the taint of being a propagandist or special pleader. Yet, even a brief review of the six or seven letters that appear each day in the *Times* and the many that are reprinted in Siegel's book shows that letters of the type that Siegel tells readers he will not print somehow manage to find their way into the paper's letters columns.

Obviously, his is a difficult and responsible position. And it seems that it is not too difficult to get a letter printed, if not in the *Times*, with its "two letters per year" limit for individual letter-writers, then in other newspapers.

Here are a few hints from us on how to get letters printed in newspapers, including the *Times*:

1. Get professional help. A well-written letter has a better chance of getting in than one with an equally important message that is not as well-written.
2. Take a position against a public person, reported by the same newspaper in a recent article: "Yesterday, in an interview with your reporter, Senator Kennedy said. . . ."
3. Pick an editorial position of the paper to support or challenge. You usually have a better chance of getting in with a challenge.
4. If you organize a letter-writing campaign, don't be obvious. Send different letters, using different language, from different writers. Most papers won't keep printing letters from the same

person, but few will analyze the letters they receive to determine who said what and when.

5. If possible, get someone important with an impressive title to write the letter. A professor, priest, or rabbi has a better chance of getting printed than a John Q. Public, all things being equal, including the letter.

Often a campaign of letters can be reprinted and distributed to others. Occasionally, letters printed in the newspaper can be used to get radio and TV time. Program producers are newspaper readers, too. Attempts to reach them by telephone may have a better chance of success if your letter to the local newspaper was just printed. You can enclose a copy of the published letter with the letter you send the producer to add some weight to your request for a meeting.

It's important not to abuse the relationship, but up to a point, a series of letters can spark a sprightly controversy. Your letter gets printed. Someone else replies. You reply to that letter. Again, a response is warranted and is printed. This can keep going until the editor decides enough is enough, the reader's interest has been served.

## *Weekly Newspapers*

The weekly newspaper is perhaps the easiest medium in which to get a letter printed. The deadline is usually a couple of days before publication, so sending your letter a week early is helpful. You can use a letter to the editor to call attention to a meeting that is important to you, to solicit support for a cause, or to discuss a local issue. Letters to weekly papers usually comment on local matters such as school problems, politics, and zoning matters.

There is no reason why you shouldn't use letters as a substitute for a news release, but sometimes, an editor will resist this approach. You'll know about it when your letter doesn't get printed. When you find that it hasn't been printed, it doesn't help to call the editor and ask if he got your letter. Just try again with another letter, expressing your point of view in different words. Calling up will only antagonize most editors.

## MAGAZINES

Letters to the editors of magazines are effective in several ways. Since most magazines have a national circulation, a letter-writer can often reach a constituency that is much broader than the one offered by the readers of a local newspaper. Also, the magazine permits selective use of material. The readers of medical journals are almost always physicians. If you are interested in sharing an experience with some environmental problem, a letter to the editor of the *Air & Water Pollution Report* will probably be seen and read by many of that publication's subscribers.

*Advertising Age*, the weekly that covers advertising and marketing, reaches more than 66,000 subscribers and perhaps three times as many "borrowers." At least one page of every issue is filled with letters, and they are often remarkable in their style and content. The *Journal of the American Medical Association* (*JAMA*), a weekly publication that reaches 240,000 physicians, also prints a varied letters section.

## LETTERS TO CONGRESSMEN

The average congressman, contrary to what you may have thought, is responsive to certain letters from constituents. Most elected officials pay attention to their mail.

Senator Clinton Anderson publicly admitted that it was the letters from his constituents and others that changed his mind about the SST aircraft vote. *Common Cause Briefs* reported that Representative Thomas O'Neill became a strong antiwar leader largely as a result of the letters he received from voters, many of whom he never knew. "I never yielded to pressure in my life," he is quoted as saying, "but when I get 400 letters a day on something, I wonder whether I'm right or wrong."

Letters to the president were the subject of one phase of the celebrated Watergate investigation that followed the 1972 election campaign. It was revealed that the president's staff thought so much of the "quotability" of letters for their press releases that they organized their own campaign to send letters to themselves in support of the president's decision to resume bombing North Vietnam. The thousands of letters that supported the action were tabulated and then shown to the press to indicate the favorable public reaction to the bombing order.

When writing congressmen, it is important that you state your feelings simply. Don't take a page to say that you are for or against a piece of legislation. But you should take plenty of time to give him a report on your views of different problems. Many congressmen and state legislators now send questionnaires to the voters back home in order to formalize the input procedure.

If you want to organize a program to influence a member of Congress be sure to avoid the printed or mimeographed form letter. The lawmaker's staff will delete them from any meaningful evaluation. It is the individually written letter bearing first-class postage or a telegram that will have more impact. Western Union now has a service that enables people to send their congressman a telegram of fifteen words or less, from anywhere in the nation, for $1.25. You can call (800) 632-2771 anytime of the day or night and send your message. The cost will be charged to your telephone.

It is important to follow up with a letter or telegram when your congressman takes an action that you have supported. They will appreciate a letter or some other notice of something that was done. Remember that the lawmaker's staff will probably keep your letters on file, so when you write or wire, don't be surprised if you get a telephone call or return letter asking for more information about a position. Be prepared so that should a call of this sort come, you can add still more information in support of the position you are advocating.

## OTHER LETTERS AND WHEN TO MAIL THEM

If you are writing to order something, seek information, complain, or request support for a campaign that you are involved with, it is best to address your letter to a specific person.

Make sure you identify yourself and, when appropriate, your organization. Along with your name and title (if any), include your address, zip code, and telephone number.

If you aren't sure of a name but know which company or organization you want to address, you can learn a specific name from a telephone call to that company or organization or from a business directory. As a last resort, write to the president of the company and address your letter to "The President's Office."

To get help in digging out the proper names, titles, and addresses, start at the library. The librarian can point out a reference book that might help, assuming telephone books in the area don't help. Local retailers may be able to provide you with information about companies that they deal with.

You must be specific in your letter. If you are complaining about something, analyze the problem before you start to write and reduce it to its most specific aspect. Talk about it with someone whose judgment you value. This also helps to clarify the central issue and focus on the point you want to make. If you are seeking to generate support for a project, again, an analysis of the subject will help you to define the key points, the so-called "button" that your letter will push to turn on wider support.

For example, if you want to get the city to help clean the street, you must come to grips with the fact that illegally parked cars are preventing sanitation crews from cleaning the street. So you deal with the problem of having the cars banned or removed before the street can be cleaned.

The problem of illegal parking can also be pursued. In large cities, whenever the subject comes up, there are those who point out that crime figures in this equation. If people weren't afraid to ride subways or buses in large cities, the reasoning goes, they would leave their cars at home and use mass-transit facilities. Therefore, make the streets safe and you will make them clean, too. There are, as we pointed out, any number of issues one can plug into.

But getting back to your street-cleaning project, you just want the street to look better: you're not going to change the world; you're interested in the cosmetics, not the cosmos. You have zeroed in on the specifics, one step at a time. You want the police tow trucks to move the cars. You want sanitation crews to be on hand for the cleanup job. They must coordinate their efforts. You know that warning signs will have to be made up and posted, placed under windshields, and tacked or taped to walls or bulletin boards. You talk over the project with your neighbors and enlist their cooperation. You have made a beginning and now you can get to work writing the letters and making the telephone calls and turning out press releases.

One must also know how to mail a letter these days. Some mailboxes work better than others. The U.S. Postal Service tells us how to help it move the mail. The suggestions:

1. Make the address easy to read and always include the zip code.

2. Try to mail no later than the last mail pickup of the day. Every mailbox includes the pickup schedule.

3. If you have missed the last pickup in your neighborhood, look for a mailbox with a white star on it. Mail is picked up later from these boxes. The schedule label on your mailbox gives the location of the nearest starred mailbox. The one-star mailboxes have a pickup at 5:00 P.M. or later, plus Sunday and holiday collections. These are usually located along busier streets and shopping districts. The two-star mailboxes have the latest pickups, none earlier than 6:30 P.M. and as close to 8:00 P.M. as possible. These are located in larger communities, in business areas, and in front of post offices.

4. Use airmail if you're mailing beyond 150 miles. Mail before 4:00 P.M. in special "Airmail Only" boxes or by 5:00 P.M. at your main post office.

# 18

# Those Who Made It

PERHAPS THIS CHAPTER, the last in the book, should have been the first. It recounts anecdotes with notes on those who have made it. By now the reader should have an affirmative answer to the question, Can a single, ordinary person, or group of people, really do anything to change the course of history, local, regional, or national?

The object of this book is to provide ways for individuals to be heard. With what we say you should know how to succeed in a fight against city hall. We hope that your campaign will be successful. At least we believe that if you follow our advice, you will be heard and noticed.

It is important to keep in mind that some of the people who started a successful effort also had little more than an idea going for them. Feeling dissatisfaction, a very personal resentment, or a selfish desire, those who succeed in being heard share a few things in common. In describing their efforts we will report what we could learn about how they did it. The most intelligent way for anyone to really learn how a Ralph Nader organized his successful campaign against General Motors or how a Marjorie Guthrie helped finance research to combat HD is to contact them directly. If your cause is interesting to them, the chances are good that they, or someone who works closely with them, will see you or respond to your letter. In fact, much of what many crusaders have done is talk to others who need their help in organizing their own campaigns to get public awareness.

## THE NATIONAL FOUNDATION—MARCH OF DIMES

From a rather small effort in 1934 organized around a few "Birthday Balls" to celebrate the birthday of President Franklin D. Roosevelt and raise money to treat other polio victims, an amazing story has emerged. Through the efforts of Roosevelt's friend and law partner, Basil O'Connor, a disease that annually infected 40,000 or more people, mostly children, is now becoming a rarity: there were only twelve cases reported in 1971. Poliomyelitis is no longer a threat because a vaccine was developed with money raised by O'Connor. From 1938, when he started his first national crusade to raise money for research into the cause of polio and search for the cure, the March of Dimes has collected almost $1 billion.

Anyone interested in mass psychology, fund-raising, and the effective use of every known tool of communication should study the history of this organization. Never anywhere else in the world has anyone succeeded in matching the success of this effort. It has become a model for all health-oriented public appeals.

From the original solicitation of a dime, to a nationwide series of hikes—"walkathons"—the parent organization has never been at a loss for ideas that produce money. When they saw polio defeated, they chose not to go out of business but to change direction and go after the defeat of birth defects—a formidable task equal only to a giant effort that because of its complex ties, can never end.

In 1973, the National Foundation raised over $22 million. They spent $15 million, of which almost $14 million was spent on programs and supporting services.

The National Foundation has mastered the art of getting individuals involved. The Mother's March, the walkathon, and the countless annual local parties to raise funds are all brilliantly organized. The use of graphics is an example. The annual selection of a "poster child" was the beginning of each year's campaign.

The young boy or girl, almost always in a wheelchair or standing with the help of crutches or a brace, would be photographed with the president of the United States. This picture would be a symbol for an entire year's effort.

Other health-oriented organizations have never been able to get anything like this publicity for their efforts. And it takes a great deal of courage to try to copy such a well-known technique, since a copy of an original publicity idea is very hard to succeed with.

The organization of the walkathons in 1973 is an example of inspired public relations. Hundreds of thousands of children in almost every town, village, and city in the nation were organized to collect money, but not by just asking for contributions. Instead the individual child asked for "sponsors" to pay so much a mile for every mile walked or bicycled. The sponsor would pledge anything from 10 cents to $10 a mile. The average walker finished at least ten miles—some did twenty. One bicycle rider in West Orange, New Jersey, did over fifty miles on his recent ride for the National Foundation.

This idea, recruiting children who in turn get their own sponsors, is in itself a good idea. What is brilliant is the way the National Foundation has organized it. Adults with no desire to do anything in the way of real involvement can give money. Children, who don't have money, can donate their most abundant asset, their energy. Competition, the driving force for almost any child, coupled with the need to conform, suddenly has a focus in the walkathon. Everyone is a winner. All get something. Most are photographed on their walk, at the finish line, or someplace along the way. Merchants can give food to the participants and drop a few dollars into the box some marchers carry.

When Basil O'Connor died in March 1972, the *New York Times* reported, "His genius was in generating large numbers of relatively small contributions for a cause; exercising undisputed control over the proceeds and determining how the funds should be spent. . . ."

An excellent booklet, *Facts 1973*, available from the National Foundation, Box 2000, White Plains, New York 10602, describes the work of the foundation. In it you can read about their entire program. The organization of the local chapters, the way they use media, and their success in fund-raising is worthy of careful study by those who want to organize a national fund-raising effort.

## THE FIRE ISLAND ASSOCIATION

Robert Moses is a legend in New York. He is responsible for the many parkways, tunnels, bridges, and developed beaches that dot the seashores and lakes in the state. Some 660 playgrounds, 75 state parks, and 100,000 housing units are there because of Moses. No one really ever suggested that this man ever moved a single truck load of dirt without thinking about the ecologic consequences. That is, no one until Moses decided that Fire Island needed a road.

In 1962 the fight began against Moses and Joseph Carlino, speaker of the N.Y. State Assembly, organizers of the Fire Island road project. These expert politicians faced a hostile crowd of over 2000 Fire Island "protectionists." A group of private citizens organized under the banner of the Fire Island Association would not be content to just stop the highway—they had decided that the thirty-two-mile-long sandbar off the south coast of Long Island needed protection against present and future encroachment by all bridge- and highway-builders; they wanted to make certain that their island would never be faced with another attempt like this one. Their goal was to see to it that Fire Island was declared a national seashore; once this was accomplished they knew no road would ever be built. As any recent visitor can testify, there is no road, there still are no autos on the island, and it is a national seashore.

The small group of people had exceptional leadership, much of it organized by a public relations professional, George Biderman. But it was still the foot soldiers of public protest, the individual citizens, who managed to defeat the powerful and politically astute leaders who had for many years championed the cause of public access to recreation areas. Robert Moses, the same man who built Jones Beach, thousands of miles of parkways, and countless golf courses and public pools, eventually put his reputation on the line to fight for the Fire Island road. He lost the battle because he did not anticipate that his adversary was a small group of very dedicated people. They fought for a vacation island free of cars.

The war against Moses lasted two and one-half years. It eventually mobilized a thousand or more people who gave up countless weekends, evenings, and a considerable amount of money. Some could well afford the time and the funds; others denied themselves things to support the effort.

The citizens' group found experts, including civil engineers, a nationally known news commentator, and naturalists who were willing to testify for their cause. Authors, Broadway and Hollywood celebrities, and ordinary Fire Island vacationers who wanted to preserve their island joined in. The leaders of the battle believe that it was the average person who did the work who is responsible for the victory. The celebrities and the like got the initial publicity, but the endless, often dull work of getting petitions signed, making appearances at local meetings, organizing marches and protests, was done by a small, very active group of ordinary people.

The Fire Island Association did its homework before it started the program of opposition to Robert Moses. This was most important. They found out that Moses's estimate of $21 million was not for the project, just the road. Their experts calculated that the true cost was likely to be $70 million and that $21 million was the value of the houses in the proposed path of the road, homes that would have to be condemned and removed. This helped them get the support of all the owners of those homes. They were able to prove that the road would not cost the Moses' estimate of $21 million but closer to $121 million. This homework eventually was a key reason many residents and taxpayers (voters) supported the association's opposition to the Moses road.

The association also managed to attract a great deal of national and international publicity for their battle. Undoubtedly one of the reasons for their success in getting into print and on television was the fact that they were a small group fighting Moses, a giant in public works. It was the man who built the Verrazano Bridge against a handful of New Yorkers who wanted to be able to continue pulling wagons across their little roadless island.

*Life* magazine, the BBC, and others picked up the story—it was good copy, a rerun of David and Goliath. This national and international coverage helped the Fire Island Association get almost every major news medium in the area to cover their battle. From the first, with the notable exception of *Newsday*, the media supported the association. Local radio stations and daily and weekly newspapers received a flood of letters about the battle, almost all against Moses and his plan. The center of the battle was not on the island, however; it was in Washington.

Perhaps the most important lesson others can learn from the battle for Fire Island is the way opponents of the road used the federal government. In effect, those organized against Moses knew that they would have an endless series of battles and eventually they had to lose. They reasoned that unless they were able to take the question of a roadless Fire Island to Congress, there was a good chance that they, or possibly their children, would eventually find a road on the island.

The decision was made not just to keep Moses from building a road, but to do it for all the future road-builders as well. The only way to do this was to get a law passed making Fire Island roadproof. *Fire Island had to be made a national seashore.*

Once this was decided, all the fighting moved from Nassau County to the halls of Congress. Powerful supporters were needed. It isn't easy to get federal money to buy land that will be set aside as a national park. This is not supposed to be a job for a few political amateurs.

To succeed, the association had to get the active support of the secretary of the interior and the New York State delegation to Congress. The leaders of almost every national ecological and environmental protection group were contacted and signed up as supporters.

The Fire Island Association needed to get Secretary of the Interior Stewart Udall and others he respected to support a bill that would pay for the land, and then make it into a national park. A federal commitment of $14 million or more was needed to swing the deal.

It was not until Senators Javits and Keating, leaders of New York's congressional delegation, joined the cause that things really started to happen. Another important lesson for any who want to go this route: Get help from the highest elected officials you can.

When these men joined the association, *Newsday*, the only important newspaper in Nassau County that had not supported the group, suddenly switched its position and joined in adding its editorial strength to the argument against the road.

But you just don't get a national seashore without authorization of the entire Congress. A bill had to be drafted, led through committee, and taken before the Senate and the House. This required skilled maneuvering, a job for experts.

The association's leaders soon found out how it's done. They were told that of the thousand or so bills introduced each year in Congress only 200 ever become law. The rest die a slow death of apathy or carefully planned neglect. The association learned that the difference between those bills that pass and those that fail are many. But most important are the public hearings. If your proposed legislation gets out of committee into a public hearing you have a good chance, for it is the public hearing that will give you the forum you need for passage. It can also give your opponents their forum. So you have to be well prepared for the hearings.

The Fire Island Association organized expert testimony. They knew that their emotional attachment to the roadless real estate had to be supported by facts if the Congress was to vote millions of dollars to buy up the needed land.

Support from over forty organizations, some local and many national, was solicited. The list of those who eventually joined in included almost every important group in the country. The Audubon Society, the National Wildlife Federation, Friends of the Land, and the Wilderness Society were all contacted and asked to lend their support. Congressmen received thousands of letters and telegrams from members of these associations. Visits to the members of Congress were organized by the association.

Finally, on August 20, 1964, after two years of work, the bill was approved by the House. It had passed the Senate fourteen days before. Then on September 11, 1964, President Johnson signed it into law. There *never* would be a road on Fire Island.

Dr. Michael Fry, a member of the association and editor of a medical magazine, recently explained the tactics of the organization. Paraphrased, here are his comments:

1. Never underestimate the strength of conservationists; once they are convinced that there is a sound reason for their support, they will go all the way.

2. Publicity is essential. A professional public relations man is best to direct it.

3. Money must be raised: $20,000 or more was collected at one time or another to fight the battle for Fire Island. This doesn't include the individual contributions in time and travel made by many.

4. The active support of elected officials is essential. To gain this, a great deal of personal contact is necessary. There are no shortcuts for visiting with the congressmen and others of importance in their offices. When you do get an appointment, go there armed with all the facts.

Secretary Udall, in an association breakfast victory celebration, made a speech that summarizes the battle and describes its high points (without Udall and his support there never would have been a Fire Island National Seashore):

> The Fire Island story is the story of a "lost cause" that somehow was won. I remember so clearly a bright early June day in 1962 when I came up to inspect this superb stretch of shoreline. I was met by the redoubtable Robert Moses and other high-minded leaders on Long Island who, after a courteous trip of reconnaissance patted me on the back and sent me back to Washington with the admonition that I was "twenty years too late."
>
> The four-lane highway plan, I was told, was supported by all right-minded citizens, and, in reality, the decision had already been made. But, as it turned out, the people had not been heard from —and the public ground swell began that brought the State of New York its first National Seashore Park.
>
> This was *your* triumph—the conservation groups, conservation-minded editors, the farsighted state and local officials who were determined that a preservation solution was best for future generations. . . . Fire Island is of the most fundamental importance, not just for the people of crowded New York—but also in the whole conservation struggle of America. For the conservation crisis in this country now centers on our urbanized areas. It is the city dweller who has the greatest stake in the preservation of nature, because it is he who has the least of it.
>
> Fire Island has proved one thing: that conservationists can be a Herculean force when they care enough to organize for action. Do you know why they can be so powerful? It is because a conservation solution always puts the interest of future generations

first. . . . Every community should have a conservation plan that looks 50 years ahead and takes into account an America with a doubled population and a doubled economy.

We must make sure that overdevelopment and contamination and blight do not destroy the joy of living in this country. Conservation should be the standard of every community in America. This does not mean—as some would have it—that development should be stopped, or that every tree is to be guarded. But it does mean that we must develop in this country a wise set of priorities for our environment.

## CORONA BEATS CITY HALL

Every property owner is aware of the finality of eminent domain. "Eminent domain" refers to the inherent right of government—local, state, or national—to force a property owner to sell his property when it is needed for public use. The sale must be for a just price and the legal process that takes place when the property owner refuses to sell is called condemnation proceedings.

Eminent domain is used to build roads, canals, military bases, harbors, dams, schools, municipal buildings, housing projects, and asylums. The right of eminent domain also can be granted to railroads or public utilities. This usage dates back to the Middle Ages and began as the rights that an overlord had over the vassal or land occupied by tenants.

Many clashes occur over eminent domain and the story of the sixty-nine homeowners in a part of Queens County, New York, known as Corona, demonstrates that it is never too late to fight city hall.

The Corona episode marked the first time in the history of New York State that a condemnation proceeding was reversed after title to property had actually passed from the homeowners to the city.

When the fight began in 1967, the Corona homeowners were told that it was no use to resist; the city needed the land on which they lived. A new high school and an athletic field would be built there.

The Corona homeowners hired a lawyer, Mario Cuomo, who had roots in the community, which consisted of second- or third-generation families of Italian descent. They argued that there were many alternate sites that would be perfect for the school and the field. They argued that the city was ignoring the alternate sites because the sites had been promised to builders of high-rise apartment houses.

The plight of the Corona residents was desperate and, to the larger community, largely unknown. They argued; they held meetings; they took their case to court, led by Lillian Manasseri, one of the homeowners, and Cuomo. In October 1969, the houses were actually condemned and the city took title to them.

The "Corona Sixty-nine" didn't give up. They painted slogans on bedsheets ("Save Our Homes") and hung them from their windows. They put up posters around their well-tended frame and cinder-block homes. Those who happened to pass through their streets became aware of the struggle, but since the media hadn't discovered the story, the resistance movement was going nowhere. And the city had taken title to their homes.

Cuomo began court actions to have the condemnation proceedings reviewed on grounds that the civil rights of the homeowners were being denied. Professional ethics prevented Cuomo from seeking publicity. He advised his clients to seek professional public relations help, but it seemed that the people wanted to fight their own fight, with no paid or unpaid consultants, only with the aid of whatever politicians they could interest.

State Assemblyman Vito Battista, supporting the Corona Sixty-nine managed to generate some media attention as he led picket lines and directed some dramatic confrontations between the homeowners and city officials. The TV stations began to discover the story, and the Corona residents found themselves on evening newscasts as they picketed and paraded. They were interviewed in front of their homes. One protest session that made the TV newscasts involved hiring a bus and riding into Manhattan to participate in a special prayer vigil at St. Patrick's Cathedral.

Battista also brought the story into the newspapers in September 1970, when the Corona group marched on city hall. Another group from another part of the city was there to demand a new school and in the ensuing brouhaha, police barricades were knocked over as the people charged up the steps of city hall. Police said Mr. Battista had incited the people in the disorder.

There were those who said, at this point, that such demonstrations were counterproductive. But a few more newsmen began visiting Corona and writing mournfully of the brave little community and its hopeless fight against the courts, the bureaucracy, and an unfeeling government. The City Planning Commission announced that the 4000-seat high school was badly needed, that the condemnation and clearing of the site was the best solution, and that further delay would deal a serious blow to education. The city went to court to have the homeowners and other families—135 in all—evicted. The Corona residents vowed a "do-or-die" effort that would take them into the courts, have them make appeals to the governor and to the people through media, and have them petitioning the State Commission of Investigation.

And then came the event that is credited with turning the situation around. The well-known writer and Queens resident, Jimmy Breslin, walked in to see Cuomo, talked to the Corona homeowners, and then left to write an article for *New York* magazine. Better than anyone else, Breslin captured the meaning of the Corona community to New York's middle-class life and the lack of concern shown for it by city hall. The impact of the article was powerful. And to add more force, Breslin telephoned reporters around the country to follow the story. He bullied other well-known newspaper columnists and friends into writing about Corona. The media barrage was irresistible.

Shortly afterward, in December 1970, Mayor John Lindsay relented. A compromise plan was worked out with Cuomo. Even though the city had taken title to the houses, the property would be returned to thirty-one homeowners. The homes of twenty-eight others would be moved to new sites just one block away. (The rest had, as the struggle continued through the years, decided to let the city keep their houses.) It would take special legislation by the state, but this would be forthcoming. The mayor called the settlement an act of "compassion" that was blended with "progress." The homeowners had won back their homes.

At this writing, homeowners still are involved in negotiations with the city over regaining title or having their houses moved. There is a notable absence of pressure. There is no deadline, no feeling of doom.

The Corona episode came to a head after the media, in the

person of a celebrated writer, became involved. The story had been around for years and seemed to be going nowhere until the dramatic values within it were unleashed boldly and clearly. If you find yourself involved with a meaningful story that is being ignored and that the local media has either tired of or cannot adequately treat, concentrate your efforts on interesting a well-known writer to look into the situation and write an in-depth magazine article. This approach can prove to be more effective than the traditional program of trying to interest all media in carrying bits and pieces of the story.

## "STORM KING FOREVER" FERVOR

Those who would affect a course of action sometimes need more than an enormous amount of energy, stamina, resourcefulness, money, communicative skills, and volunteer workers all blessed with thick skins. They also need patience, for the fight can take a long, long time.

One of the great recent examples of sustained combat involves the residents of towns, cities, and villages along New York's Hudson River. Since 1963 they have been fighting to prevent Consolidated Edison, the utility that supplies electrical power to New York City and Westchester County, from building a power plant at Storm King Mountain in Cornwall, New York.

Storm King Mountain is regarded as something sacred by environmentalists; it is spoken of in reverential tones, written about in poetry and song, and considered inviolate as a scenic landmark and forest preserve by area residents. It is located in what is called the Hudson Highlands, some fifty miles north of Manhattan.

And that is where Con Ed decided to build a new power plant. During the past ten years, the struggle has taken dozens of twists and turns. There have been triumphs and defeats for both sides and the story still hasn't ended; it is still before the courts at this writing.

In order to carry their fight this far, the people of the area have had to raise well over $500,000. It has been estimated that Con Ed has spent more than $22 million during that same period. The anti–Con Ed forces used their funds for legal fees, professional public relations support, publications, publicity, research, and what ultimately became a full-time, staffed organization, Scenic Hudson Preservation Conference, Inc., with an office at 545 Madison Avenue, New York, New York 10022. Barbara Curry is executive secretary.

The combat began after Con Ed announced its Cornwall plan. In September 1962, the newspapers reported that Con Ed was planning to spend $115 million to build the nation's third largest hydroelectric plant along the Hudson. The utility said it would soon file an application with the Federal Power Commission (FPC) and anticipated no delays. Con Ed didn't think it would need the approval of the U.S. Corps of Engineers, which must be consulted where navigational concerns are raised, and anticipated no difficulties in connection with the Cornwall water supply or in acquiring the land. At that point, media paid little attention to the plan, for it seemed to be cut and dried, virtually a *fait accompli.*

In April 1963, Leo Rothschild, a prominent New York attorney and chairman of the conservation committee of the New York–New Jersey Trail Conference, a parent organization of various hikers' groups, read Con Ed's 1962 annual report with keen interest. For the first time, he saw a drawing of the proposed Cornwall plant. And for the first time, as *Audubon Magazine* reported, "the jargon of engineers and public relations writers was translated into a picture of the finished project. And all of the glowing words could not disguise the scar on Storm King, northern gateway to the Hudson River gorge."

Rothschild was finally moved to write a letter to the editor of the *New York Times*, which was published on April 11, 1963. His letter stated: "The Hudson must be preserved. We cannot allow the most beautiful part of one of the most beautiful of the world's rivers to be desecrated."

The media then began paying attention to the controversy. The residents of the Cornwall area, on both sides of the Hudson, began mobilizing to do battle. And on May 22, 1963, the *Times* carried a lengthy article that was headlined:

POWER PLAN STIRS
BATTLE ON HUDSON

Conservation Groups Rally
to Protest Construction of
Hydroelectric Projects

GOVERNOR GETS PLEA

Storm King Mountain Area
in Highlands Said To Be in
Danger of Defacement

Written by John C. Devlin, the article told how nature-lovers, including conservation groups, garden clubs, and hikers' organizations, were rallying to fight the Con Ed project. Spearheading the fight was the New York–New Jersey Trail Conference, headed by Harry Nees at that time. Rothschild had sent a telegram to Governor Rockefeller in which, after citing Rockefeller's "interest in the scenic and historic landmarks of our state," called on him to "do everything in your power to preserve the Highlands."

The "easy approval" that Con Ed had hoped for was fast turning into a pipedream.

A week after the *Times* news article appeared, the *Times* carried an editorial entitled "Defacing the Hudson," the first of many editorials critical of Con Ed's plan.

Rothschild and the Trail Conference reprinted the *Times* article and editorial on a flyer and distributed thousands of copies, along with appeals to the people of Cornwall and surrounding communities to "Do Your Part to Save the Hudson." The flyer suggested that letters be written to Rockefeller, to the state conservation commissioner, to state senators and assemblymen, to Con Edison, and to local newspapers.

The residents of the Hudson Highlands area rallied together with Rothschild, Nees, and author Carl Carmer and on November 8, 1963, the Scenic Hudson Preservation Conference was founded.

The campaign to mobilize public support against the Storm King plan was stepped up. Scenic Hudson argued that the project would deface the mountain, perhaps open other mountains to similar power projects along the Hudson valley, and mar the hills of two counties across which high-tension wires would have to be strung.

Con Ed maintained that its plan to suck up 6 billion gallons of river water a day and pump it through Storm King by way of a two-mile-long, 40-foot-wide tunnel to a storage reservoir constructed behind the mountain was a necessity if the utility was to provide for the needs of its customers, present and future. Con Ed promised to take every precaution to "minimize" the physical scarring of Storm King. An intensive advertising campaign was conducted by Con Ed to tell the public of its plans.

For its part, Scenic Hudson raised money to support the "Save Storm King" drive. Its solicitation of funds involved other conservation organizations across the country and overseas; it organized protest demonstrations, auctions, antique sales, garage sales, art sales, and picnics, and its members traveled around the area to have petitions circulated and signed.

One protest demonstration generated publicity. Residents of Croton-on-Hudson, to dramatize their opposition to Con Ed, turned out their lights at ten o'clock one night. At the time, Con Ed was using the slogan Dig We Must in its advertising. Bumper stickers began appearing that read, Dig They Won't. Save Storm King.

In February 1964, as the battleground shifted to the hearing rooms, Scenic Hudson hired a former FPC member, Dale Doty, to represent it before the FPC hearing examiner in Washington. The hearing-examiner system applies to federal agency operations; the examiner listens to testimony and then makes a recommendation to the full commission, which can accept or reject. Doty won the status of an "intervenor" at the hearing, meaning he would have the right to present and cross-examine witnesses.

Scenic Hudson, organizing for the mighty battle, also hired a full-time executive director, Rod Vandivert, and a prominent Manhattan public relations firm, to help counter Con Ed's campaign and influence.

Vandivert began his work by first conducting a thorough research of the Storm King controversy, thereby equipping himself with arguments or responses to each Con Ed proposal. Having done his homework, he sought public platforms from which to present his case against Con Ed. By word of mouth and by reading newspapers and periodicals, he developed a calendar that listed the meeting dates of every organization in the Kingston-Cornwall area. He dealt with fishermen clubs, boating groups, garden clubs, service clubs, game hunters, and school organizations. He wrote letters to them or made telephone calls to request that he be invited to speak about Storm King. As a result, he was out almost every night. He developed a powerful presentation against the Con Ed project and always merchandised his appearances. That is, he made certain to inform the local media about each appearance. He tried to prepare a press release before every speaking appearance and certainly to send one out immediately after the meeting if no reporters were present. Often, he was able to prepare a press release beforehand and deliver it to reporters at the meeting. He would write letters to the editors of the area newspapers in order to explain Scenic Hudson's position, or challenge opposing views. He appeared at public hearings to present testimony as a Scenic spokesperson. When media committed what Scenic Hudson deemed to be a major distortion, Vandivert would try to correct the matter with a telephone call, a letter, or a meeting with a reporter to discuss Storm King in detail. He learned the different deadlines of area media and doled out his press material accordingly.

Scenic Hudson also employed the public relations firm of Selvage & Lee (now Manning, Selvage & Lee), which assigned three account executives—James Cope, Michael Kitzmiller, and Louis Frankel—to the Storm King–Scenic Hudson account. The public relations campaign was budgeted at $10,000, which was raised in part through the professional fund-raising firm of Harold Oram Associates. The Oram organization helped nationalize the Storm King controversy through a mailing to influential persons in the United States and Europe and to conservation groups.

For the FPC hearings, Scenic Hudson also gathered together experts on fish life, biologists, conservationists, and authorities on power plants.

The public relations firm set up a series of press conferences and issued numerous press releases and photographs to wire services; to newspapers, large and small, daily and weekly; to magazines; and to radio and TV stations. Every time Con Ed issued a statement or a report on Storm King, the Scenic Hudson organization published a rebuttal. Reporters soon began to call Scenic Hudson spokespersons whenever Con Ed put out a press release, in order to provide "equal time" in the bitter controversy.

When it became known that Con Ed lobbyists had referred to the Scenic Hudson group as "nature fakers," "land-grabbers," and "bird-watchers" before members of the New York State legislature, one resident was moved to say at a public meeting, "Yes, I am a bird-watcher, and I have been watching buzzards and vultures."

The question of disruption of Hudson River fisheries became a crucial one. Scenic Hudson produced a 1957 study that told of the spawning habits of striped bass and noted that the principal spawning area was near West Point, two miles south of Storm King, and that the area extended southward for seven and a half miles. Fishermen used this to bolster their claim that the power plant, set in the midst of this spawning ground, would destroy fish life in the river.

Scenic Hudson may have been helped in its fight to win public sympathy and support by the fact that electric utilities do not generally enjoy a good reputation. (As the Storm King controversy raged, *Fortune* magazine published an article in 1965 that was entitled "Con Ed: The Company You Love to Hate.")

In July 1964, the hearing examiner recommended that the FPC issue a license to Con Ed. Still, the Scenic Hudson group refused to give up. The recommendation still would require a vote by the full FPC. Along with the Scenic Hudson experts, numerous conservation groups, boat-owner associations, fishermen, and taxpayer groups also asked for permission to testify before the FPC. Scenic Hudson filed a petition to intervene, a legalism that would allow it to function before the FPC as it did before the examiner.

The FPC voted in March 1965 to permit Con Ed to build the Storm King plant. But it said that another hearing would have to be held in order to determine the best route for the high-tension wires.

Scenic Hudson turned to the courts. It asked the Federal Circuit Court of Appeals in August 1965 to have the FPC license set aside. The Scenic Hudson case rested on the belief that the FPC had appeared to ignore certain material, such as the striped-bass study. In December 1965, the court of appeals set aside the FPC license and there was great jubilation along the banks of the Hudson. Con Ed sought a review, but the U. S. Supreme Court denied the request. New hearings before the FPC were called.

Con Ed presented a revised plan in November 1966. The new plan involved blasting inside the mountain to create a cavern that would hold the water. Nearly thirty organizations, including Scenic Hudson, testified against the new plan, along with cartographers, naturalists, and ecologists. The hearings lasted into the spring of 1967, and in August 1968, the examiner again recommended that the FPC license Storm King.

The New York City government then was heard from. It intervened to charge that by blasting rock from Storm King, Con Ed could imperil an aqueduct that the city relied upon for its water supply.

The FPC recommended that the proposed plant site be moved. But the proposed new location would place the plant within an interstate park system, and this necessitated further hearings.

A complicated, drawn-out, costly struggle? Unquestionably. The case has taken several other turns since then, including an investigation into the need for new sources of power in the New York metropolitan area in view of an energy crisis. Con Ed remains determined to go ahead with the long-delayed project.

The point of this narrative is to show how residents of the Hudson River Valley managed to band together in an effort to impress government with the argument that scenic values of an area and the ecology as well as the area's historical role are as important as the proposed commercial use when considering building applications.

The Scenic Hudson campaign is noteworthy because of its thoroughness, its clear enunciation of the issues as seen by Scenic Hudson, the steady flow of information that was provided to media, its refusal to be intimidated, and its employment of local talent to spread the word.

Vandivert, now an environmental consultant says organizations must remain flexible in order to react quickly to events. Small grass-roots organizations that are formed to do battle with larger, well-established forces have this fast action in their favor. Vandivert finds that large corporations move slowly because they require approvals through elaborate decision-making echelons. He recommends that the grass-roots group "mold itself" to every available platform, as Scenic Hudson did—that is, bring its case into meeting rooms throughout the area. And he also makes this comment:

"The main trouble with many groups is that they're too civilized. You've got to be a gut fighter. You've got to be ready to kick your opponent in the crotch. He'll be civilized about things and he'll assume that you will be civilized, too." Such civility, Vandivert implies, works to the advantage of the opponent. Above all, however, he recommends "staying loose; being ready to move quickly."

Another example of how Vandivert moved quickly: When actor James Cagney, a resident of the area, sent out telegrams to prominent Americans and urged them to join the protest campaign against Storm King construction, Vandivert saw to it that copies of Cagney's telegrams were released to the media.

Also helping to spread the word was Robert Boyle, an ardent fisherman who is a senior editor at *Sports Illustrated* and a resident of Croton-on-Hudson, who saw to it that readers of the magazine were kept informed about Storm King. One such article featured a photograph of dead fish. It was taken at Con Ed's nuclear power plant at Indian Point, fifteen miles south of Storm King. The article was entitled, "A Stink of Dead Stripers." He also wrote editorials for a weekly newspaper in his home town and, in 1969, published, The *Hudson River: A Natural and Unnatural History* (W. W. Norton), which explained the uniqueness of the river's many fabled stretches and included a twenty-eight-page chapter on the Storm King fight.

Given enough time, as in the Storm King case, partisans can get around to touching every base.

## ONE MAN AGAINST CIGARETTES

In the spring of 1970, Congress passed the Public Health Cigarette-Smoking Act. The measure, which imposed a ban on all TV and radio commercials for cigarettes, was the culmination of a campaign that effectively started in 1954 with the publication of an American Cancer Society study on the relationship between cigarette smoking and health.

The 1970 law came about largely because one man, a private citizen, knew how to employ both the law and the media. John F. Banzhaf III organized his energies and talent and, with limited funds, mobilized a one-man campaign that was to drive cigarette commercials from the airwaves.

Banzhaf decided that the FCC's "fairness doctrine" should apply to cigarettes. The FCC has, in matters of political issues, election campaigns, and editorial content aired by stations, held that in fairness, all sides must be given access to the airwaves. Being a lawyer, Banzhaf knew that FCC licenses were granted, not to networks, but to individual stations, and he set out to test his "equal time" concept against WCBS-TV, New York. He requested, in a simple letter to the station management, that free time be made available for antismoking messages in order to balance the effect of commercials by the cigarette advertisers.

He sent out mimeographed press releases about his action to newspapers, magazines, and the news desks of radio and TV stations. He followed up with telephone calls to reporters and editors whom he had never met. When he didn't know which editor to ask for, switchboard operators directed his calls to the proper desks, and Banzhaf, without special "pull," help, or influence, took it from there, making certain that the reporters understood the full significance of his action.

His request, as expected, was denied by WCBS-TV. Banzhaf publicized his failure in the same fashion, with calls to newspapers, wire services, and the like. And then he went on to his next move—the filing of a petition with the FCC to ask it to intervene and see to it that reply time would be made available for the airing of messages dealing with the dangers of cigarette smoking.

Supporting his claim that smoking was a controversial matter were the various scientific studies and reports that had been published through the years. Again, Banzhaf took it upon himself to keep media informed through press releases and telephone calls and, occasionally, meeting with reporters and editors.

In June 1967, the FCC ruled in his favor and stated that radio and TV stations were obliged to provide "a significant amount of time" to those who sought to publicize the hazards of smoking. The ratio of one free anticigarette message for every three cigarette commercials was decided upon. By this time, Banzhaf did not have to make calls or send out as many press releases to the media. His personal crusade was on assignment books at news desks, which meant that the course of his unique legal maneuver was now being covered by the press as a routine matter. His telephone number was in the notebooks of reporters.

Banzhaf set up an organizational structure called Action on Smoking and Health, not much more than a small office in midtown Manhattan, with a telephone, law books, typewriter, access to copying machines, and a letterhead. ASH, as the organization was known, solicited public support and funds.

Knowing that the broadcasters and the tobacco industry would appeal the FCC ruling, Banzhaf didn't wait for their inevitable counterattack. He outflanked the tobacco industry lawyers by selecting the court in which the appeal from the FCC decision would be heard. This was done by his filing the petition that challenged the FCC decision. He filed his petition with the U.S. Court of Appeals in Washington, D.C., a court more accessible to Banzhaf than, say, a Los Angeles court, which the broadcasters and cigarette companies conceivably could have selected in order to make Banzhaf's fight more difficult and more costly to pursue (Banzhaf was then moving to Washington from New York).

Anticipating the need for monitoring TV stations in order to see whether the 3:1 commercial ratio was being honored, Banzhaf and friends spent two weeks monitoring station WNBC-TV, New York. They found that the station was running one anticigarette spot for every ten cigarette commercials. (The antismoking commercials were supplied to the stations by the ACS and the National Tuberculosis Association.)

Banzhaf then filed a petition that called on the FCC to revoke the station's license on grounds that the station was in violation of the fairness doctrine. When the station challenged the results of his monitoring, Banzhaf was able to offer facts and figures that prevailed. Instead of revoking the station's license, the FCC ruled that the number of antismoking spots would have to be increased. And, said the FCC, these spots would have to be aired during peak viewing hours—7:30 P.M.–11:00 P.M.—instead of the 2:30 A.M.–6:30 A.M. off-hour airings that Banzhaf had shown to be the practice. One by one, stations across the country began to comply with the FCC decision.

By February 1969, the FCC was announcing that it planned to seek a prohibition against all cigarette commercials on radio and TV because a health hazard was involved. Despite determined and costly efforts by the tobacco industry and broadcasters to counter the pressures from the antismoking forces, the law was enacted.

Bear in mind that Banzhaf, fired by his revulsion to cigarette smoking, had carried out his fight on his own time and with limited funds. He learned to work the channels of publicity and maintained close contact with media—mostly print media, since radio and TV stations weren't inclined to publicize his campaign, let alone put him on news shows.

## THE NOW CAMPAIGN

In August 1970, members of the National Organization for Women (NOW) decided that a public-service advertising campaign dealing with the equal rights for women theme would do much to raise the level of awareness of the problem.

The NOW members included a number of talented advertising professionals, men as well as women, who were eager to donate their time and their talent to work up some possible approaches to radio and TV commercials. They prevailed upon friends and associates in the radio and TV stations to produce the commercials after obtaining funds to pay for the production charges from two foundations, the Rockefeller Family Fund and the John and Elizabeth Bates Cowles Foundation. To help complete the project, engravers, TV-commercial producers, photographers, actors, models, and a company that sells mailing lists volunteered to help with the campaign. The NOW people next arranged a meeting with members of the Advertising Council, a private, nonprofit organization that is supported by the advertising industry and businessmen. The council conducts national advertising campaigns that are deemed to be for "the public good." Some of the council's campaigns are for forest-fire prevention (Smokey the Bear), the American Red Cross, jobs for veterans, aid to higher education, the Urban Coalition, and U.S. Savings Bonds.

The NOW members were told that a campaign must be noncommercial, politically nonpartisan, not designed to influence legislation, national in scope, and carry a message that can be addressed to all Americans if it is to qualify for council support.

And, of course, the subject must be of sufficient seriousness and importance to justify its acceptance by media.

The NOW Legal Defense and Education Fund was ultimately accepted as the vehicle for the Advertising Council campaign and in the fall of 1972, the council approved the equal rights for women campaign.

Every three months, the council sends out its *Advertising Council Bulletin*, listing approved campaigns and including order forms with which the newspapers, magazines, and radio and TV stations can place orders. The May–June 1973 *Bulletin* described the NOW materials and many orders for the actual print advertisements, radio commercial tapes, and TV commercials, began to come in. The NOW staff also mailed advertising kits directly to leading publications and radio and TV stations.

In addition, each chapter president of NOW was sent a full report on the campaign. The report also urged each chapter president to appoint a campaign committee coordinator who would work with other NOW members to promote the equal rights campaign locally. It was suggested that the coordinator, the chapter president perhaps, call a meeting and explain the campaign to the membership.

Instructions on how to approach the media were also included in the kit by Midge Kovacs, campaign coordinator for the NOW Legal Defense and Education Fund. Her instructions included this advice: "Contact the advertising manager or managing editor of your leading local newspaper. . . . Make an appointment with the public affairs director. Take the enclosed radio disk to the station."

Referring to the purpose of the campaign, NOW said, "We believe that the campaign will open doors previously closed to us. It will help us to attract new NOW members, raise funds, help to raise the public's consciousness and above all, it is excellent public relations for NOW and for the women's movement. It shows what we are doing for all women." The campaign slogan was, Womanpower. It's Much Too Good to Waste.

Certainly, the NOW campaign is a remarkable example of alert, intelligent, persistent, and hard-working "civilians" banding together to seek to affect public attitudes.

## "THIS IS MY LIMIT"

In San Francisco, Kay Pachtner became so frustrated by constantly rising meat prices that she tried to do something about it. Her organization, San Francisco Consumer Action (SFCA), began circulating to consumers cards that read, "This is my limit." The SFCA directed people to give one card to the butcher "to jog his memory a bit on the subject of reasonable prices."

The card bore this information: "These are the top prices I'll pay for these meats: Full cut round steak, $1.30 lb. Regular ground beef, 76¢ lb. Loin or rib pork roast, 79¢ lb. Beef liver, 84¢ lb. Blade or center chuck roast, 89¢ lb. Whole chicken, 49¢ lb." The cards were mimeographed—nothing fancy—and printed in duplicate stubs, one to hand to the butcher, the other to be carried in the shopper's wallet.

By issuing press releases, calling radio and TV stations, distributing handbills and the "limit" cards, the group organized a series of meat boycotts. While meat prices didn't retreat very noticeably, Kay Pachtner came away from the venture with some definite conclusions that can be of help to others who are seeking to make a point: "It's just a question of organizing consumers and convincing them that together, they can swing a very large stick in the marketplace." She found that the media played a "huge" role in focusing attention on the problem, in this case, rising meat prices. "With that kind of attention and exposure in the press, radio, and television, a mass movement is easily created," she explained.

## THE LEARNING EXCHANGE

A graduate student in education at Northwestern University in Evanston, Illinois, decided that the process of teaching and learning need not be confined to formal classroom meetings at school. The student, Denis Detzel, felt that it would be beneficial if people who want to learn could be put in contact with people who want to teach, outside of classroom disciplines. Detzel and five friends put together a kitty of $25 and formed the Learning Exchange.

The exchange would enroll people who wanted to instruct

others, people who wanted to learn something, or people who simply wanted to meet in a discussion group.

Leaflets were printed and distributed. Detzel and a friend, Bob Lewis, also visited newspaper offices and radio stations to appeal for publicity, which they received. Other students made posters that were placed in libraries, stores, and coin-operated laundries. The leaflets and posters invited people to telephone a number and register. When enough calls were in, the matching-up process began. One retired teacher helped a hospital worker prepare for a high school equivalency test that would lead to a promotion. A Puerto Rican who wanted to pursue a career in radio in Puerto Rico was matched with a radio broadcaster who taught him about newscasting. Lewis's wife gave piano lessons to the children of a Chinese woman who was, in turn, teaching the art of Chinese cooking to Mrs. Lewis. Says Detzel, "Anyone with a telephone and a box of file cards can start his own Learning Exchange. It costs almost nothing."

## THE TELEPHONE RANGER

Florence Rice, a resident of Harlem in New York City, had long been interested and involved in the consumer problems of her neighbors, specifically those arising from installment buying, rent increases, poor or nonexistent services, and unsophisticated shopping habits.

She formed an organization called the Harlem Consumer Education Council and for years has been operating it virtually on a shoestring. In the beginning, she wrote her own letters, did her own telephoning, and arranged for meetings, all without much publicity or the aid of a staff. By paying attention to available literature, city laws, and state activities, she was able to disseminate a constant supply of shopping tips to her neighbors.

When another black activist, Florynce Kennedy, convinced Mrs. Rice that public utilities were a major source of consumer complaints, especially in ghetto areas, Mrs. Rice began educating telephone-company customers about billing practices and complaint procedures.

From her position as an unpaid volunteer worker who depended on a part-time job for her income, Mrs. Rice has gone on to set up community workshops at which telephone-company personnel have appeared and participated in programs aimed at imparting information to the public.

There are other such organizations—they are called "the phone rangers" by telephone companies—that keep an eye on rates, billings, and general business practices of these companies. Among these organizations are the Ad Hoc Committee for Utility Efficiency, which represents senior citizen groups, and the Center for United Labor Action, an organization that favors free telephone service. An organization that gets into a more commercial aspect of telephone service is the American Telephone Consumers Council. This council advises businesses on ways to save on telephone bills and also represents organizations that would be affected by increased rates when rate hearings are conducted.

## OPERATION POCKETBOOK

Mrs. Bernice Davidson of Oceanside, New York, like Mrs. Pachtner in San Francisco, got tired of complaining about increased prices every time she went to the supermarket. And she got tired of writing to the president. "He responds with a form letter thanking you for your support," she reported.

And so, in September 1972, when her brother-in-law suggested that she do more than complain, she was open to suggestions. He went on to explain that she would do better to organize a consumer protest, something he called Operation Pocketbook, which would dramatize how the dollar is shrinking. Mrs. Davidson's husband, Reuben, and her sister, Belle, went along with the idea of organizing a march, and Operation Pocketbook was under way.

A leaflet was prepared that pointed out the various touchstone statistics that spell inflation—the rising prices, unemployment rate, growth of welfare rolls, and so on. Maps were drawn, printed, and distributed that charted the route of the march in two communities, Oceanside and Forest Hills.

On the day of the march, old people, youngsters, mothers with babies in strollers or carriages, white-collar and blue-collar workers, handicapped people, and professional people marched in the streets carrying a variety of placards, some reading, "Meat is a luxury item," and "I used to be a meat eater." Mrs. Davidson's husband and brother-in-law designed and produced the posters and placards. The marches took place for a period of time on Thursdays, food-shopping day, and the media picked up the story.

In the September 29, 1972 edition of the *New York Times,* Mrs. Davidson wrote, "We've been getting enthusiastic calls and inquiries on how to get started. We even got a call from the *New York Times.* We were covered by *Newsday* in Oceanside and the *Long Island Press* in Forest Hills. We're hoping other towns will walk against inflation, too; especially our friends in Harlem, East Bronx and Fort Greene, and let the government know that we're no fools."

The walks certainly didn't succeed in ending inflation, but for many people, Operation Pocketbook served as a means of letting off steam and began to teach them about the process of getting involved, of dealing with media in seeking to spread the word about a problem.

## THE RERUN BATTLE

If we ever return to the time when fewer reruns are shown on TV, it will be because of a man named Bernard Balmuth, a fifty-two-year-old devotee of the TV series, "The FBI."

Mr. Balmuth exercised his rights.

He resented the fact that early in 1971, while viewing TV in his Los Angeles home, he was confronted by a rerun of his favorite series. He was probably more irritated because he was not warned about the repeat performance in advance. After all, he reasoned, isn't March a bit early to begin the expected summer repeat schedule?

All Mr. Balmuth did was to type out a single-citizen petition to the Federal Communications Commission. In it, he asked that the FCC make TV stations show thirty-nine weeks of original, or first-run, programs, confine the rerun period to thirteen weeks in the summertime, and plainly label reruns as such.

So far, according to an article by Bill Davidson in the June 9, 1973 issue of *TV Guide*, this action by a private citizen has a good chance of success. Mr. Balmuth, a film editor, had his petition accepted by the FCC. His campaign also attracted a wide array of allies, including TV performers who earn their living from films shown on TV. The actors unions, craft unions, and even President Nixon, have rallied to the cause of fewer reruns. Mr. Nixon wrote a letter that called upon the networks to solve the problem voluntarily or face possible regulatory actions. The TV networks have joined to combat Mr. Balmuth's proposals, which would return programming practices to where they were in the 1950s.

The battle has some big-money implications. It costs a TV network $200,000 or more to produce a film for a one-hour show. A commercial message on a prime-time show costs about $55,000 per minute. One of the reasons the networks like reruns is that they receive the same $55,000 per commercial minute while the rerun's production cost drops to about $30,000.

The stakes in the dispute are important, and it was one man's petition that triggered it. Mr. Davidson said of Mr. Balmuth: "No other individual, Ralph Nader included, has ever stirred up such a fuss in the broadcasting industry."

## PEP TALK

We close this book with some final words of advice and encouragement.

We hope that more people will be encouraged to make themselves heard in their communities as a result of reading this book. It isn't as hard as it seems. And there are many people out there who will help you to be heard.

We have tried to go beyond mere instructions on how lay people can gain access to media; we have suggested some structures for messages, what to say when you are finally going to be "heard," how to make the most of that opportunity and then, if necessary, sustain interest in the message.

As this book neared completion, there appeared in the July 23, 1973 issue of *The New Yorker* an interview with John Gardner, written by Elizabeth Drew. Mr. Gardner, founder and head of Common Cause, the citizens' lobby, and a person who clearly understands the dynamics of electoral power and communicative skills, offered views on citizen action that were as inspiring as they were insightful and informative. We commend Mr. Gardner's words to all and, because they are so pertinent to the purpose of this book, single out these: "The type of citizen action we are trying to create is a new ingredient in the political process —highly organized, tough-minded citizen action to hold government continuously accountable, a means of voting between elections. . . ." Mr. Gardner added:

> There are in any population a lot of people who are very busy just living, just surviving, just getting through the day. . . . But there is always a segment of the population that has the time and energy to worry about the community and the nation. You find these people in all parts of society—in the ghettos, in the labor unions, in the suburbs. Since you can't know where these vigorous, concerned citizens will come from, you have to keep the channels of a free society open, so that they can step forward and make themselves felt.

And Mr. Gardner also commented:

> The tasks of citizen action are never-ending. The battles are never over. Nothing is finally safe. There will always be issues of freedom and government.

He went on to say:

> The first requirement for effective citizen action is stamina. Arthur Vanderbilt said court reform is no sport for the short-winded. The same is true of citizen action.

This is the exhilarating stuff that enriches life in the United States and gives meaning to our freedoms.

Obviously, although we have tried to cover the inside aspects of dealing with media, there always will be the unexpected experience, the episode for which no amount of briefing or coaching can prepare one. We trust that such moments will be few for our readers. Perhaps the feeling of confidence, of competence, and of being in control that this book engenders among its users will also provide them with a veneer of deftness that will take them through a nasty media experience, a hasty editorial judgment that seems inexplicable.

Again returning to Mr. Gardner's interview in *The New Yorker*, we find this:

As I listen to people listing all the great problems they intend to solve, I think of people sitting in an ancient automobile by the side of the road. The tires are flat and the steering wheel is broken and the drive shaft is bent, but they're engaged in a great argument as to whether they should go to Phoenix or San Francisco, or the Oregon coast. And in my imagination I am standing by the road saying, "You're not going anywhere till you fix the goddam car."

To our way of thinking, this book can be considered one of the replacement parts for that "ancient automobile." Happy motoring along the media highways. We hope this book takes you where you want to go.

Ted Klein and Fred Danzig

# References and Notes

## CHAPTER 1

### *Books and Articles*

Bliss, E. W., Jr., and Patterson, J. M. *Writing News for Broadcast.* New York: Columbia University Press, 1971.

Bluem, A. W. et al. *Television and the Public Interest.* New York: Hastings House, 1961.

Chester, Giraud, et al. *Television & Radio.* 4th ed. New York: Appleton-Century-Crofts, 1971.

Dary, David. *Television News Handbook.* Thurmont, Md.: TAB, 1971.

Epstein, E. J. *Television News from Nowhere.* New York: Random House, 1973.

Fang, Irving E. *Television News: Writing, Filming, Editing, and Broadcasting.* New York: Hastings House, 1968.

Feldman, Albert, ed. *Inside News Broadcasting.* Washington Depot, Conn.: Public Relations Plus, 1972.

Goodall, George S. *Television Tape Recording Primer.* New York: Cahners, 1970.

Graf, Richard. "Special Delivery—How National News Gets to Local Stations." *TV Guide,* July 8, 1972.

Green, Maury. *Television News Anatomy and Process.* Belmont, Calif.: Wadsworth, 1969.

Kopkind, Andrew. "Video Revolution—Is Anyone Out There Watching?" (article on the videotape projects of protest groups). *Boston After Dark*, July 11, 1972.

MacGregor, James. "Once Over Lightly: How Av Westin Decides What Evening News Is." *Wall Street Journal*, Nov. 22, 1972.

Shayon, Robert C. *Television: The Dream and the Reality.* Milwaukee, Wis.: Marquette University Press, 1960.

Skorina, Harry J. *Television and the News.* Palo Alto, Calif.: Pacific, 1968.

Skorina, Henry J. *Television & Society–An Inquest and Agenda for Improvement.* New York: McGraw Hill, 1965.

"CATV: What It Means to Advertising," *Marketing Communications*, Apr. 1971, pp. 26–31.

"Information Technology." *Science*, 176, 1392–1405 (1972).

## *Booklets*

*If You Want Air Time.* National Association of Broadcasters, 1771 N St. N.W., Washington D.C. 2006 (free).

*Science News Communications.* National Association of Science Writers, P.O. Box 44, Seacliff, N.Y. 11579 ($2.00).

*Television Contacts.* Names of local people to contact in fifty top cities. Available from PR Aids, Inc., 305 E. 45 St., New York, N.Y. 10017 ($60.00).

## *Other*

"Guerrilla Television." Michael Shamberg & Radiance Corporation, Holt, Rinehart & Winston, New York, 1971. A TV version of *Don't Steal This Book.* This is an innovative approach to do-it-yourself TV production using your own videotape recorder. Not likely to do much toward replacing commercial TV for the next few years, still a fairly good guide to starting your own TV production unit. No commercial station or educational outlet is likely to let you put your own footage on their channel, unless you have exclusive coverage of a riot. The section on cable TV is good.

*Radical Software*, a periodical published in 1970–1971 by Michael Shamberg and Ira Schneider, 24 E. 22 St., New York, N.Y. 10010. Issue no. 3 (Spring 1971) contains a breakdown of total production costs for publishing the issue and articles on Grass Roots Television, Hardware Design and Consequences, Distribution Plans.

## CHAPTER 2

Day, David. *Radio News Handbook*. Thurmont, Md.: TAB Books, 1970.

## CHAPTER 3

Charnley, Mitchel. *Reporting*. New York: Holt Rinehart & Winston,
Doing, Ivan, and Doing, Carole. *News: A Consumers Guide*. Englewood Cliffs, N.J.: Prentice-Hall, 1972.

## CHAPTER 5

Epstein, Edward Jay. *News from Nowhere*. New York: Random House, 1973.

*Editor & Publisher Yearbook*. *Editor & Publisher*, 850 Third Ave., New York, N.Y.

Profile on Peter S. Willett, Vice-president, Broadcast Services, UPI article in *Broadcasting*, Jan. 15, 1973, p. 73.

"Health/Medicine Makes the News," *PR Doctor*, Nov.–Dec. 1970.

Feldman, Albert, ed. *Inside News Broadcasting*. Booklet published by Public Relations Plus, Inc., Washington Depot, Conn. 06794.

## CHAPTER 6

Bagdikian, Ben. *The Effete Conspiracy*. New York: Harper and Row, 1972.

Fabun, Don. *Communications: The Transfer of Meaning*. Beverly Hills, Calif.: Glencoe, 1968.

## CHAPTER 10

An excellent article about how the American Cancer Society organizes their annual seminars was printed in *Science*, 180, 722–764 (1973).

## CHAPTER 14

Aylesworth, Thomas. *This Vital Air, This Vital Water: Man's Environment Crisis*. Chicago: Rand McNally, 1968.

Behrman, A. S. *Water is Everybody's Business*. New York: Doubleday, 1968.

Borgstrom, G. *The Hungry Planet*. New York: Collier, 1965.

Carson, Rachel. *Silent Spring*. Boston: Houghton Mifflin, 1962.

Carona, Philip. *Water*. Chicago: Follett, 1967.

Commoner, B. *Science and Survival*. New York: Viking, 1966.

——. *The Changing Circle*. New York: Knopf, 1971.

Council of State Governments. *The Book of States*, Lexington, Ky., 1970.

Cox, G., ed. *Readings in Conservation Ecology*. New York: Appleton, 1969.

Debell, Garrett. *The Environmental Handbook*. New York: Ballantine, 1970.

Dubos, Rene. *So Human an Animal*. New York: Scribner's, 1970.

Ehrlich, Paul. *The Population Bomb*. New York: Sierra Club-Ballantine, 1971.

Fuller, R. Buckminster. *Utopia or Oblivion: The Prospects for Humanity*. New York: Bantam, 1969.

Goldman, Marshall. *Controlling Pollution: The Economics of a Cleaner America*. Englewood Cliffs, N.J.: Prentice-Hall, 1967.

Herber, Lewis. *Crisis in Our Cities*. Englewood Cliffs, N.J.: Prentice-Hall, 1965.

Holtzman, A. *Interest Groups and Lobbying*. New York: Macmillan, 1966.

Jeffers, R. *Not Man Apart*. New York: Sierra Club-Ballantine, 1969.

Kavaler, Lucy. *Dangerous Air*. New York: Day, 1967.

Kormonday, Edward J. *Concepts of Ecology*. Englewood Cliffs, N.J.: Prentice-Hall, 1968.

Lane, Edgar. *Lobbying and the Law*. Berkeley and Los Angeles: University of California Press, 1964.

Leinwand, Gerald, ed. *Air and Water Pollution*. New York: Washington Square, 1969.

McClosky, Maxime, and Gilligan, James P., eds. *Wilderness and the Quality of Life*. New York: Sierra Club, 1969.

Marx, Wesley. *The Frail Ocean*. New York: Sierra Club-Ballantine, 1969 (paperback).

Mayers, W., and Rinard, P. *Making Activism Work*. New York: Gordon and Breach, 1972.

Morris, D. *The Naked Ape*. New York: Dell, 1969.

Moss, Frank. *The Water Crisis*. New York: Praeger, 1967.

Nadel, M. V. *The Politics of Consumer Protection*. New York: Bobbs-Merrill, 1972.

National Association of Attorneys General, *State Progress in Consumer Protection*, Raleigh, N.C., 1971.

O. M. Collective. *The Organizers Manual*. New York: Bantam, 1971.

*The Sierra Club Handbook*, San Francisco: Sierra Club, 1970.
Storer, J. *Man in the Web of Life*. New York: Signet, 1968.
Terry, Mark. *Teaching for Survival*. New York: Ballantine, 1971.
Udall, Stewart. *1976: Agenda for Tomorrow*. New York: Holt, Rinehart & Winston, 1969.
Vosburgh, John. *Living with Your Land*. Bloomfield Hills, Mich.: Cranbook Institute of Science, 1968.
Winter, R. K. *The Consumer Advocates vs. the Consumer*, Washington, D.C.: The American Enterprise Institute, 1972.

## *Environmental Publications*

*Audubon Magazine*, National Audubon Society, 950 Third Avenue, New York, N.Y. 10022.
*Air and Water*, McGraw Hill, 1221 Avenue of the Americas, New York, N.Y. 10020.
*Catalyst for Environmental Quality*, 274 Madison Ave., New York, N.Y. 10016.
*Clear Creek*, One South Park, San Francisco, Calif. 94107.
*The Ecologist*, 73 Kew Green, Richmond, Surrey, England.
*Eco-News*, 235 E. 49 St., New York, N.Y. 10017.
*Environment*, 428 N. Skinner Boulevard, St. Louis, Mo. 63130.
*The Environment Monthly*, 420 Lexington Ave., New York, N.Y. 10017.
*Environmental Action*, Room 731, 1346 Connecticut Ave. N.W., Washington, D.C. 20036
*The Living Wilderness*, Wilderness Society, 729 Fifteenth St. N.W., Washington, D.C.
*National Parks and Conservation Magazine*, 1701 Eighteenth St. N.W., Washington, D.C. 20009.
*Natural History Magazine*, American Museum of Natural History, Central Park West at 79 St., New York, N.Y. 10024.
*Our Daily Planet*, Room 223, 51 Chambers St., New York, N.Y. 10007.
Rodale Press, Inc., 33 E. Minor Street, Emmaus, Pa. 18049.
*The Saturday Review*, 380 Madison Ave., New York, N.Y. 10017.
*The Sierra Club Bulletin*, 1050 Mills Tower, San Francisco, Calif. 94104.
*Smithsonian*, 900 Jefferson Drive S.W., Washington, D.C. 20560
*Voluntary Action News*, 1735 I St. N.W., Washington, D.C. 20006.

## CHAPTER 15

O. M. Collective. *The Organizer's Manual.* New York: Bantam, 1971 ($1.25). An excellent manual for anyone who wants nuts and bolts information on how to organize for social change. The chapters on Mass Education and Communication are excellent, including "how-to" information on the use of speakers, bureaus, mobile units, coffee houses, films, and guerrilla theater. The manual has excellent chapters on Zaps, Marches, Pickets, Sit-ins, Harassments, Boycotts, and Tax Resistance. The section on Defense provides information on how to get legal protection and medical aid and what to do for self defense. The extensive and annotated directory is worth ten times the price of the book. It gives names and addresses of everything from publishers of books and newsletters on fund-raising and addresses of legal defense funds who help organizations and individuals engaged in "movement" activities.

Office of Consumer Affairs, *Forming Consumer Organizations*, Washington, D.C. 20506: U.S. Government Printing Office, 1972 (35¢) 0–514–170 (42). Compiled by Virginia H. Knauer, Director, Office of Consumer Affairs, Executive Office of the President, this valuable pamphlet explains in detail how consumer organizations are organized, from bylaws to committees and officers. Sample constitution and bylaws are included along with a sample press release. It is one of the finest publications of its kind ever printed.

## CHAPTER 16

Barton, Roger, Ed. *Advertising Handbook.* Englewood Cliffs, N.J.: Prentice-Hall, 1950.

Berelson, B., and Steiner, G. *Human Behavior, An Inventory of Scientific Findings.* New York: Harcourt Brace Jovanovich, 1967.

Frey, Albert W., and Halterman, Jean C. *Advertising.* 4th ed. New York: Ronald, 1970.

McCaffrey, Maurice. *Advertising Wins Elections.* Minneapolis, Minn.: Dillon, 1962.

# Appendix I

# Media Information

*Author's note:* This information is accurate as of 1973. Sources used include various organizations of media—National Association Broadcasters—publications, and newspaper sales presentations. All Figures are for the United States only.

## *Television*

- Of over 67 million households, 97% have TV (64 million).
- There are a total of 230 TV markets that include all households:
  60 have one station
  30 have two stations
  74 have three stations
  66 have four or more stations.
- There are 904 TV stations, including 205 educational stations.
- On an average at any given time 27% of all homes watch daytime TV
  50% of all homes watch early evening TV
  62.2% watch from 7:00 to 10:00 P.M.
  30% watch late evening TV.
- The average cost per minute for a network daytime TV spot of one minute is $7500; the average cost per minute for a network nighttime TV spot of one minute is $50,000.

## *Radio*

- Over 99% of all households have at least one radio—the average home has over five sets.
- Of 336 million radios in the United States, 240 million are portable or need to be plugged in; 85 million cars have radios.
- There are 7130 radio stations: 4354 are AM; 2777 are FM.
- 80% of the country has access to an FM radio.

## *Magazines*

- A total of 130 million Americans read magazines: 48% are men, 52% women. *Reader's Digest* reaches over 42 million people each issue. *TV Guide* reaches over 35 million.

## *Newspapers*

- There are 1749 daily newspapers: 339 are morning, 1425 are evening, 590 have Sunday editions.
- There are 7567 weekly newspapers.

## *Outdoor Billboards*

- It would cost over $240,000 a month to reach over 90% of the population in the top ten markets (over 37 million people).
- It would cost over $120,000 per month to reach 50% of the people in the same markets.

## *Direct Mail* (*Source*: National Research Council)

- The best medium is a letter. The most effective use of the letter is one with a request for a reply. Those with two colors outpull one-color letters.
- Insertion of a reply envelope increases returns to a mailing.
- A two-page letter printed on two separate pages usually outpulls a one-page letter.
- Third-class postage will usually pull as well as first-class postage.
- Use of postage meter usually outpulls postage stamps.
- Follow-up campaigns need about five separate letters; a twelve-month program with a mailing every thirty days is usually the best use of mail promotion.
- Handwritten addressing usually reduces returns. Where possible always address letters to an individual.

# Appendix II

# National Public Listener-Sponsored Radio Member Stations

*Alaska*

| | |
|---|---|
| College | KUAC (FM) |

*Arizona*

| | |
|---|---|
| Phoenix | KMCR (FM) |
| Tucson | KUAT (AM) |
| Yuma | KAWC (AM) |

*Arkansas*

| | |
|---|---|
| Jonesboro | KASU (FM) |

*California*

| | |
|---|---|
| Long Beach | KLON (FM) |
| Los Angeles | KUSC (FM) |
| Northridge | KEDC (FM) |
| San Bernardino | KVCR-FM |
| San Diego | KPBS-FM |
| San Francisco | KALW (FM) |
| San Francisco | KPFD |
| San Francisco | KQED-FM |
| San Mateo | KCSM-FM |
| Santa Monica | KCRW (FM) |
| Stockton | KUOP (FM) |

*Colorado*

| | |
|---|---|
| Greeley | KUNC (FM) |

*District of Columbia*

| | |
|---|---|
| | WAMU-FM |
| | WETA-FM |

*Florida*

| | |
|---|---|
| Boynton Beach | WHRS (FM) |
| Jacksonville | WJCT-FM |
| Tallahassee | WFSU-FM |
| Tampa | WUSF-FM |

*Georgia*

| | |
|---|---|
| Atlanta | WABE (FM) |

*Illinois*

| | |
|---|---|
| Carbondale | WSIU (FM) |
| Chicago | WBEZ (FM) |
| DeKalb | WNIU (FM) |
| Edwardsville | WSIE (FM) |
| Lincoln | WLCC (FM) |
| Urbana | WILL (AM) |

*Indiana*

| | |
|---|---|
| Bloomington | WFIU (FM) |
| Indianapolis | WIAN (FM) |
| W. Lafayette | WBAA (AM) |

*Iowa*

| | |
|---|---|
| Ames | WOI (FM) |
| Cedar Falls | KHKE (FM) |
| Iowa City | WSUI (FM) |

*Kansas*

| | |
|---|---|
| Lawrence | KANU (FM) |
| Manhattan | KSAC (AM) |
| Wichita | KMUW (FM) |

*Kentucky*

| | |
|---|---|
| Lexington | WBKY (FM) |
| Louisville | WFPK (FM)<br>WFPL (FM) |
| Morehead | WMKY (FM) |
| Murray | WKMS (FM) |
| Richmond | WEKU (FM) |

*Louisiana*

| | |
|---|---|
| New Orleans | WWNO (FM) |

*Maine*

| | |
|---|---|
| Bangor | WMEH (FM) |

*Maryland*

| | |
|---|---|
| Baltimore | WBJC (FM) |

*Massachusetts*

| | |
|---|---|
| Amherst | WFCR (FM) |
| Boston | WBUR (FM)<br>WGBH-FM |
| Worcester | WICN (FM) |

*Michigan*

| | |
|---|---|
| Ann Arbor | WUOM (FM) |
| Berrien Springs | WAUS (FM) |
| Detroit | WDET (FM) |
| East Lansing | WKAR-FM<br>(AM) |
| Flint | WFBE (FM) |
| Houghton | WGGL (FM) |
| Interlochen | WIAA (FM) |
| Kalamazoo | WMUK (FM) |
| Marquette | WNMR-FM |

*Minnesota*

| | |
|---|---|
| Collegeville | KSJR (FM) |
| Minneapolis/St. Paul | KSJN (FM) |
| Minneapolis | KUOM (AM) |
| Northfield | WCAL-FM |

*Mississippi*

| | |
|---|---|
| Senatobia | WNJC (FM) |

*Missouri*

| | |
|---|---|
| Buffalo | KBFL (FM) |
| Columbia | KBIA (FM) |
| Kansas City | KCUR (FM) |
| Maryville | KXCV (FM) |
| Point Lookout | KSOZ (FM) |
| St. Louis | KWMU (FM) |
| Warrensburg | KCMW (FM) |

*Nebraska*

| | |
|---|---|
| Omaha | KIOS (FM) |

*New Mexico*

| | |
|---|---|
| Las Cruces | KRWG (FM) |

*New York*

| | |
|---|---|
| Albany | WAMC (FM) |
| Buffalo | WBFO (FM) |
| Canton | WSLU (FM) |

| | |
|---|---|
| New York City | WNYC-FM (AM) |
| | WBAI (FM) |
| Schenectady | WMHT (FM) |
| Syracuse | WCNY (FM) |
| *North Carolina* | |
| Durham | WAFR (FM) |
| Winston-Salem | WFDD (FM) |
| *North Dakota* | |
| Fargo | KDSU (FM) |
| Grand Forks | KFJM (AM) |
| *Ohio* | |
| Athens | WOUB-FM (AM) |
| Bowling Green | WBGU-FM |
| Cincinnati | WGUC (FM) |
| Columbus | WCBE (FM) |
| | WOSU-FM (AM) |
| Oxford | WMUB-FM |
| Wilberforce | WCSU (FM) |
| Youngstown | WYSU (FM) |
| *Oklahoma* | |
| Stillwater | KOSU (FM) |
| *Oregon* | |
| Corvallis | KOAC (AM) |
| Eugene | KLCC (FM) |
| | KWAX (FM) |
| Portland | KBPS (AM) |
| | KOAP-FM |
| | KBOO (FM) |
| *Pennsylvania* | |
| Erie* | WQLN (FM) |
| Hershey | WUHY (FM) |
| Philadelphia | WITF (FM) |
| Pittsburgh | WDUQ (FM) |
| *Puerto Rico* | |
| Hato Rey | WIPR (AM) |
| *South Carolina* | |
| Greenville | WEPR (FM) |
| *South Dakota* | |
| Vermillion | KUSD (AM) |
| *Tennessee* | |
| Collegedale | WSMC (FM) |
| Knoxville | WUOT (FM) |
| Memphis | WKNO-FM |
| Murfreesboro | WMOT (FM) |
| Nashville | WPLN (FM) |
| *Texas* | |
| Austin | KUT (FM) |
| Dallas* | KVTT (FM) |
| El Paso | KTEP (FM) |
| Houston | |
| Killeen | KNCT-FM |
| *Utah* | |
| Logan | KUSU (FM) |
| Provo | KBYU (FM) |
| Salt Lake City | KUER (FM) |
| *Virginia* | |
| Richmond | WRFK (FM) |
| *Washington* | |
| Pullman | KWSU (AM) |
| Seattle | KRAB (FM) |
| | KOUW (FM) |
| Tacoma | KTOY (FM) |
| *West Virginia* | |
| Buckhannon | WVWC (FM) |
| *Wisconsin* | |
| La Crosse | WLSU (FM) |
| Madison | WHA (AM) |
| Milwaukee | WUWM (FM) |

* Provisional.

## *Associated Stations:*

*Illinois*

| | |
|---|---|
| Urbana | WILL-FM |

*Iowa*

| | |
|---|---|
| Ames | WOI-AM |
| Iowa City | KSUI-FM |

*Michigan*

| | |
|---|---|
| Grand Rapids | WVGR (FM) |

*Minnesota*

| | |
|---|---|
| Moorhead | KCCM (FM) |
| Northfield | WCAL-FM |

*Puerto Rico*

| | |
|---|---|
| Hato Rey | WIPR-FM |

*South Dakota*

| | |
|---|---|
| Vermillion | KUSD-FM |

*Wisconsin*

| | |
|---|---|
| Auburndale | WLBL (AM) |
| Brule | WHSA (FM) |
| Chilton | WHKW (FM) |
| Colfax | WHWC (FM) |
| Delafield | WHAD (FM) |
| Highland | WHHI (FM) |
| Holmen | WHLA (FM) |
| Madison | WHA-FM |
| Rib Mountain Park | WHRM (FM) |
| Suring | WHMD (FM) |

# Appendix III

# Groups That Can Help

Before you embark on a program it is best to locate others you may be able to help. In Chapter 15 we talked about how to attract members. Chapter 18 provided examples of how others made it. Here is a potpourri of names and addresses of organizations who have in one way or another helped citizens achieve certain goals. How you should approach anyone, what to ask for, and what to do with what you get is up to you. Our purpose in listing them is to bring together in the book in this one place people who may help other people get heard.

## *Environmental Organizations*

The U.S. Environmental Protection Agency (Office of Public Affairs, Washington, D.C. 20040) publishes a series of booklets on what is happening with people who want to do something to protect the environment. For 15 cents the GPO will send you a list of organizations; ask for Publication 5501-00418, title *Groups That Can Help,* or get the *Directory of Government Agencies Safeguarding Consumer and Environment* (4th ed. Alexandria, Va.: Serina Press). Here is a shortened list, from that publication and some others, of groups interested in the environment:

## I. GENERAL INFORMATION

Environmental Health Service
Office of Public Affairs HEW
Washington, D.C. 20204

Environmental Protection Administration
2345 Municipal Building
New York, N.Y. 10007

Environmental Protection Agency
Office of Public Affairs
Parklawn Building, Room 17B17
5600 Fishers Lane
Rockville, Md. 20853

Fund for New Priorities in America
415 Lexington Avenue
New York, N.Y. 10017

National Industrial Pollution Control Council
U.S. Department of Commerce
14 H Street and Constitution Avenue NW
Washington, D.C. 20230

National Oceanic and Atmospheric Administration
U.S. Department of Commerce
6010 Executive Boulevard
Rockville, Md. 20852

Office of Solid Waste Management Programs
Environmental Protection Agency
Waterside Mall, 41 M Street SW
Washington, D.C. 20460

Coordinator for Environmental Education
U.S. Department of Health, Education, and Welfare
400 Maryland Avenue SW
Washington, D.C. 20202

Superintendent of Documents
U.S. Government Printing Office
C Street NW
Washington, D.C. 20590

Urban Mass Transit Administration
U.S. Department of Transportation
400 Seventeenth Street SW
Washington, D.C. 20590

### LAND AND WATER

Bureau of Outdoor Recreation
U.S. Department of the Interior
Washington, D.C. 20240

National Park Service
U.S. Department of the Interior
1701 Eighteenth Street NW
Washington, D.C. 2009

New York City Planning Commission
2 Lafayette Street
New York, N.Y. 10007

Parks, Recreation, and Cultural Affairs Administration
830 Fifth Avenue
New York, N.Y. 10021

## II. RESOURCES

Council on Environmental Quality
722 Jackson Place NW
Washington, D.C. 20006

New York State Department of Environmental Conservation
50 Wolf Road
Albany, N.Y. 12201

Office of Conservation Education
U.S. Department of the Interior
C Street
Washington, D.C. 20009

National Parks and Conservation Association
1701 Eighteenth Street NW
Washington, D.C. 20009

New York City Planning Commission
2 Lafayette Street
New York, N.Y. 10007

The Parks Council
80 Central Park West
New York, N.Y. 10023

## *III. ENVIRONMENTAL ORGANIZATIONS*

Air Pollution Control Association
4400 Fifth Avenue
Pittsburgh, Pa. 15213

Citizens for Clean Air
502 Park Avenue
New York, N. Y. 10022

New York State Action for Clean Air Committee
105 East Twenty-second Street
New York, N.Y. 10019

### BEAUTIFICATION

Garden Club of America
598 Madison Avenue
New York, N.Y. 10022

Keep American Beautiful Inc.
99 Park Avenue
New York, N.Y. 10016

### FORESTRY AND CONSERVATION

American Forestry Association
919 Seventeenth Street NW
Washington, D.C. 20006

New York State Conservation Council
Room 505
5 Broadway
Troy, N.Y. 12180

The Society of American Foresters
1010 Sixteenth Street NW
Washington, D.C. 20036

The Wilderness Society
729 Fifteenth Street NW
Washington, D.C. 20005

Citizens for a Quieter City
150 Amsterdam Avenue
New York, N.Y. 10023

Citizens League Against the Sonic Boom
19 Appleton Street
Cambridge, Mass. 02138

### POPULATION

Planned Parenthood
515 Madison Avenue
New York, N. Y. 10022

Population Crisis Committee
1730 K Street NW
Washington, D.C. 20006

The Population Institute
100 Maryland Avenue NE
Washington, D.C. 20002

Zero Population Growth
367 State Street
Los Altos, Calif. 94022

TREES

Forest History Society
P.O. Box 1581
Santa Cruz, Calif. 95060

International Shade Tree Conference
3 Lincoln Square
P.O. Box 71
Urbana, Ill. 61801

The Parks Council
80 Central Park West
New York, N.Y. 10023

Tree Pest Information Services
State University College of Forestry
Syracuse, N.Y. 13210

WATER AND LAND

Committee to Save the Waterfront
167 Columbia Street
Brooklyn, N.Y. 11231

Isaak Walton League of America
1326 Waukegan Road
Glenview, Ill. 60025

National Association of Soil & Water Conservation Districts
1025 Vermont Avenue NW
Washington, D.C. 20005

The Oceanic Society
680 Beach Street
San Francisco, Calif. 94109

Regional Plan Association
230 West Forty-first Street
New York, N.Y. 10036

Resources for the Future
1755 Massachusetts Avenue NW
Washington, D.C. 20036

Soil Conservation Society of America
7515 Northeast Ankeny Road
Ankeny, Iowa 50021

Water Pollution Control Federation
3900 Wisconsin Avenue NW
Washington, D.C. 20005

Water Resources Council
2120 L Street NW
Washington, D.C. 20037

## *IV. GENERAL ENVIRONMENT PROTECTION AND INFORMATION*

Boy Scouts of America
North Brunswick, N.J. 08902

Camp Fire Club of America
19 Rector Street
New York, N.Y. 10006

Citizens Committee for the Hudson Valley
P.O. Box 146
Ardsley on Hudson, N.Y. 10503

Citizens Committee on Natural Resources
1346 Connecticut Avenue NW
Washington, D.C. 20036

Conservation Law Society of America
220 Bush Street
San Francisco, Calif. 94104

Conservation Education Association
Box 450
Madison, Wis. 53701

The Conservation Foundation
1717 Massachusetts Avenue NW
Washington, D.C. 20036

Committee for Environmental Information
439 North Skinner Boulevard
St. Louis, Mo. 63130

Conservation Services, Inc.
S. Great Road
Lincoln, Mass. 01773

Consumer Action Now (CAN)
30 East Sixty-eighth Street
New York, N.Y. 10021

The Council on the Environment
Room 228
51 Chambers Street
New York, N.Y. 10007

Environmental Action Committee
Room 200
2000 P Street NW
Washington, D.C. 20036

The Environmental Clearinghouse, Inc.
137 D Street SE
Washington, D.C.

The Environmental Defense Fund
162 Old Town Road
East Setauket, N.Y. 11733

Friends of the Earth
30 East Forty-second Street
New York, N.Y. 10017

National Center for Resources Recovery, Inc.
1211 Connecticut Avenue NW
Washington, D.C. 20036

National Parks and Conservation Association
1701 Eighteenth Street NW
Washington, D.C. 20009

National Recreation and Park Association
1700 Pennsylvania Avenue NW
Washington, D.C. 20006

National Trust for Historic Preservation
Decatur House
748 Jackson Place NW
Washington, D.C. 20006

Pratt Institute Center for Community Environmental Development
642 Hall Street
Brooklyn, N.Y. 11203

Scientists' Institute for Publication Information (SCIP)
30 East Sixty-eighth Street
New York, N. Y. 10021

The Sierra Club
220 Bush Street
San Francisco, Calif. 94104

Student Conservation Association, Inc.
Olympic View Drive
Route 1, Box 573A
Vashon, Wash. 98070

## V. WILDLIFE AND ANIMALS

Defenders of Wildlife
2000 N Street NW
Washington, D.C. 20036

Ducks Unlimited
P.O. Box 66300
Chicago, Ill. 60666

Friends of Animals, Inc.
11 West Sixtieth Street
New York, N.Y. 10023

Izaak Walton League of America
1800 North Kent Street
Arlington, Va. 22209

National Audubon Society
950 Third Avenue
New York, N.Y. 10022

National Wildlife Federation
1412 Sixteenth Street
Washington, D.C. 20036

Sport Fishing Institute
719 Thirteenth Street NW
Washington, D.C. 20005

Trout Unlimited
25–26 State Street
P.O. Box 1807
Saginaw, Mich. 48605

Wildlife Management Institute
709 Wire Building
Washington, D.C. 20005

## VI. ENVIRONMENT CAMPAIGNS

If you are primarily concerned about the environment and want to get involved in an organizational effort, there are a number of ways to begin.

The Conservation Foundation (1717 Massachusetts Ave. NW, Washington, D.C. 20036) offers a free booklet, *A Citizen's Guide to Clean Air.*

For $1, the Conservation Foundation offers *Law and Taxation—A Guide for Conservation and Other Non-Profit Organizations.*

The Regional Plan Association of Southern California (621 South Virgil Avenue, Los Angeles, Calif. 90005) offers for $5 *A Guide to Citizen Participation in Environmental Action.*

The Izaak Walton League (1800 North Kent Street, Arlington, Va. 22209) offers a free booklet, *Clean Water—It's Up to You.*

The U.S. Environmental Protection Agency (Washington, D.C. 20460) also offers a free booklet, *Citizen Action Can Get Results.*

The Citizens Advisory Committee on Environmental Quality has prepared the brochure *Community Action for Environmental Quality*, available at 60¢ from the Government Printing Office (Washington, D.C. 20402).

The League of Women Voters' Education Fund (1730 M Street NW, Washington, D.C. 30036) offers a free booklet, *How to Plan an Environmental Conference*.

## *Other Groups That Can Help*

American Civil Liberties Union (ACLU)
22 E. Fortieth Street
New York, N.Y. 10016

Founded in 1920 this organization now has 170,000 members. With 48 state affiliates and over 350 local chapters, it is the organization that often is the only one to provide legal representation for all groups who are seeking rights denied them. From the ultraleft to the far right, the ACLU will find an attorney when almost no one else can.

Rights of everyone from children to mental patients, homosexuals, and even Nazis have been fought for in the courts by the ACLU. In the recent past the organization has fought court battles for the right to privacy and against book censorship, loyalty oaths, and unreasonable searches.

Accuracy In Media, Inc.
425 Thirteenth Street NW
Suite 1232
Washington, D.C. 20004

Since 1969 this self-appointed watchdog for truth in media has specialized in finding errors in the *New York Times*, NBC, and other media.

# Appendix IV

# Women's Organizations

There is so much that is needed to help women in their fight for equal rights that we can do no more than hope that this book will be useful. The organizations that represent women are many. Here are a few that should be consulted before starting out on any battle.

National Organization for Women (NOW)
Legal Defense & Education Fund
127 East Fifty-ninth Street
New York, N.Y. 10022

Women's Law Fund
17210 Parkland Drive
Shaker Heights, Ohio 44120

Women's Equity Action League
610 Glenn Road
State College, Pa. 16801

The Columbia Missouri Women's Center
501 Rollins Street
Columbia, Mo. 65201

Women's National Abortion Action Coalition
150 Fifth Avenue
New York, N.Y. 10010

National Association of Minority Women in Business
Suite 500
906 Grand Street
Kansas City, Mo. 64106

Stewardesses for Women's Rights
P.O. Box 3235
Alexandria, Va. 22302

The National Women's Health Coalition
222 East Thirty-fifth Street
New York, N.Y. 10016

# Appendix V

# Environmental Defense Fund Cases As of August 1972 (Supplied by Environmental Defense Fund)

Here is a list of cases from the files of the Environmental Defense Fund, with a description of the action. It is printed here so that the reader can see what kind of action is being initiated in this one area of citizen concern. Write the Environmental Defense Fund, 162 Old Town Rd., East Setauket, N.Y. 11733 for the latest listing.

*Abbreviations*

AEC——Atomic Energy Commission
EPA——Environmental Protection Agency
FAA——Federal Aviation Administration
FCC——Federal Communications Commission
FDA——Food and Drug Administration
FPC——Federal Power Commission
FTC——Federal Trade Commission
HUD——Housing & Urban Development
NEPA—National Environmental Policy Act
TVA——Tennessee Valley Authority
USDA—United States Department of Agriculture

## *Power/Energy:*

| | |
|---|---|
| Atomic Energy Commission (regulatory proceedings) | Consultation with AEC to make their licensing rules more responsive to environmental needs. (Consolidated Edison, Indian Point Plant 2, Hudson River, New York; Consumers Power Co., Midland, Michigan) |
| Electric utilities pricing structure | Participation in rate-making proceedings to modify the present rate structure, which encourages maximum consumption of power by lowering the cost per unit as consumption increases. |
| Indian Point Nuclear Power Plant #2 (Hudson River, N.Y.) | Suit to enforce NEPA in nuclear power reactor case. |
| Trans-Alaska Pipeline | Suit to minimize or avoid environmental hazards of transporting oil from the North Slope of Alaska. |
| Four Corners Power Plants (Arizona, Nevada, New Mexico, Utah) | Petition to expand FPC jurisdiction over fossil fuel plants and petition to Dept. of Interior to enforce NEPA denied. Appeal has been filed. |

## *Land Use:*

| | |
|---|---|
| Amendments to grazing regulations | Comments submitted to Depts. of Interior and Agriculture regarding enforcement of proposed regulations |
| Connecticut wetlands | Conn. Environmental Protection Statute of 1971 violated by proposed development of land along the Saugatuck River. EDF intervened in support of local group. |
| Half Moon Bay, Coastide County, California | Complaint filed based on the California Environmental Quality Act, alleging absence of adequate environmental studies and planning for development of an expanded water system. |

| | |
|---|---|
| Joyce Kilmer Memorial Forest–Slickrock Creek Drainage Area (North Carolina) | U.S. Forest Service petitioned to designate this area as a wilderness-study area and halt all road construction, logging, and other development. |
| Kosanke Sand Corp. (California) | Action to intervene in the granting of land patent for strip-mining, because no impact statement had been prepared. |
| New Orleans Bridge | Petition to deny permit for construction of bridge and connecting highway because of potential environmental damage to residential areas. |
| 160-acre limitation (California) | Suit filed to enforce the 160-acre limitation as a means of curtailing intrusion of large corporations into agriculture. Such intrusions allegedly cause, among other things, overdevelopment of water resources. |
| TVA–strip-mining | Suit filed to compel TVA to comply with requirements of NEPA before letting contracts for strip-mining. |

*Environmental Health:*

| | |
|---|---|
| Airborne lead pollution | Petition submitted to set federal standards for atmospheric lead emission. |
| Airborne lead pollution (California Air Resources Board, CARB) | Suit filed to compel CARB to adopt necessary regulations to phase out lead additives in motor fuel to achieve air-quality standards adopted by CARB. |
| DDVP (pesticide); Hexachlorophene (germicide); freedom of information | Efforts to make the toxicological and safety data available to the public by the manufacturer of these products. |
| Diethylpyrocarbonate (DEP, beverage preservative) | FDA petitioned to ban DEP as a known carcinogen. Successful. |
| Diethylstilbestrol (DES, cattle feed additive) | Action to prevent further approvals of applications for DES as additive to cattle feed because of its carcinogenic characteristics. Successful. |

| | |
|---|---|
| Lead Poisoning | Case being investigated regarding regulations on the use of lead-base paints in public housing. |
| Long Island water (New York) | Petition filed to require environmental impact statement to be filed regarding relationship of sewage system to County's water table. |
| Noise research | Participation in the writing of the Noise Pollution Control Act of 1972. |
| | Staff testified before Senate Sub-Committee on Air & Water Pollution. |
| | Prepared an independent report for N.Y. Environmental Protection Agency, relating to proposed New York City Noise Code. |
| Polychlorinated biphenyls (PCB, heat transfer materials and food packaging) | Negotiations with Monsanto Chemical Co. resulted in the release of relevant data on PCB's for scientific study to determine possible environmental hazards in the use of this persistent chemical. |
| Sodium nitrite (freedom of information) | Suit challenging FDA's interference with the public's right to safety data on chemical food additives. Successful. |

*Water Resources:*

| | |
|---|---|
| Truman Reservoir (Missouri) | Suit filed to stop construction because of potential disruption of farm communities and environmental destruction. Most construction has been postponed pending compliance with NEPA. |
| Cache River (Arkansas) | Channelization of 232 miles of the free-flowing Cache River and tributaries will cause destruction of wetlands and wildlife habitat. Original motion for injunction was denied. The decision has been appealed. |

| | |
|---|---|
| Gillham Dam (Arkansas) | Suit filed to stop the damming of the last free-flowing stream in the Ouachita Mtns. Preliminary injunction won on basis of inadequate impact statement. Injunction was dissolved following filing of new impact statement. Decision being appealed. |
| Tennessee–Tombigbee (Mississippi) | EDF believes the proposed Tennessee–Tombigbee waterway to be superfluous, since it would parallel the Mississippi River at great cost to taxpayers and cause extensive environmental damage. Preliminary injunction was granted and after transferral of case to another district court, the injunction was dissolved. Appeal is being taken. |
| Tocks Island-Delaware River (Pennsylvania, New Jersey, New York) | Moratorium was called on project because of potential eutrophication and regional waste-treatment problems. EDF study revealed project would perpetuate the already complex water-resource problems. |
| Discount rate, Water Resource Guidelines Hearings, District of Columbia | The low discount rate used by federal agencies to evaluate the benefit–cost ratio of water-resource projects has been an issue in several EDF cases. Discount rates can make or break a project because of their effect on the benefit–cost ratios. Suit filed against Water Resource Council, alleging the current discount-rate policy is arbitrary and capricious. |
| Tellico Project (Tennessee) | Suit filed against proposed TVA dam on the Little Tennessee River because EDF believes project economically unjustifiable and damaging to archaeological, historical, and environmental treasures. Preliminary injunction granted. |
| Falmouth Dam (Licking River, Kentucky) | Valuable woodland and farmland threatened by construction of this project. The project is being reconsidered. |

| | |
|---|---|
| Duck River Project (Tennessee) | Suit filed against construction of two dams on the Duck River because EDF feels water supply is adequate and project is economically questionable. |
| Oakley Dam (Illinois) | Suit filed against dam on Sangamon River, which would threaten Allerton Park. |
| California Water Plan | Suit filed asking Bureau of Reclamation to file an environmental impact statement on proposed California Water Plan (large-scale transport plan to supply water to the San Joaquin Valley). Statement was filed, but construction of Folsom Dam (part of project) has not been halted. EDF requested Pres. Nixon to stop construction. |
| Cross-Florida Barge Canal | Construction of this project was halted by presidential order in 1971, following successful EDF litigation. Project was partially complete at that time. EDF was successful in getting Rodman Pool (one of the completed reservoirs) lowered five feet, which, it is believed, will save 25,000 hardwood trees. |
| East Bay Municipal Utilities District (MUD) (California) | Suit to force East Bay MUD to recycle water, treat effluent properly, and change water pricing structures and rates. The proposed Auburn Folsom South Dam on the American River would not be needed and pollution of San Francisco Bay would be greatly reduced. |

*Highways:*

| | |
|---|---|
| Century Freeway (Los Angeles) | Action to require filing of environmental-impact statement before highway construction begins. |

| | |
|---|---|
| Interstate 78 (Lehigh Valley, Pennsylvania) | Suit filed to enjoin construction of proposed Interstate bypass of Allentown–Bethlehem, pending correction of substantial omissions and defects in environmental-impact statement and in public hearings. |

*Pesticides:*

| | |
|---|---|
| Aldrin-dieldrin | Petition to EPA for cancellation and suspension of this carcinogenic pesticide. |
| DDT | Ruling obtained from EPA to ban all use of DDT except in narrow specified instances. |
| Gypsy moth control program (Northeastern U.S.) | Petition to U.S. Forest Service to provide adequate NEPA requirements for gypsy moth control programs. |
| Mirex—fire ant control (Southeastern U.S.) | Suit to modify USDA aerial spray program to control the imported fire ant. |
| 2,4,5,-T (herbicide) | Plans to file petition requesting suspension of objectional uses of this powerful herbicide known to have teratogenic effects. |

*Special Cases:*

| | |
|---|---|
| Amchitka—sea otters | Protest to AEC on the killing of otters following nuclear testing and suggesting restitution to provide funds for wildlife study program for the State of Alaska. |
| Agency for International Development | EDF maintains that the National Environmental Policy Act applies to AID-funded international projects as well as those within national boundaries. |
| Fairness doctrine | Views filed with the FCC on the application of the fairness doctrine as it applies to the broadcasting of both sides of controversial issues. |

| | |
|---|---|
| Predator control | Preparation of legal and scientific comments on the predator control program submitted to the Dept. of the Interior. |
| Railroad freight-rate case (Interstate Commerce Comm.) | Freight rates challenged in compliance with NEPA because tariff restrictions and freight costs handicap the shipping of recyclable materials across state lines. |
| Washington National Airport (Noise) | Scientific data supplied for case against expansion of Washington National Airport. |
| Whale preservation | Successful addition of certain species of whales to the Dept. of Interior's list of endangered species. EDF currently involved in efforts to curtail international use of whale products. |
| Nuclear power plant safety | Negotiations with AEC for promulgation of new rules protecting the occupational safety and health rights of employees of AEC licensees. |
| Gasoline octane (FTC Rule-Making) | Participation in FTC rule-making proceedings for requirements to post levels of octane in gasoline, thus reducing lead pollution levels in urban air. |
| Interstate Highway System | Suit to compel inclusion of environmental impact statement with Secretary Volpe's submission of biennial *Needs Report on the Federal Aid Highway System to Congress* in early 1972. Suit dismissed, in part, on undertaking by Volpe to include such a statement with proposed draft legislation based in Need Report. |
| Yerba Buena Center | Suit filed to compel HUD to file environmental impact statement on downtown redevelopment project. The Oakland Redevelopment Agency agreed to file an impact statement on redevelopment project in Oakland. |

| | |
|---|---|
| SST (supersonic transport) | Petition to FAA requesting promulgation of environmental standards to govern the supersonic transport. Subsequently, plans to develop the SST were dropped. Efforts continue to assure that the Concorde will be required to meet the same noise and pollution standards as subsonic jets. |
| Obion and Forked Deer channelization project (Northwestern Tennessee) | EDF helped in preparation of scientific evidence and presented testimony concerning economic and hydrologic effects of this project. |
| Mineral King (California) | Amicus curiae brief filed in support of Sierra Club's standing in its suit to prevent development of a large private resort in the Mineral King Valley. As a result of the case, it will be necessary in the future to show that members of litigating organizations have substantial connection with the area of environmental concern. |
| Montrose DDT (California) | Suit filed against Montrose Chemical Co. to halt the discharge of DDT effluent into the Los Angeles sewage system, which flows directly into the ocean. Montrose agreed to disconnect its operation from the sewage system altogether. |
| Nerve-gas disposal | U.S. Army sued in August 1970 over plan to dump nerve gas into the Atlantic Ocean. Suit was unsuccessful but Dept. of Defense promised not to dump such hazardous materials in the ocean again. |
| Operation Snowy Beach (Maine) | Suit filed to stop a U.S. Marine maneuver exercise that would damage the natural environment of Reid State Park. Exercise was then modified to minimize damage. |

| | |
|---|---|
| Phosphate Detergent (Indiana & Erie Co., N.Y.) | Intervention in cases to support legislation prohibiting sale of phosphate detergents. |
| Santa Cruz long-toed salamander (California) | Request made to assistant secretary of interior to stop plan to rezone the last breeding ground of this endangered amphibian to allow construction of a trailer park. Petition to rezone was denied following this action and pressure from local citizens. |
| Alaska native claims | EDF joined other environmentalists to impel secretary of interior to set aside a substantial amount of Alaskan land for wilderness areas; 135 million acres were withdrawn for preservation and control. |
| Assateague Island (Maryland) | Recommendation that proposed research pier on Assateague Island National Seashore not be built resulted in abandonment of plans. |
| Lead tinsel | Suit to stop a District of Columbia drugstore chain from selling Christmas tinsel containing lead. After suit, company agreed to stop selling lead tinsel. |
| Midland nuclear power (Michigan) | Suit filed to force Consumers Power Co. to submit environmental-impact statement to conform with NEPA guidelines. |

Additional information on any of the above cases is available on request from the Environmental Defense Fund, 163 Old Town Rd., East Setauket, N.Y. 11733.

# Appendix VI

# The People's Yellow Pages

* To get a copy send $1.00 to Vocations for Social Change, 351 Broadway, Cambridge, Mass. 02139.

An unusual publication appeared in the early 1970s that has been widely copied. It is called *The People's Yellow Pages* and was published by the Vocations for Social Change, an organization supported by the American Friends Service Committee in Boston.* This 126-page directory is described in the flyleaf as "an attempt to share with you the many efforts that are being made to build a new culture. . . . *The People's Yellow Pages* is a step in building a non-exploitative alternative way to meet our daily needs."

To give you an idea what this telephone-book-sized directory, mostly about Boston services, is all about, here are some random entries from the noncopyrighted volume.

*Abortion—see also Pregnancy Counseling, Liberation Struggles: Women, Birth Control*

Boston Women's Abortion Action Coalition
522 Mass. Ave., Cambridge 02139
547-1818

The Boston Women's Abortion Action Coalition is part of the national campaign to repeal all abortion and contraception laws, with no forced sterilization. The campaign is being coordinated nationally by the Women's National Abortion Action Coalition, and includes working through legislation, legal actions, women's speak-outs, and public demonstrations. As such, BOWAAC is working closely with Women vs. Mass. (see below), supporting activities at area-wide schools and speak-outs in suburban areas, and working on national demonstrations for repeal of all abortion laws.

Mass. Organization for Repeal of Abortion Laws
Box 238, Boston 02134
237-9493

This is a group which does community organizing to mobilize support for the repeal of abortion laws. They organize meetings, operate a speakers bureau, file legislative and court action, and hold at least one conference a year. They are encouraging the formation of similar groups elsewhere in the state. They have a membership fee of $3 which puts you on their newsletter mailing list.

Female Liberation
Box 303, Kenmore Square Station, Boston 02215
491-1071

Putting out a booklet examining all aspects of the abortion question and the medical and moral issues involved. Articles will also discuss the relationship between the campaign to repeal abortion laws and the feminist movement.

Women vs. Mass.
Civil Liberties Union of Mass.
3 Joy St., Boston 02108
227-9459

A group of women in Mass. are bringing a lawsuit against Massachusetts' anti-abortion law. They have put out a booklet which summarizes their basic reasons for bringing suit, what it means to bring suit in this case, the legal arguments for it and legal information for plaintiffs. If you are interested in being a plaintiff you should contact them. They feel that bringing a lawsuit against Massachusetts' anti-abortion law is an important step toward a responsive health care system and women's control over their bodies. Available at above address or from Mass. Lawyers Guild, 595 Mass. Ave., Cambridge 02139, 661-8898.

## *Mimeo Machines—Cambridge*

Cambridge Ministry in Higher Education

Rm. 105, basement of Memorial Hall at Harvard. Office hours: 1 PM to 5 PM. Office phone: 495-3945. They ask that you bring decent paper, since very cheap paper or ditto paper messes up the machine. Another machine is also available to CMHE at MIT: 864-6900 ex. 2983. The machine at Harvard is a Gestetner.

Mass. PAX

67 Winthrop St., Cambridge (near Harvard Sq.) phone: 492-5570. Ask for Jean Rubenstein. They're open 9 AM to 6 PM. They have an A.B. Dick machine and they say that anyone can use it "as long as they're not fascists."

University Christian Movement
1145 Mass. Ave., Cambridge
354-6583. Dee Hopkins or Helen Ewer.

Open 10 AM–5 PM. Staff must be present when the machine is being used. A.B. Dick. Bring heavy paper—cheap paper is hard on the machine.

Urban Planning Aid
639 Mass. Ave., Cambridge
661-9220

Office hours: 9:30–5:30, but non-UPA users of mimeo are asked to use the machine after 5 PM or on weekends, except in emergency. Between 5 and 7 PM is probably most convenient. Gestetner machine.

Cambridge Tenants Organizing Committee
595 Mass. Ave., Cambridge
354-2064

There are usually people in the office in the evenings and often during the day. Two other groups regularly use machine and it can't be used during meetings. Gestetner.

United States Servicemen's Fund
94 School St., Cambridge
547-4546

Open noon–7 PM, M–F. Have a 7-hole Rex Rotary machine. Ask for Jay at USSF.

Vietnam Veterans Against the War
67A Winthrop St., Cambridge
492-5570

A.B. Dick machine.

## *Mimeo Machines—Boston*

Civil Liberties Union of Massachusetts
3 Joy St., Boston
227-9459

Open 9–5 but lunch time is not usually good since they often have meetings in the mimeo room. A.B. Dick. Parking is hard on Beacon Hill so plan to bring small jobs by MTA or arrange to be dropped off or picked up later.

South End Neighborhood Action Program
109 W. Brookline St., Boston
267-7400

Call for an appointment 3–4 days in advance. A.B. Dick. When you call ask to speak to the secretary or to the director.

People's Coalition for Peace and Justice
173 Mass. Ave., Boston
262-3681 Contact: Lydia Sargent

Open 9:30–4:30 M–F. A.B. Dick.

Citizens for Participation Politics
11 South St., Boston
462-3040 Contact: Carolyn Stouffer

Open 10 AM–7 PM, M–Sat. A.B. Dick. CPP is across from South Station.

## *Mimeo Machines—Brighton*

Allston-Brighton Tenants Union
111A Brighton Ave., Brighton
254-3050

Rex Rotary machine and needs Rex Rotary stencils and ink. Open 6–8 PM, M–F.

## *Mimeo Machines for Emergency Use Only*

Roxbury Multi-Service Center
317 Blue Hill Ave., Roxbury
427-4470

Contact: Mrs. Gloria Thomas. A.B. Dick.

## *Police*

Citizens Committee for Police Brutality
Contacts: Joanne Pelham, Saundra Graham
547-6811, 9–5 PM, M–F.

Anyone who wants to register a complaint against a Cambridge policeman should report it to this committee, which meets every Thursday at 8:30 AM at the Cambridge City Hospital. (If you go to the police station they will refer you to this committee.) The committee includes 2 people from the Cambridge black community, 1 policeman, 1 person picked by the City Manager, and another person decided upon by these 4. For information on this committee's actual effectiveness concerning the occurrence of police brutality in Cambridge, get in touch with Joanne Pelham or Saundra Graham, spokeswoman for the black community.

Police on the Homefront: They're Bringing It All Back Home

A book published by NARMIC (see Military-Industrial Complex) about police surveillance and infiltration of radical organizations. The book and a supplement (copies of a xeroxed FBI file liberated in the March raid on Media, Pa.) are available for $1.35 from Cambridge AFSC, 48 Inman St., 02139.

## *Political Science*

Manas
Box 32112, El Sereno Station, Los Angeles
CA 90032

Weekly, $5/year, samples free. One of the earlier alternative efforts, *Manas* is a journal of independent inquiry concerned with the study of the principles which move world society on its present course.

## *Pottery—see also Arts, Crafts*

Norman Bacon and Sabra Segal
Eclipse, on Route 6A
P.O. Box 55, East Sandwich, Mass. 02537

Show stoneware clay hanging pots for plants; both artists show their sculpture and other handbuilt clay pieces. Open year-round 10 AM–5 PM, although their hours are irregular during the winter. Call if you are making a special trip.

## *Poverty*

National Rural Coalition Inc.
J. A. Hammer, 13 Hamilton St., Holyoke, Mass. 01040

The purpose of this group is to unite the different organizations and individuals concerned with the preservation of rural America and its culture. Also, to eliminate poverty thru economic development that does not exploit but enriches the lives of the rural poor, and to bring the rural people together to overcome problems of transportation, water, education, etc.

New England Poor People's Congress
c/o J. Hammer, 13 Hamilton St., Holyoke, Mass. 01040
(413) 536-6575

Attempting to offer mutual unity and support to poor people by providing a powerful voice to identify their needs to society and by educating the nonpoor about poverty. Membership is $1 a year. Members are actively working toward a national poor people's congress, uniting with poor all over the country; are presently meeting monthly throughout New England. Ideas and donations welcome.

# Index

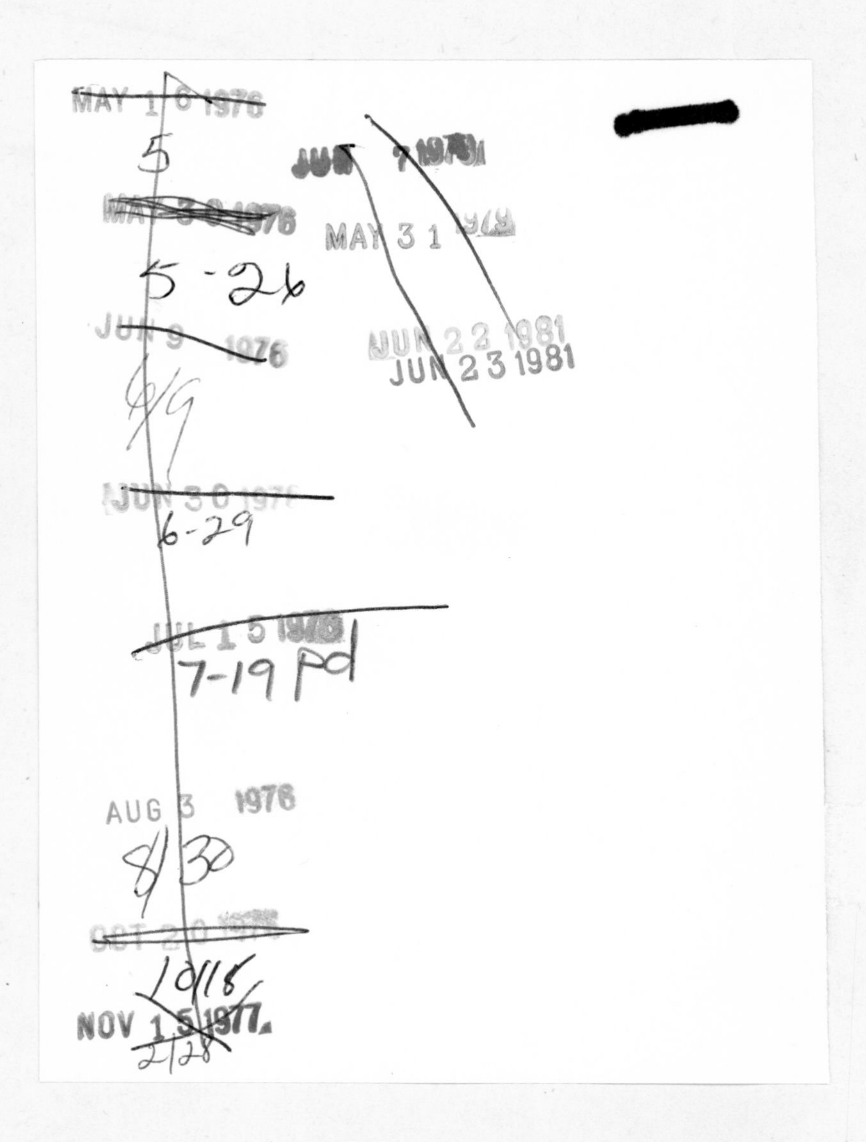
MAY 1 6 1976
JUN 7 1979
MAY 3 0 1976
MAY 3 1 1979
JUN 9 1976
JUN 2 2 1981
JUN 2 3 1981
JUN 3 0 1976
JUL 1 5 1976
AUG 3 1976
NOV 1 5 1977